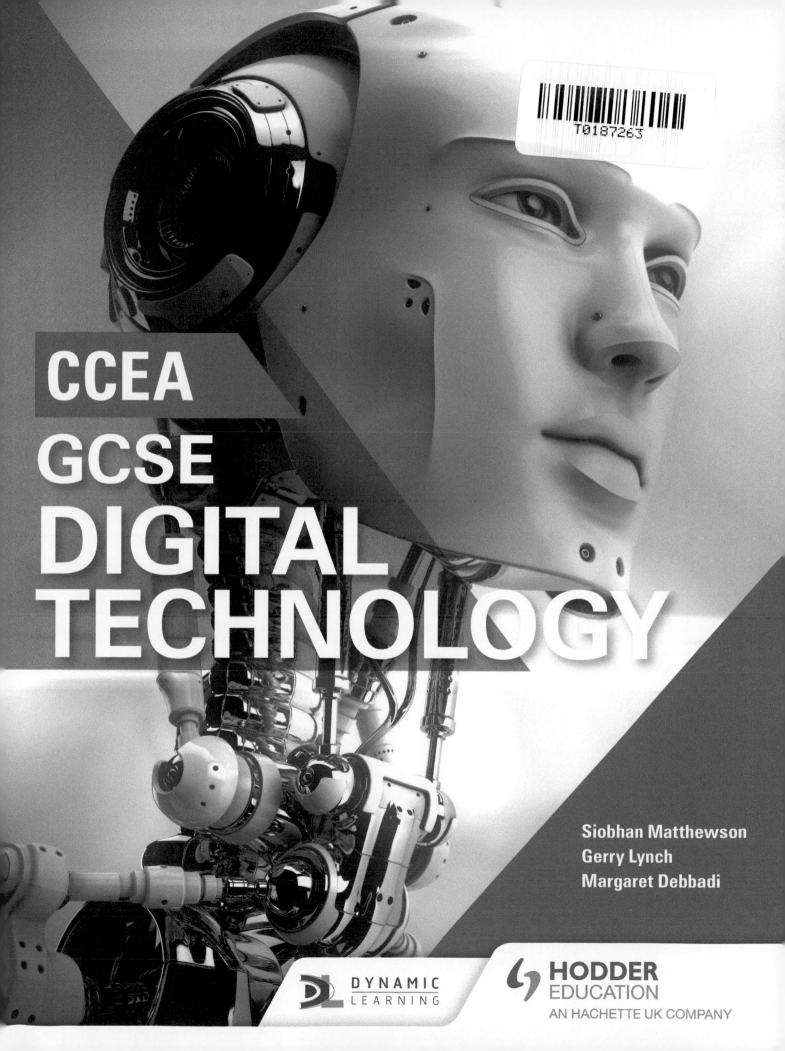

CCEA

GCSE

DIGITAL TECHNOLOGY

Siobhan Matthewson

Gerry Lynch

Margaret Debbadi

DYNAMIC LEARNING

HODDER EDUCATION
AN HACHETTE UK COMPANY

The publisher would like to thank the following for permission to reproduce copyright material:

Photo credits:

p. 12 © Jmiks/Shutterstock.com; **p. 35** *top* © Coprid/Fotolia; *bottom* © Mpanchenko/Shutterstock.com; **p. 36** *top* © ImYanis/Shutterstock.com; *bottom* © Sergey Nivens/Fotolia; **p. 37** © Robert Milek/Shutterstock.com; **p. 38** *top* © Scanrail1/Shutterstock.com; *bottom* © Mingis/iStock/Thinkstock; **p. 42** © a-image/Shutterstock.com; **p. 44** *top* © Christoph Burgstedt/Shutterstock.com; *bottom* © Marc Dietrich/Fotolia; **p. 62** © Roger Bamber/Alamy Stock photo; **p. 66** © Photo Researchers/Science History Images/Alamy Stock Photo; **p. 67** © Aey/Fotolia; **p. 68** © Mama_mia/Shutterstock.com; **p. 70** © Bplanet/Shutterstock.com; **p. 85** © Javier Larrea/ Age fotostock/Alamy Stock Photo; **p. 86** © Alexey Boldin/Shutterstock.com.

Although every effort has been made to ensure that website addresses are correct at time of going to press, Hodder Education cannot be held responsible for the content of any website mentioned. It is sometimes possible to find a relocated web page by typing in the address of the home page for a website in the URL window of your browser.

Orders: Please conatct Hachette UK Distribution, Hely Hutchinson Centre, Milton Road, Didcot, Oxforshire, OX11 7HH. Telephone: +44 (0)1235 827827. Email education@hachette.co.uk. Lines are open from 9 a.m. to 5 p.m., Monday to Friday. You can also order through our website: www.hoddereducation.com

ISBN 9781510414969

© Margaret Debbadi, Gerry Lynch, Siobhan Matthewson 2017

First published in 2017 by

Hodder Education
An Hachette UK Company,
Carmelite House, 50 Victoria Embankment
London EC4Y 0DZ

Impression number 5 4

Year   2022

Cover photo © Vladislav Ociacia/Getty Images/iStockphoto/Thinkstock

Illustrations by Integra Software Services Pvt. Ltd.

Typeset in Caecilia LT Std 55 Roman 10/14, Integra Software Services Pvt. Ltd., Pondicherry, India

Printed and bound by CPI Group (UK) Ltd, Croydon, CR0 4YY

A catalogue record for this title is available from the British Library

CONTENTS

UNIT 1 DIGITAL TECHNOLOGY

UNIT 2 DIGITAL AUTHORING CONCEPTS

UNIT 3 DIGITAL AUTHORING PRACTICE

UNIT 4 DIGITAL DEVELOPMENT CONCEPTS

UNIT 5 DIGITAL DEVELOPMENT PRACTICE

Chapter 1 Digital data

What this chapter covers

▶ Representing data
▶ Representing images
▶ Representing sound
▶ Data portability

Representing data

Difference between information and data

Data consists of raw facts and figures with no meaning attached. When data is processed (or given meaning) it provides us with **information**. Therefore, we can define information as 'data with meaning'.

For example, in the table in the margin, the number 62351 is data, but when we add meaning to this sequence of figures, such as 'Product number 62351 is a 2 Tb portable hard drive', we provide information.

An information system, consisting of hardware and software working together, takes data as input and converts it into information. Therefore, an information system *processes* data and produces information.

Product number	Product description
24315	32 Gb USB flash drive
62351	2 Tb portable hard drive

Input **data** → Information system will **process** the data. → Output **information**

▲ An information system

Storing data

Computers store data in digital format. This is done using a number system known as binary. A **Binary digIT** (also known as a bit) has a value of 0 or 1 and is the smallest unit of computer storage. When bits are grouped together (typically in groups of eight) they are referred to as a byte. A single **character** (such as a letter or a digit) is represented by one byte (or 8 bits). Therefore two letters (or two characters) are represented by two bytes (or 16 bits). A nibble is four bits, therefore two nibbles is equal to one byte (or 8 bits).

The storage capacity of a computer's memory is measured in bytes. Multiples of bytes are referred to as shown in the table.

These terms are usually used to describe data storage capacity and computer memory. Therefore we use these terms to describe the capacity of USB flash drives and hard drives used in typical computers.

1024 bytes	1 kilobyte (kB)
w1024 kilobytes	1 megabyte (MB)
1024 megabytes	1 gigabyte (GB)
1024 gigabytes	1 terabyte (TB)

Characters are classified as letters, digits and punctuation marks. Each character is a byte (or 8 bits). A commonly used character set is ASCII (American Standard Code for Information Interchange). Every character in the set has a unique binary pattern (or byte) as shown below.

01000001 A	01100001 a
01000010 B	01100010 b
01000011 C	01100011 c
01000100 D	01100100 d
...	...

Data types

In order to optimise a computer's processing power, data needs to be stored in the most appropriate way. In order for this to happen, data must be defined as a certain type before it is processed.

Data type	Description
Numeric	**Integer numbers**: an integer can be a positive or negative whole number, which has no decimal or fractional parts. **Real numbers**: real numbers include whole numbers (integers) and numbers with decimal/fractional parts. Real numbers can be positive or negative.
Date/Time	This determines the way that the date or time appears when it is displayed or printed by a computer. You can use a predefined format that already exists in the software or create your own customised date and time formats. Examples of predefined formats: Long date Displayed as Saturday, April 1, 2018 Medium date Displayed as dd-mmm-yyyy Example: 1-Apr-2018 Short date Displayed as dd/mm/yyyy Example: 01/04/2018 Long time Displayed as hh:mm:ss Example 13:26:34 Medium time Displayed as hh:mm PM/AM Example 01:26 PM Short time Displayed as hh:mm Example 13:26
Character/String	A character is a single letter or digit represented by codes from the character set used by the computer (such as ASCII). A string is textual data in the form of a sequence of characters from a character set. This could be in the form of a word. A string will have a variable number of characters.

Tasks

1. How many bits are there in 5 kilobytes?
2. How many characters are there in the word 'digital'?
3. Which of these numbers are 'real numbers'? 2, 3.5, -4.6, 7, 21, 99.2
4. Which of these are 'integers'? 5.34, -4, -89, 2.1, 678

Representing images

A **pixel** (usually represented by a dot or square) is the smallest unit of a digital image that can be displayed and edited on a computer screen. Each pixel can have its own individual colour and when pixels are combined together they produce a complete image. The number of pixels on a typical computer screen depends on the size of the screen and the graphics card used by the processor.

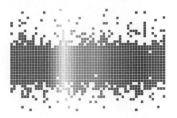

▲ A number of pixels are put together to provide an image. Each pixel can be a different colour.

When an image is created using pixels, each pixel is stored as a series of binary digits. The number of bits used to store a pixel depends on the range of colours used. For example, to use 256 different colours for a pixel will require 8 bits for a pixel to be stored ($2^8 = 256$).

Image **resolution** tells us the quality of an image. The greater the number of pixels used in an image, the higher the resolution and the sharper the image. However, higher resolution images need more storage space. Image resolution is represented by two numbers, such as 1280 x 720. The first number is the number of pixels displayed horizontally and the second number is the number of pixels displayed vertically. The position of a pixel in an image is given using a system similar to (X, Y) coordinates.

Bitmap and vector-based graphics

Bitmap graphics

Bitmap graphics are made up of a grid of pixels. If you use your mobile phone to take a photograph, or you scan a picture into your computer, you are creating a bitmap image. The higher the resolution of the mobile-phone camera you are using to capture the image, the higher the quality of the image will be. In other words, the more pixels, the better the resolution of the image. This will also require more storage space to save the image.

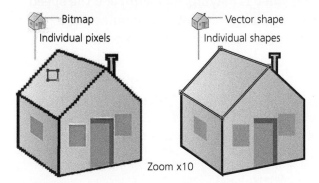

▲ Bitmap and vector-based graphics

Bitmap graphics store details about every individual element (pixel) of the image and since each pixel could have a different colour, this means an image can be very complex. Because the computer has to store every pixel, the file size of a bitmap image can be very large. Large bitmap images can take a long time to load from the computer's memory. Bitmap images can be compressed to reduce the file size but this may result in a loss of quality.

When you zoom in to or enlarge a bitmap image, pixelation can occur. This means that the pixels become larger on screen and look like a number of small blocks put together. This is the reason why bitmap images are poor quality when enlarged too much.

Vector-based graphics

Vector-based graphics are not made up of a grid of pixels. Instead vector-based graphics store information about the components that make up an image. These components are based on mathematical objects such as lines, curves and shapes. This means it is possible to edit these objects separately, for example by changing the colour, size or the position of the object.

Vector-based graphics do not depend on resolution for quality. Because they store details about the shape of individual image objects they require less storage capacity compared to using pixels. This means they can be saved as smaller files and can be easily edited without loss of quality. Since vector-based images are not made up of a grid of pixels, they can be enlarged and not lose image quality.

Buffering and streaming a video

A large video can take a long time to download from the internet. **Streaming** is a process that allows video to be viewed on a website or app straight away, without having to wait for the full video to be downloaded. Using streaming, the user can start watching the video as it downloads in 'real time' rather than downloading and permanently storing the complete video to be watched later.

A **buffer** is an allocated part of memory that is used to store a downloaded part of the video before it is watched. When a user is watching a video, a buffer is used to download the next part. This helps to prevent possible disruptions in streaming while the video is playing, for example if the speed of the internet connection is inconsistent or if the internet connection is temporarily lost. Buffering helps to improve the streaming experience.

Representing sound

Factor	Description
Sample rate	This is the number of audio sound samples captured every second to represent the sounds digitally and is measured in Hertz (Hz). The more samples that are taken per second the more accurate the digital representation of the original sound (resulting in higher quality sound) and the shape of the sound wave is captured more accurately.
Bit depth	Bit depth is the number of bits used to store each sound sample. Higher quality sound requires a higher bit depth. Bit depth is usually 16 bits on a CD, which has a resolution of 65 536 possible values (2^{16}). Bit depth is higher on a DVD which is usually 24 bits.
Bit rate	Bit rate refers to the quantity of data measured in bits that is processed in a given amount of time. This is usually in kilobits per second. For example, a typical iTunes song stores 256 kilobits of data in every second of a song.

▲ Factors affecting the quality of sound when it is recorded using a computer

Analogue to digital conversion

An **analogue signal** is described as a continuous varying signal that represents a physical quantity such as sound. Before a computer can process analogue signals (in this case, sound waves) they need to be converted into a digital format (binary). For this to happen, the sound first needs to be captured by an input device, such as a microphone, and then converted to a digital signal using an analogue to digital converter (ADC).

An analogue to digital converter will sample a sound wave at regular time intervals. If the number of sound samples per second (sample rate) is low, there will be a loss of audio quality because the samples do not show what the sound wave is doing in between each time sample. To ensure the original sound is maintained, sampling per second should be increased. The frequency at which samples are taken is known as the sample rate, measured in Hertz (Hz) (see above).

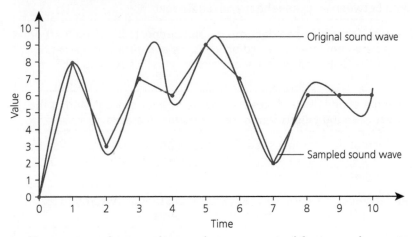

▲ How a sound wave alters when converted from analogue to digital

Data portability

Data portability is the ability to transfer data from one computer to another or from one software application to another without having to re-enter the data. Different types of data need to be stored using particular formats to ensure data is portable between different software applications or different computer systems.

File format	Detail
JPEG	JPEG (Joint Photographic Expert Group) files support the compression of images. The level of compression can vary and can be controlled by the user. Higher compression will reduce the quality of the image but decrease the file size (hence making the image load quicker). JPEG images are often used on web pages.
TIFF	TIFF (Tagged Image File Format) files store bitmapped images. This file format allows the image to be portable so it can be moved between a Windows (PC) and an Apple environment. TIFF image files retain their quality but larger file sizes compared to JPEGs.

File format	Detail
PNG	PNG (Portable Network Graphics) allows data compression of bitmapped graphics. PNG format was developed to support the sharing of graphics via the internet whilst maintaining the quality of the image.
PICT	PICT files are the standard file format for Apple graphics. They can support graphic interchange between both bitmapped and vector-based graphics.
GIF	GIF (Graphics Interchange Format) supports bitmapped image file formats. This format uses a form of compression that does not degrade the quality of the image. These file sizes are relatively small and therefore take up less storage space. They are also suitable for inclusion on web pages. Animated GIFs combine a series of GIF images and display them one after the other.
TXT	TXT file is a plain text document that contains no text formatting. It is stored as a 'text' file and can be opened by any word-processing program to allow for text editing.
CSV	A CSV (comma-separated value) file is a text format file used by database and spreadsheet applications. For example, in a spreadsheet, each line in the CSV file corresponds to a row in a worksheet. Within the line of CSV text, columns are separated by commas. The CSV files are often used for moving tabular data between a spreadsheet and a database.
RTF	RTF (Rich Text Format) format is used for text-based documents and supports basic formatting. It allows the movement of text files between different word processors and different operating systems. Documents scanned using the OCR facility of a scanner are usually saved as RTF documents.
MP3	MP3 is a file format for compressing a sound file to decrease the file size for storage and at the same time keeping the original level of sound quality when the sound file is played.
MP4	MP4 is similar to MP3 but is a file format that compresses both sound and video to decrease the storage size. It can also be used to store other data such as still images and text subtitles. This file format also allows data streaming across the internet.
MIDI	MIDI (Musical Instrument Digital Interface) is a communication protocol that allows sound samples to be interchanged between different digital musical instruments.
MPEG	MPEG (Moving/Motion Picture Experts Group) refers to a group of experts who developed standards for compressing digital video.
AVI	AVI (Audio Video Interleaved) is a multimedia file format created by Microsoft® for Windows® software. AVI files can contain both audio and video content allowing synchronous audio-with-video playback.
PDF	PDF (Portable Document Format) is a file format developed by Adobe Systems®. A PDF file can be created from a range of files including Microsoft Word® documents and PowerPoint® presentations. The PDF captures formatting used within a document so that when the document is opened the original fonts, images and the layout of the file is the same. Files are usually 'read only' and the contents cannot be edited. The PDF file generated is usually smaller in file size than the original file. A special piece of software is required to view or print the PDF file.
WAV	WAV (Windows Audio Waveform) is a file format standard for storing an audio bit stream on PCs. A WAV file is uncompressed audio file format.
WMA	WMA (Windows Media Audio®) is an audio data compression file format developed by Microsoft for Windows Media Player®.

Data compression

When we include images on webpages it is important that these images can be downloaded in an acceptable time. When creating and editing graphical images it is important to consider how the final graphic will be distributed when deciding what file format to save the graphic image in.

To ensure that we maximise the potential of these aspects it is important to reduce the storage requirements of image files and audio files data, allowing uploading or downloading to and from the internet at faster transfer speeds.

Data compression is used to convert digital data to as small a size as possible while still maintaining the quality of the data contained in the file. Data that has been compressed takes less time to upload and download. There are two main types of data compression: lossy and lossless.

Lossy compression reduces the file size by removing some of the data, for example by reducing the number of colours used in an image. This can result in a small reduction in quality of an image. Once a file has been compressed using this method data is permanently lost. JPEG is an example of a lossy compression method.

Lossless compression maintains the quality of the file, so no data is lost. An example of this form of compression is the use of WinZip® software, which reduces file size by 'zipping' up a file, so it can be sent over the internet. The file can then be recreated (unzipped) exactly as it was before it was compressed.

Tasks

1 Distinguish between bit depth and bit rate when capturing sound for a digital device.
2 Define the purpose of an ADC.

Checkpoint

▷ Data is raw facts and figures. Information is data with meaning.
▷ Computers store data in digital format using the binary number system.
▷ ASCII is a character set used to represent letters, digits or punctuation marks in binary format.
▷ A bitmap graphic can be formed as a number of pixels. The more pixels the better the resolution of the image.
▷ A vector-based graphic is formed using mathematical objects such as lines and curves.
▷ Videos that are streamed can be viewed straight away as opposed to downloading before viewing.
▷ An analogue signal is a varying signal that represents a physical quality such as a sound wave.
▷ Text and graphics use standard formats to allow data to be portable.
▷ Data compression is the act of reducing the file size which will decrease transmission speeds.

Practice questions ?

1 Using an example, distinguish between data and information. [4 marks]

2 Why does a computer use ASCII codes? [2 marks]

3 State three ways in which a date could be formatted as a data type. [3 marks]

4 Describe two differences between vector-based graphics and bitmap graphics. [3 marks]

5 Describe what is meant by the term 'pixelation'. [3 marks]

6 Explain how the number of pixels can affect the resolution of an image. [4 marks]

7 Explain how a buffer can assist in the process of video streaming. [4 marks]

8 Name and describe two graphic file formats. [6 marks]

9 Name and describe two text file formats. [6 marks]

10 Explain how data compression can assist in uploading a file to the internet. [4 marks]

Chapter 2 Software

What this chapter covers

▶ System software

▶ Modes of processing

▶ Utility software

▶ Role of anti-virus software

System software

System software is often described as the interface between computer hardware and user application programs. It enables the computer to operate its hardware and applications software. **Application software** enables the computer to do a particular task such as word processing.

Types of system software include the operating system and **utility programs**. The **operating system** is an essential piece of software that manages all other programs being used on a computer. Microsoft Windows is a common operating system.

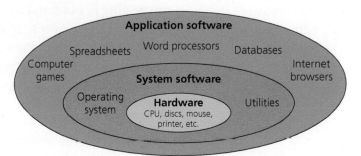

▲ The key components of a computer: hardware, system software and application software

Allocating memory	The operating system organises the use of main memory between programs and data files. Programs and data files that a user wants to access need to be transferred from a hard disc into main memory (such as RAM) before they can be used. The operating system does this by locating free memory space in RAM and then allocating this to the program or the data file. When programs and files are no longer required by the user they are transferred back out of main memory to the hard disc.
Storage	The operating system can manage the storage of data and files. Data and files need to be saved, and data and files that are no longer required need to be deleted.
Processing time	System software allocates processing time between the running programs and the users. It divides the time into a number of time slices and depending on the priority of the tasks to be processed, each task is allocated a number of time slices. System performance includes response time and processor usage and this is monitored by the system software.

▲ The main functions of system software

> **RAM is discussed in more detail in Chapter 5 Computer hardware (Unit 1).**

Modes of processing

Real-time processing

In **real-time processing**, data is processed immediately after it is input. The output generated is processed quickly which influences the next input received.

Applications that use real time processing include:

▶ airline/concert booking systems

▶ online stock control systems

▶ air traffic control systems.

In computer-controlled systems, such as air traffic control, real-time processing is essential to avoid a disaster. For example, the current position of an aeroplane needs to be shown on the operator's screen. As an aeroplane changes its position, the output on the screen must be updated immediately to show the actual 'real' position of the aeroplane. This ensures the pilot gets the correct information and avoids other aircraft.

Tasks ✎

Use the internet to research how applications use real-time processing.

Batch processing

Batch processing involves collecting groups (or batches) of similar data over a period of time (days, weeks, months) and then inputting the data at an agreed time. These batches of data are then processed collectively without human involvement. This type of processing suits applications where data does not have to be processed immediately. All the processing can be done at a convenient time when a computer system is least busy (such as at night or the weekend). Applications that use batch processing tend to have huge volumes of data to collect and process.

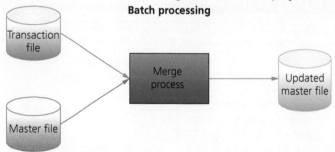

▲ Batch processing

While the computer system is processing 'a batch of data' it cannot be used for any other activity. Therefore if the computer is used for batch processing overnight it can be used for other activities during the day, such as an enquiry system to answer customer billing queries.

Applications that make use of batch processing include:

▶ billing systems (electricity/gas/telephone)

▶ payroll systems (weekly/monthly)

▶ banking systems (monthly customer statements).

Consider an electricity billing system that is used to collect meter readings from houses and produce quarterly bills for electricity usage. The computer has almost all the information required to produce the bill such as the customer account number, customer name, address details and a history of meter readings. This information does not change in the short term (from one billing period to the next) and is stored in the customer **master file**.

When a meter reading has been collected, the customer account number and the meter reading are entered into the computer. This data is used to create a **transaction file** (or a temporary file). Using the customer account number on the transaction file and the same customer account number on the master file, records are matched to allow other customer details to be retrieved (such as customer name and address) and the calculation of the bill takes place.

The bill is then calculated by multiplying the number of units used by the price per unit.

Finally, batch processing then occurs when a 'batch' of bills are produced and sent to customers. Once a bill is paid, the customer master file is updated using the transaction file to produce a new master file ready for the next billing quarter.

> **Tasks** 🖎
>
> Use the internet to research how applications use batch processing.

Multi-user system

A multi-user system involves many users at different computers sharing the processor of a powerful computer. It is also referred to as a 'time-sharing' system. It works by the operating system switching at high speed between the computers giving each one in turn a small amount of processor time known as a 'time slice'.

Utility software

A utility application is a program that carries out a specific task to assist the operating system such as:

▶ disc defragmentation

▶ task scheduling

▶ data backup and restore.

Disc defragmentation

Before a file is stored on a disc it is broken down into a number of data blocks by the operating system. Each block is then stored in a free block space on a disc. It is not always possible for the operating system to locate enough adjacent free block spaces for the blocks to be stored together. Therefore a single file may be broken up and stored in different parts of the disc. This is known as file fragmentation.

Over a period of time as new files are saved to a disc and older files are deleted from the same disc, a number of free blocks which are spread across the disc will be available to store new files. Therefore a large file will be more than likely stored in a fragmented way.

As part of the disc maintenance process a utility known as a disc defragmenter can be used. This rearranges the data on the disc so that:

▶ files are stored in blocks that are all together.

▶ all the free blocks (free storage space) are together in the same part of the disc.

The process of defragmentation also speeds up the time it takes to access files because all the data is stored in the same area of the disc.

Task scheduling

Task scheduling is a method by which the processor time is divided amongst a number of tasks. The aim is to make maximum use of the processor time, therefore making the system more efficient.

In multi-user systems that use time slices, this is accomplished using a 'round robin' method. The processor deals with a task from the first computer and then moves to the next in sequence, and so on. When it reaches the last computer it automatically starts over again with the first computer. Due to the high speed of the processor, each user appears to have uninterrupted access to the powerful computer. So it attempts to process as many tasks as possible in a given timeframe.

Data backup and restore

A **backup** is a copy of the original data or file in case it gets damaged or lost. A business or an organisation should have more than one copy of their data in case a:

▶ hard disc fails

▶ virus destroys the data stored

▶ user accidently deletes a file

▶ fire destroys the building where the data is stored.

The backup should always be stored off site in a secure location. It can then be used to restore the original data to its previous state by uploading the latest backup file onto the system. If the data is not backed up then the situation could be disastrous for an organisation. It would be difficult for a hospital to tell the public that they have lost all patient records.

▲ The process of data backup

In some organisations, data does not change often so backups may take place at the end of each day. In other organisations that use real-time processing, the backups take place as soon as a transaction is processed. Backups can be scheduled to take place during the night, when network traffic is low and bandwidth is high.

A backup procedure may involve backing up the complete data file (full backup) or just backing up the data that has changed (incremental backup).

Role of anti-virus software

Anti-virus software is not part of a typical computer's operating system. It is normally installed on computers connected to the internet. Its main purpose is to detect, locate and remove a virus that can infect a computer system.

A virus is a program that can attach itself to a file and once the file is opened it can then spread to other files and to other computers linked to the internet. A virus can intentionally damage a computer system, prevent it from booting up or even slow down the performance of a computer.

▲ Computer viruses can damage the performance of a computer.

Anti-virus software can scan files stored on a computer and data entering a computer system and compare these to a known database of viruses. It is important that the database of viruses is regularly updated so that the anti-virus software can detect all known viruses including any new viruses that have been created. The software can scan all storage devices connected to a computer such as the internal hard drive and all external storage devices.

Tasks

Use the internet to compare different types of anti-virus software available for home users.

Checkpoint ✓

▷ Software is classified as systems software or applications software.
▷ The operating system manages the functions of the hardware providing an interface to allow users to communicate with the computer system.
▷ Real-time processing applications need to process data immediately it is received and update files before the next input occurs.
▷ Batch processing collects data over a period of time and then processes it together at a later stage.
▷ Utility programs include disc defragmenters, task schedulers and backup and restore programs.
▷ Anti-virus software is a utility that detects and removes viruses that can affect the performance of a computer system.

Practice questions ?

1 Distinguish between system software and applications software. [4 marks]
2 Describe three main functions of an operating system. [6 marks]
3 Using an application, describe the main features of real-time processing. [4 marks]
4 Using an application, describe the main features of batch processing. [4 marks]
5 What is meant by a multi-user system? [3 marks]
6 Name and describe two utility programs. [4 marks]

Chapter 3 Database applications

What this chapter covers

▶ Database concepts

▶ Data types

▶ Data validation

▶ Logical operators

Database concepts

Tables, records and fields

When data is organised into files, and each file is organised into a number of rows and columns this is referred to as a **table** or 'flat file'. A table is two-dimensional hence the description 'flat file'. The table below can be referred to as a 'customer' table.

CustomerID	Surname	FirstName	DOB	Gender	TelephoneNumber	Email
1	Bradley	Alec	17/08/72	M	02966474911	abradley@blue.com
2	Sloan	Jenny	05/07/61	F	02937667891	jsloan@vortel.com
3	Coary	Ben	01/12/80	M	02994467914	bcoary@blue.com
4	McGlone	Alice	06/05/56	F	02990875432	amcglone@yellow.eu
5	McKelvey	Jude	12/11/60	M	02986334556	jmckelvey@one.com
6	Stewart	Catherine	30/06/75	F	02990909876	cstewart@one.com
7	Kelly	Brian	01/05/95	M	02990987602	bkelly@fast.co.uk
8	Noble	Bernard	15/11/80	M	02966786311	bnoble@openup.com
9	Girr	Tracey	09/09/98	F	02982763209	tgirr@educ.co.uk
10	McNally	Mary	17/04/78	F	02990001166	mmcnally@email.com

Record

Field

A file or table such as the one above consists of a number of records. A **record** is represented as a row in a table. A record consists of data items related to an object or person.

A **field** is part of a record that stores a single data item. In a table, each field is represented by a column and is referenced by its field name (the column title). The **key field** (or primary key) is the field used to uniquely identify one record. In the table above the key field is CustomerID; each customer has a unique ID.

Queries, forms and reports

While tables store data, a database uses a number of tools that allow you to interact, extract and present information that is required. Queries, forms and reports are three such tools available in a database software package.

A **query** is a way of searching and extracting data from a database to find the answer to a question. The query/search checks each record and produces a list of data that satisfies the query criteria. To create a query, criteria are added to one or more fields in the table.

Field:	CustomerNumber	Surname	FirstName	Gender
Table:	Customer	Customer	Customer	Customer
Sort:				
Show:	☑	☑	☑	☑
Criteria:				"M"
or:				

⌃ Query designed to extract male customers from the table above

CustomerID	Surname	FirstName	DOB	Gender	TelephoneNumber	Email
1	Bradley	Alec	17/08/72	M	02966474911	abradley@blue.com
3	Coary	Ben	01/12/80	M	02994467914	bcoary@blue.com
5	McKelvey	Jude	12/11/60	M	02986334556	jmckelvey@one.com
7	Kelly	Brian	01/05/95	M	02990987602	bkelly@fast.co.uk
8	Noble	Bernard	15/11/80	M	02966786311	bnoble@openup.com

⌃ The result of the query

Forms are a common way to collect data from people. They can be used to enter a new record, modify an existing record or to view records already stored in a table. When data is entered into a form, it is automatically added into the specified table and stored as part of the database.

When there are a number of different tables in a database, forms make it easier to enter data as one form may include fields from different tables. When the user enters data into the form the database software will ensure the data is stored in the correct table.

Another advantage of using forms to enter data into tables is that the database designer can control the type and format of the data ensuring that it is kept consistent and accurate. Forms can also be customised to include a logo and colour.

	Customer and activity bookings		
CustomerNumber	2		Next Record
Surname	Sloan		
First Name	Jenny		Previous Record
Date of Birth	05-Jul-61		
Gender	F		
TelephoneNumber	02937667891		
Email	jsloan@vortel.com		

BookingNumber	BookingDate	ActivityDate	Location
7	30-Mar-13	04-Apr-15	Outdoor
9	12-Jul-13	14-Jan-15	Indoor

⋏ This form includes fields from a customer table and a booking table and is designed to allow customers to enter events they would like to book. These details are then added to both tables in the database.

A **report** allows tables and results from queries to be presented in a user-friendly way. The layout of the report can be customised, making it visually attractive and easy to read for the intended person or organisation. The data can also be presented by grouping similar data or sorting it in ascending or descending order.

Activity Bookings

Location	BookingDate	ActivityDate	Activity	Surname	FirstName
Indoor					
	15-Sep-14	23-Mar-16	Archery	Turner	Ciaran
	07-Oct-14	30-Dec-15	Karting	Quinn	Michael
	12-Jun-13	16-Jun-15	Archery	McElhone	Liz
	14-Feb-14	16-Feb-16	Archery	Carroll	John
	10-Nov-13	13-Nov-15	Karting	McKelvey	Jude
	05-May-14	07-May-15	Archery	Stewart	Catherine
Outdoor					
	17-Mar-14	21-Mar-16	Quad Biking	Doherty	Ciara
	30-Mar-14	02-Apr-16	Horse Riding	Murray	Gareth
	17-Mar-14	20-Mar-16	Quad Biking	McNally	Mary

⋏ Report showing bookings made by customers grouped by location

Macros

A **macro** is a small program written to perform a repetitive database task automatically. In a database, macros allow functionality to be added to both forms and reports such as adding a new record, deleting an old record or updating an existing record. Instead of entering multiple instructions each time a task is performed, the user only needs to perform a single operation, such as clicking on a button, and the instructions stored within the macro are executed.

Database relationships

It is possible to link together two tables in a database using a **relationship**. To do this, a common field has to exist in each table to allow the link to be made; the key field from one table is stored in another table as a non-key field (also called a **foreign key**). In the example below, 'customer number' is the key field in the customer table and a foreign key in the activity table to create a relationship. The degree of relationship can be categorised as a one-to-one, one-to-many or a many-to many. In the example below the degree of relationship is one-to-many and this can be described in words as 'one customer can book many activities'.

To ensure that the data entered is consistent in both tables, a feature called 'enforce **referential integrity**' can be applied to the relationship between the tables. This feature also ensures that when a customer record is deleted in the customer table, then all records in the activity table linked to that customer will also be deleted.

Importing data

Spreadsheets are useful for importing data as they allow easy manipulation and analysis of numerical data. However, a database package can store several linked tables which makes consolidating and organising data an even easier task. It is possible to import a number of worksheets from a spreadsheet to a database package or vice versa which gives organisations more flexibility in handling their data.

> **Tasks**
>
> Using a spreadsheet saved in your documents, import it into a database package.

> **Tasks**
>
> Identify the features used in both the form and the report above.

> **Tasks**
>
> Use the internet to research different ways a macro could be used in a database.

> Database relationships are also explored in Chapter 11 Designing solutions (Unit 2).

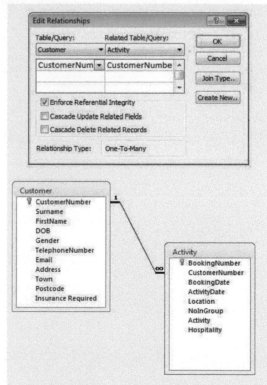

▲ Here, referential integrity prevents the addition of a new record to the activity table that cannot be linked to a record in the customer table.

Data types

When a database is created, each field within the record structure is named and an appropriate **data type** is attached to the field name. The data type defines the type of data associated with the field.

Data Type	Use
Text	Text and data that is a mixture of text and numbers, such as a postcode. Numbers that do not require calculations. 'Short text' is used for a small number of characters. 'Long text' is used for a large number of characters (such as a product description field).
Number	Numeric data that requires a mathematical calculation.
Date/Time	Dates and times (for example, a date from a pop-up calendar).
Currency	Monetary data such as 'item price'. (This data type includes two decimal places.)
Autonumber	To create a key field the computer generates sequential numbers which are automatically inserted for each new record created.
Yes/No	The data entered into the field contains one of two possible values such as Yes/No or True/False. This data type is called a Boolean value.
OLE object	Object linking and embedding, such a word-processed document or a spreadsheet. These objects have been created using a software package other than a database.
Hyperlink	The data type is a link to web address (URL) or an email address.
Attachment	Files are attached to a record, for example a digital image.
Calculated	For the result of a calculation produced from another field in the record.
Lookup wizard	To create a list of values. A value can be selected from the list and entered into the field.

Data validation

A computer automatically checks data at the input stage to ensure it is reasonable, sensible and within acceptable limits. **Data validation** guarantees that data is present and the correct type, range or length.

Data that does not conform to specified rules is rejected. When the computer checks input data it either accepts the data or displays an error message giving a reason why the data was rejected. A number of data validation checks exist: presence, length, type, format and range checks.

Presence check

A **presence check** ensures that data is present; the area cannot be left blank. This type of check is mainly used when you complete an online form. In the database table below, the description for 'Town' must be entered for each customer. To ensure this, there is a presence check in the field description for field name 'Town' ('Required' is set to 'yes' and the validation rule states 'Is not Null').

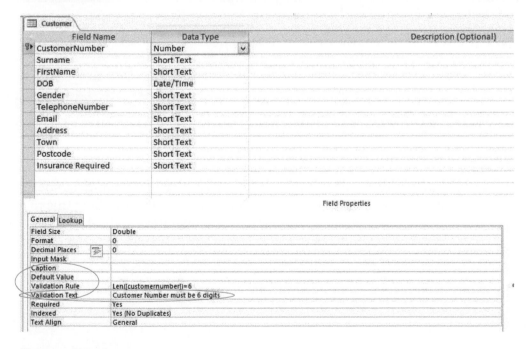

Customer	
Field Name	**Data Type**
CustomerNumber	Number
Surname	Text
FirstName	Text
DOB	Date/Time
Gender	Text
TelephoneNumber	Text
Email	Text
Address	Text
Town	Text
Postcode	Text
Insurance Required	Text

General	Lookup
Field Size	20
Format	@
Input Mask	
Caption	
Default Value	
Validation Rule	Is Not Null
Validation Text	
Required	Yes
Allow Zero Length	Yes
Indexed	No
Unicode Compression	No
IME Mode	No Control
IME Sentence Mode	None
Smart Tags	

Length check

A **length check** ensures that data entered is the correct number of characters. In the example below, every CustomerNumber in the database must contain six characters.

Customer		
Field Name	**Data Type**	**Description (Optional)**
CustomerNumber	Number	
Surname	Short Text	
FirstName	Short Text	
DOB	Date/Time	
Gender	Short Text	
TelephoneNumber	Short Text	
Email	Short Text	
Address	Short Text	
Town	Short Text	
Postcode	Short Text	
Insurance Required	Short Text	

Field Properties

General	Lookup
Field Size	Double
Format	0
Decimal Places	0
Input Mask	
Caption	
Default Value	
Validation Rule	Len([customernumber])=6
Validation Text	Customer Number must be 6 digits
Required	Yes
Indexed	Yes (No Duplicates)
Text Align	General

Type check

A **type check** is used to ensure that the data entered is of the correct type. There are several different data types including: numeric, text and date (see example above).

Tasks

Use the internet to research how data types are used in data collection forms.

Format check

A **format check** ensures that data entered matches a predetermined pattern. For example, a postcode would have a pattern such as BTXX XXX. The database would only allow data to be entered in this format.

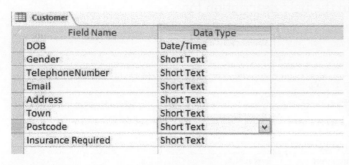

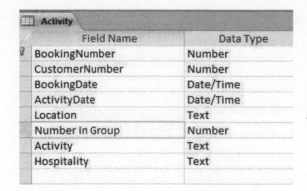

Range check

A **range check** ensures that data entered is within a lower limit and upper limit. In the example below, the number of people included in a group activity booking must be between 2 and 15.

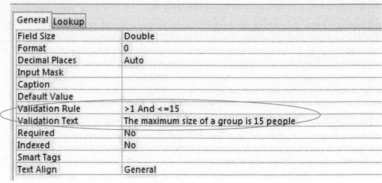

Comparison operators	
<	Less than
<=	Less than or equal to
>	Greater than
>=	Greater than or equal to
=	Equal to
<>	Not equal to

Logical operators

Comparing a value against other data is a typical operation when data is queried in a database. Comparison operators allow this to be done. For example, the comparison operator < indicates that the data entered must be less than a specified value for the result to be correct.

Logical operators are also used to analyse two values and return either a true or a false result. When there are only two possible results (true/false or yes/no) these are called Boolean operators. These operators are denoted by words such as AND, OR and BETWEEN.

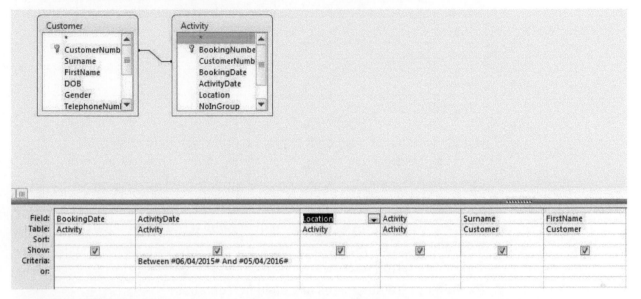

▲ Here, the activity date must be between the two values shown if the result is to be true.

Checkpoint ✓

▷ A database file (or table) is a number of records. Each record has a number of fields.

▷ The field that uniquely identifies a record is the key field.

▷ Different data types are used when defining fields, for example, currency is used for a field 'product price'.

▷ A query is a way of searching and extracting required data from the database.

▷ Forms allow data to be collected and entered into a database.

▷ A report allows tables and results from queries to be presented in a user-friendly manner.

▷ Macros allow users to perform a single operation by clicking on a button that represents a set of instructions.

▷ Data validation checks that data is reasonable, sensible and within acceptable limits.

▷ Logical operators are used to analyse two values and return either a true or a false result.

Practice questions ?

1 Complete this table. [8 marks]

Field Name	Data Type	Validation Check
Customer ID		
Date of birth		
Gender		
Email address		

2 Using the table above, identify and justify which field is suitable for a key field. [2 marks]

3 State three features that should be included in an on-screen form design. [3 marks]

4 Explain the difference between a query and a report as used in a database. [4 marks]

5 Define the term 'macro'. [2 marks]

6 Explain how relationships are used in a database. [4 marks]

7 What is meant by 'importing data to a database'? [4 marks]

8 Explain how logical operators are used in designing database queries. [6 marks]

Chapter 4 Spreadsheet applications

What this chapter covers

▶ Spreadsheet structure

▶ Cell formatting

▶ Worksheet presentation

▶ Formulas and functions

▶ Using spreadsheets for data modelling

Spreadsheet structure

A spreadsheet contains one or more **worksheets** which are used to present and manipulate data. A worksheet is presented as a grid in the form of rows and columns. Spreadsheets are mainly designed to allow applications to perform calculations and recalculations automatically. A **cell** has a column reference (a letter) and a row reference (a number). When referring to a cell, the column reference is always stated first. For example, H8. It works the same way as co-ordinates in mathematics.

Cells can store data in a variety of forms: text, number, date, formula or a reference to another cell.

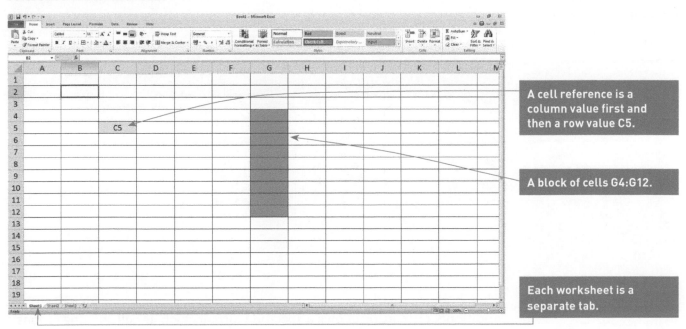

A cell reference is a column value first and then a row value C5.

A block of cells G4:G12.

Each worksheet is a separate tab.

Spreadsheet data can be formatted as general, number, currency, date, time and percentage as can be seen below.

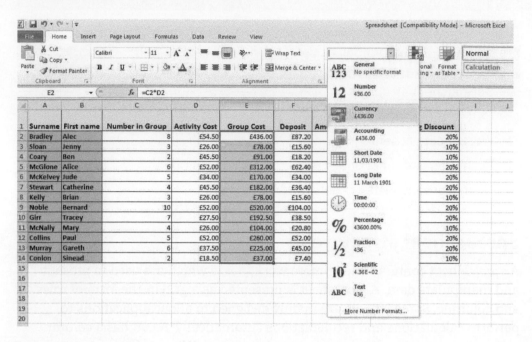

Cell formatting

 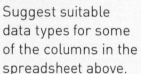
Formatting allows a user to control the contents and appearance of a cell, for example aligning text, changing the font, adding a border or adding background colour.

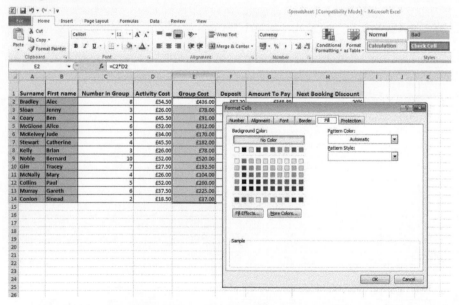

Conditional formatting allows a specified format, such as cell shading or font colour, to be applied to a cell or group of cells if a specified condition is met. In the example on the next page, if the number in the group is greater than 5 then the cells will be displayed as 'Light Red Fill with Dark Red Text'. If the condition is not met then nothing will happen to the formatting of the cells selected.

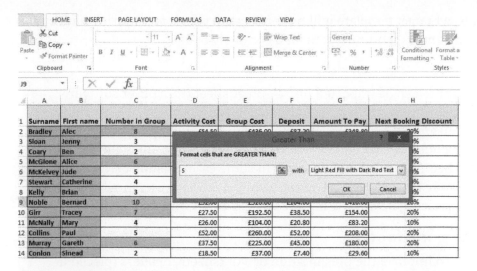

	A	B	C	D	E	F	G	H
1	Surname	First name	Number in Group	Activity Cost	Group Cost	Deposit	Amount To Pay	Next Booking Discount
2	Bradley	Alec	8	£54.50	£436.00	£87.20	£348.80	20%
3	Sloan	Jenny	3					%
4	Coary	Ben	2					%
5	McGlone	Alice	6					%
6	McKelvey	Jude	5					%
7	Stewart	Catherine	4					%
8	Kelly	Brian	3					%
9	Noble	Bernard	10	£52.00	£520.00	£104.00	£416.00	20%
10	Girr	Tracey	7	£27.50	£192.50	£38.50	£154.00	20%
11	McNally	Mary	4	£26.00	£104.00	£20.80	£83.20	10%
12	Collins	Paul	5	£52.00	£260.00	£52.00	£208.00	20%
13	Murray	Gareth	6	£37.50	£225.00	£45.00	£180.00	20%
14	Conlon	Sinead	2	£18.50	£37.00	£7.40	£29.60	10%

Data validation

It is possible to control the value input to a given cell(s) by using the data validation tool. For example, if the number in a group must be at least 1 and no greater than 10, a range check where the values lie between 1 and 10 can be created in the validation criteria. It is also possible to define the data type to be used in this range. In the example below, the number is defined as a whole number.

Tasks

Research how different validation checks could be used in a spreadsheet.

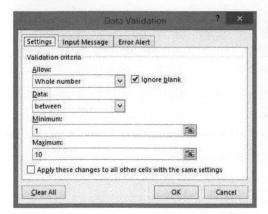

To guide and inform the user, a suitable error message can be created as part of the validation check. This error message can be set to pop up as a dialogue box to encourage the user to retry entering **valid data**.

Worksheet presentation

Templates

A **template** is a document that has been formatted using a predetermined layout for the user. It serves as a starting point for a new document. For example, a budget template will have allocated places for entering data such as income and expenditure data for a company budget.

Importing data

Data can be imported into a spreadsheet from other software sources (such as a database table) using a **wizard**, which guides the user through a series of steps. Each step involves asking the user a question, through the use of dialogue boxes, until the data has been successfully imported. In some cases the file being imported may have to be in a certain format such as csv (comma separated variable) before the import process can begin.

Headers and footers

To improve the presentation of worksheets, headers (placed at the top of the worksheet) and footers (placed at the bottom of the worksheet) can be added. These can be used to add page numbers, filenames or dates.

Formulas and functions

Formulas

Formulas allow a spreadsheet to perform calculations, and automatic recalculations if values in the associated cells change. A formula tells the computer what mathematical operation(s) needs to be performed on a specific cell(s). Simple formulas calculate totals for rows or columns.

A spreadsheet formula must begin with an equals sign (=), followed by an inbuilt function, followed by a cell reference(s) and/or a value(s). When a formula is entered into a cell it can be replicated quickly down a column or across a row using the Fill function.

	A	B	C	D	E	F
	F2		f_x =C2*E2			
1	**Surname**	**First name**	**Number in Group**	**Activity**	**Activity Cost**	**Group Cost**
2	Bradley	Alec	8	Bowling	£2.50	£20.00
3	Sloan	Jenny	3	Archery	£5.75	£17.25
4	Coary	Ben	2	Fencing	£4.50	£9.00
5	McGlone	Alice	6	Fencing	£4.50	£27.00
6	McKelvey	Jude	5	Archery	£5.75	£28.75
7	Stewart	Catherine	4	Horse Riding	£6.50	£26.00
8	Kelly	Brian	3	Swimming	£3.25	£9.75
9	Noble	Bernard	10	Fencing	£4.50	£45.00
10	Girr	Tracey	7	Fencing	£4.50	£31.50
11	McNally	Mary	4	Bowling	£2.50	£10.00
12	Collins	Paul	5	Archery	£5.75	£28.75
13	Murray	Gareth	6	Fencing	£4.50	£27.00
14	Conlon	Sinead	2	Bowling	£2.50	£5.00

Fill
- Down
- Right
- Up
- Left

Simple functions

Function	Example	Meaning
SUM	=SUM(C3:C10)	The cells in the range C3 to C10 are added together and total calculated.
AVERAGE	=AVERAGE(C3:C10)	The cells in the range C3 to C10 are added together and the average calculated.
MAX	=MAX(C3:C10)	The highest value in the cell range from C3 to C10 is returned.
MIN	=MIN(C3:C10)	The lowest value in the cell range from C3 to C10 is returned.

▲ Table of simple functions that you need to know

Tasks

Use Excel to find other simple functions that could be used. For each function found suggest an example of how it could be used.

More complex functions

Using the IF statement

This function allows a condition to be examined resulting in one of two actions being carried out.

```
IF <condition is true>
  THEN
    <action 1 is carried out>
  ELSE
    <action 2 is carried out>
ENDIF
```

Consider this example:

```
IF 'Group Cost' is less than or equal to £150
  THEN
    Give 10% discount off next booking
  ELSE
    Give 20% discount off next booking
ENDIF
```

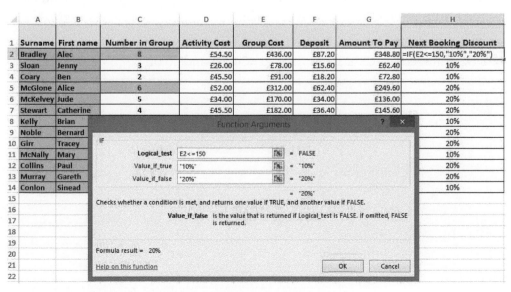

	A	B	C	D	E	F	G	H
1	Surname	First name	Number in Group	Activity Cost	Group Cost	Deposit	Amount To Pay	Next Booking Discount
2	Bradley	Alec	8	£54.50	£436.00	£87.20	£348.80	=IF(E2<=150,"10%","20%")
3	Sloan	Jenny	3	£26.00	£78.00	£15.60	£62.40	10%
4	Coary	Ben	2	£45.50	£91.00	£18.20	£72.80	10%
5	McGlone	Alice	6	£52.00	£312.00	£62.40	£249.60	20%
6	McKelvey	Jude	5	£34.00	£170.00	£34.00	£136.00	20%
7	Stewart	Catherine	4	£45.50	£182.00	£36.40	£145.60	20%
8	Kelly	Brian						10%
9	Noble	Bernard						20%
10	Girr	Tracey						20%
11	McNally	Mary						10%
12	Collins	Paul						20%
13	Murray	Gareth						20%
14	Conlon	Sinead						10%

Function Arguments

IF

Logical_test   E2<=150   = FALSE

Value_if_true   "10%"   = "10%"

Value_if_false   "20%"   = "20%"

= "20%"

Checks whether a condition is met, and returns one value if TRUE, and another value if FALSE.

Value_if_false   is the value that is returned if Logical_test is FALSE. If omitted, FALSE is returned.

Formula result = 20%

Help on this function   OK   Cancel

▲ Spreadsheet showing the IF statement function

Using the VLookup function

The VLookup function uses the value in a selected cell to 'lookup' a match in a column of a lookup table (vertical lookup). It then returns a value from a specified column from the same row of the lookup table. Consider the example below where the activity number is used to lookup an activity table to find its cost.

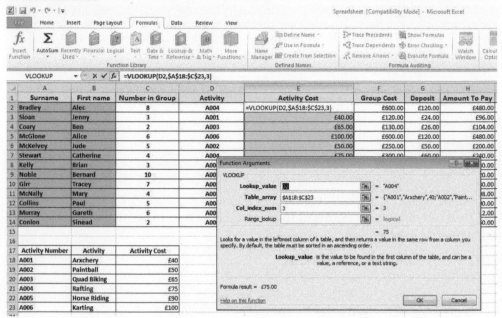

Lookup table

To use this function, click on the Formulas tab and select the Lookup & Reference **menu**, and then the VLOOKUP function. Then enter the cell reference that will collect the lookup value, the table cell range and the table column number where the activity cost will be found. The value from the table will be automatically copied into the seleted cell (E2).

Relative and absolute cell reference

When a formula is automatically copied down a column or across a row using the Fill function, a **relative cell reference** adjusts and changes the formulas to make sure it refers to the correct cell(s).

For example, in the spreadsheet below, when 'filled down' the formula =C2*D2 changes to =C3*D3 and then to =C4*D4 and so on.

	A	B	C	D	E
1	Surname	First name	Number in group	Activity cost	Group cost
2	Bradley	Alec	8	£54.50	=C2*D2
3	Sloan	Jenny	3	£26.00	=C3*D3
4	Coary	Ben	2	£45.50	
5	McGlone	Alice	6	£52.00	
6	McKelvey	Jude	5	£34.00	
7	Stewart	Catherine	4	£45.50	
8	Kelly	Brian	3	£26.00	

9	Noble	Bernard	10	£52.00	
10	Girr	Tracey	7	£27.50	
11	McNally	Mary	4	£26.00	
12	Collins	Paul	5	£52.00	
13	Murray	Gareth	6	£37.50	
14	Conlon	Sinead	2	£18.50	

In some cases, the cell reference must remain the same when it is copied. This is called an **absolute cell reference**. For instance, to convert the amount to pay from pounds into Euros, the same exchange rate for each group calculation would need to be used.

In this example, each group is offered one of two exchange rates depending on the total amount to pay. As the formula is copied from group to group, the cell references B18 and B19 (which give the two possible exchange rates) must remain the same. To create an absolute cell reference a $ sign is used (B18) to ensure that this cell reference does not change. This means the cell is locked into the calculation as the formula changes.

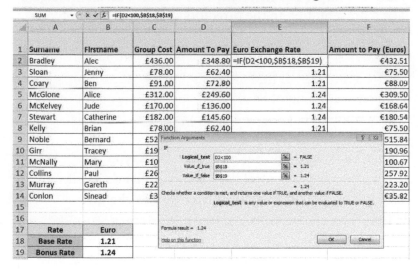

Using charts to display results

Using charts can help visualise the data from a selected worksheet. Once data has been selected, users can choose their preferred chart (bar chart, pie chart etc.) from the charting tool to enable data to be displayed graphically.

Using charts can greatly assist in the communication of information when an organisation is doing a presentation for its clients. The presentation of the chart can be enhanced by adding chart titles, legends and colour.

Using macros in spreadsheets

When using a spreadsheet, a macro (a small program written to carry out a task) can eliminate the need for the user to repeat the steps of commonly performed tasks over and over again. Automating these repetitive tasks saves the user time. These tasks could range from adding a date to a worksheet to sophisticated calculations that require complex formulas.

> **Tasks**
>
> What are the advantages of using charts to display information?

> **Macros are also explored in Chapter 3 Database applications (Unit 1).**

Using spreadsheets for data modelling

Spreadsheet software is increasingly being used in organisations for **data modelling**, whereby the model is controlled by a set of rules defined by formulas. By changing the formulas, the rules of the model can be varied. For example, an organisation could find out what would happen to the income from product sales by changing the product price of one or more items. When the product price is changed the formulas will automatically recalculate the values for income and sales as the spreadsheet is continually updated.

Being able to answer 'what if' questions, such as 'What if we increase the number of employees by 10 per cent; will it decrease our profits?', allows organisations to predict future outcomes. Therefore using a spreadsheet to model data can help answer key questions when making predictions and allow managers to make better-informed decisions for future planning.

Using graphs makes it easier for managers to understand the outcomes of spreadsheet modelling and allows an organisation to see trends over a period of time. For example, a bar graph could be used to show possible sales for the next five years within an organisation. This will also assist managers if they have to make a presentation to the directors of the organisation on future sales.

Checkpoint

▷ A spreadsheet consists of a number of worksheets.

▷ A worksheet has a number of rows and columns and each cell is identified by a column reference and a row reference.

▷ Data entered into a cell can be formatted using a data type.

▷ Data validation can be used to control the data entered into a cell.

▷ A template can be used to determine the layout of a worksheet.

▷ Formulas and functions can be used to carry out automatic calculations.

▷ An absolute cell reference is used to ensure the cell reference remains the same when it is copied.

▷ Graphs and charts can be used to enhance presentation of results.

▷ Macros can be built and used to carry out a particular task in the spreadsheet.

▷ Spreadsheets are used in applications that carry out data modelling.

Practice questions ?

John is planning a party to celebrate a special birthday for his mother.

	A	B	C	D	E
1	Party venue	Club 2020			
2	Available money	£400.00			
3	Party costing				
4	Item	Estimated cost	Actual cost	Difference	Within budget
5	Hire of Venue	£100.00	£110.00	–£10.00	No
6	DJ	£120.00	£100.00	£20.00	Yes
7	Food	£60.00	£75.00	–£15.00	No
8	Prizes	£50.00	£70.00	–£20.00	No
9	Decorations	£50.00	£45.00	£5.00	Yes
10	Tickets	£25.00	£30.00	–£5.00	No
11	Insurance	£35.00	£30.00	£5.00	Yes
12	Other	£60.00	£90.00	–£30.00	No
13	Total costs	£500.00	£550.00	–£50.00	
14	Over budget	£150.00			

1   How have the cells in row 3 been formatted?

2   How can the data in cells B5 to B12 be used to help John plan the party?

3   In the table below, write down the formula used to calculate the values in the cells.

Cell	Formula
D5	
B13	
B14	

4   John's spending does not match his available money. What information is available to him in column E?

5   Complete the IF statement which provides the information in E11.

=IF(_____ < _____ ,'Yes','No')

6   John wants to show the information about party costs on a graph. By making reference to cells, explain how a bar graph could be produced.

7   Explain an advantage of presenting information on a graph.

8   John wants to create a macro to print the graph. What is a macro?

Chapter 5 Computer hardware

What this chapter covers

▶ Central processing unit (CPU)

▶ Fetch–execute cycle

▶ Factors that influence the speed of processing

▶ Computer hardware devices

▶ Internal memory

Central processing unit (CPU)

The CPU (central processing unit) is often referred to as the 'brain' of the computer. The CPU is a microprocessor; its main role is to process **programs** and data. It does this by repeatedly fetching an instruction from memory and executing it (carrying out the instruction). This is known as the **fetch–execute cycle**.

There are three main components of a CPU:

▶ control unit

▶ arithmetic and logic unit (ALU)

▶ immediate access store (IAS).

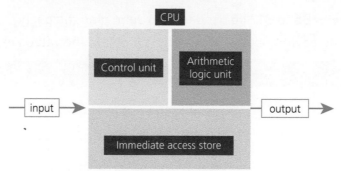

▲ The main components of a CPU

Control unit

This component manages the execution of instructions (usually one at a time), which are usually in some sort of order, using the fetch–execute cycle. This is done by sending control signals to other parts of the CPU. It has three main jobs:

1 To decide which instruction to carry out next and fetch it from memory.

2 To decode the instruction (work out what needs to be done to carry the instruction out).

3 To execute (or follow) the instruction.

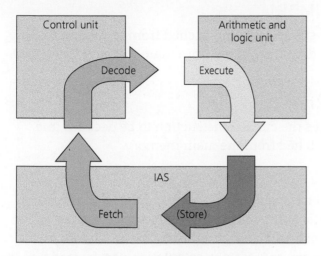

▲ Simple layout of the fetch–execute cycle

The arithmetic and logic unit (ALU)

This component processes data that requires arithmetic calculations to be carried out, such as addition, multiplication, subtraction or division. It also performs logical comparisons to assist with decision making by using logical operators AND, OR and NOT.

> Logical comparisons are discussed in more detail in Chapter 22 Digital data (Unit 4).

Immediate access store (IAS)

Immediate access store is also referred to as main memory. This component stores all programs and data temporarily whilst they are in use. (These programs and data are also stored permanently on an external storage device such as a hard disc.) During the fetch–execute cycle, instructions are fetched from their specific storage location in the IAS using an address. Each memory location has a unique address assigned to it.

Fetch–execute cycle

The CPU includes a number of **registers**. These are high-speed memory locations, each used for specific purposes. The registers below have an important role during the fetch–execute cycle.

Program counter (PC)

A program counter is a CPU register that stores the address (memory location reference) of the next instruction to be fetched. As many program instructions are ordered in sequence, the program counter is automatically incremented by 1 every time an instruction is fetched. Therefore the program counter points to the next instruction address in sequence.

Memory address register (MAR)

All program instructions are stored in the main memory of the CPU in a number of memory locations. Each memory location contains a unique address. The address of the current instruction or data being executed is temporarily stored in the MAR.

Memory data register (MDR)

This register will temporarily store data being fetched from or written to the main memory of the CPU. All data transferred from main memory to the CPU goes via the MDR.

Instruction register (IR)

This register temporarily stores the current instruction to be decoded and then executed, having been fetched from the main memory.

Accumulator

The accumulator is a dedicated register which is part of the ALU. When calculations take place on data, the results are initially stored in the accumulator before being transferred and stored in the main memory. Therefore it is the default location to store any calculations performed by the ALU.

Factors that influence the speed of processing

Clock speed

The clock speed is an indicator of the speed at which the CPU can operate. The standard unit of measurement for clock speed is **gigahertz** (GHz) and this is a representation of how many instruction cycles the CPU can deal with in a second. For example, a 5 GHz CPU performs five billion instruction cycles a second.

The default setting on a computer's clock is normally set to the maximum clock speed. Although clock speed is one way to measure computer power, increasing the clock speed does not automatically increase the performance of the processor. If the speed capability of the hardware used by the processor does not change, then doubling the clock speed of the processor will not increase the overall speed of processing.

Cache

Cache memory can be used to store temporarily frequently used instructions and data. It is a small capacity memory which is situated between the processor and RAM. The control unit of the CPU will automatically check the cache memory first when fetching an instruction. It is quicker to search cache memory rather than RAM because cache memory has a significantly lower storage capacity than RAM, resulting in reduced search times. Therefore, using cache memory results in an increase in processor speed.

Processor core

A core can be defined as a single processor (or a processing unit) with its own control unit, ALU and registers. More advanced CPUs contain more than one core which will increase their ability to run many programs at the same time. For example, a 'dual core' CPU has two processors whilst a 'quad core' processor will have four processors.

Tasks ✎

Use the internet to research the speeds of processors produced by different computer manufacturers.

Computer hardware devices

Microphone

The purpose of this device is to accept sound input or human voice into a computer system. A voice recognition system converts sound to text or accepts spoken commands. These systems require a user to train a computer to recognise their voice and match spoken words and phrases with those stored in a database. Microphones are also used to record music in analogue format and store it in digital format.

Headsets which include a microphone and headphones are used in gaming applications where a user plays with others online via an internet connection. They are also used in applications such as Skype, where people speak to each other over the internet using **VOIP** (**Voice over internet protocol**).

▲ A headset incorporating a microphone and headphones

Advantages of using a microphone

▶ Faster to speak using a microphone than keying words using a keyboard.

▶ It is hands free allowing users to carry out other activities at the same time as voice input.

Disadvantages of using a microphone

▶ The recognition rate of spoken words can be low if there is background noise.

▶ Sound files require greater storage capacity than a text file.

Mouse

A mouse is also referred to as a 'pointing device'. It is designed to fit under the hand and when moved controls the **pointer** on a visual display unit (VDU). A mouse uses built-in sensors to detect movements and send corresponding signals back to the computer. A mouse can also use infrared or wireless technology which removes the need to connect the mouse to a computer with a **USB** cable.

▲ A mouse uses sensors to detect movement.

A mouse includes two or three buttons which are used to make selections on the screen. On a typical mouse, the left-hand button is used to make selections such as selecting options from menus, selecting icons and positioning the **cursor** on the screen, while the right-hand button is used to display a pop-up menu at the position of the cursor. The middle button is used to scroll up and down the VDU.

Advantages of using a mouse

▶ Easy to use and requires little or no training.

▶ Quicker to select menus and icons compared to using a keyboard.

Disadvantages of using a mouse

▶ Experienced users find it slow compared to using 'hot keys'. For example pressing ctrl + P to print is quicker than selecting a menu and the print option.

▶ They need a flat surface (additional space) to function properly.

Graphics digitiser

A graphics digitiser allows a user to hand-draw images or pictures in a similar way to how we draw with a pencil on a sheet of paper. In some ICT applications, they are also used to capture handwritten signatures. The device consists of a flat surface and a stylus. The stylus works in the same way as a pencil. It allows the user to input data using a 'freehand' mode. The image does not usually appear on the tablet itself but is displayed on the computer's VDU.

▲ A graphics digitiser

Advantages of using a graphics digitiser

▶ More natural to draw diagrams with a stylus than with a mouse.

▶ Produce more accurate and detailed drawings using a stylus.

Disadvantages of using a graphics digitiser

▶ Not suitable for selecting menus and pointing at menu items.

▶ Compared to a mouse the graphics digitiser is much more expensive.

Touchscreen

Touchscreens avoid the need for a mouse. Touching the screen is the same as clicking your mouse at the same position on the screen. You can tap the screen twice to perform a double-click operation and you can drag your finger across the screen to perform 'drag-and-drop' operations.

▲ Touchscreens are used in mobile phones, tourist information offices, online tests and interactive whiteboards.

A touchscreen looks similar to ordinary computer screens but consists of a clear glass panel with a touch-sensitive surface. There are several different touch-sensing technologies in use today. Touchscreens generally have an electrical current going through them. Touching the screen causes a change in voltage which is used to determine the location of the touch to the screen. Built-in computer software processes the user request by manipulating the position on the screen as a (x,y) co-ordinate.

Advantages of using a touchscreen

▶ Little ICT competence required compared to using a keyboard.

▶ Selecting and entering options much faster than using a keyboard.

Disadvantages of using a touchscreen

▶ Limited number of options available on screen.

▶ Screens can become dirty quickly.

Speaker

The majority of computers are fitted with at least one small internal speaker as a standard output device. To allow sound to be output through a speaker requires a sound card to be fitted inside the computer. The quality of the sound can be improved by using external speakers which can be connected to a computer by USB connections or wireless technology. Speakers can output music as well as the spoken word. They also allow sound output when designing **multimedia** solutions. On a daily basis the speaker communicates with the user by producing a sound alert if an error occurs or it needs the user to carry out an activity.

Advantages

▶ Useful for visually impaired users where text or figures can be spoken by the computer.
▶ Natural way to communicate with users.

Disadvantages

▶ External speakers require additional desk space compared to using headphones.
▶ Speakers can distract other users in the same office who are doing other tasks.

Laser printers

Laser printers produce high-quality output of both text and graphics. A computer sends the printer 'a stream of bits' which represents the page to be printed. A **laser beam** is then used to scan the image of the page onto a drum by building a pattern of static electricity. This in turn attracts toners (printer ink) to reproduce the page. Laser printers can print around 40 pages per minute.

Advantages

▶ Faster to print in bulk compared to an inkjet printer.
▶ Produce high-quality text and graphic output.

Disadvantages

▶ Colour laser printers are expensive to purchase and use.
▶ Because they are non-impact printers, multipart stationery cannot be used.

▲ Laser printers are used in school networks and in offices as they are suitable for large volumes of data.

3D printer

A 3D printer can print onto a variety of surfaces including ceramic, plastic and metal. It gradually prints a solid 3D object one layer at a time. 3D printing works alongside specialist applications software such as CAD (computer aided design) software where the printer takes the data from a computer-generated model. 3D printers are mainly used to create prototypes of real world objects that can be tested before they are mass produced.

▲ 3D printers work alongside specialist CAD software.

Tasks

Use the internet to find applications which use the input and output devices included in this section.

▲ A hard disc drive

Advantages of 3D printers

▶ Time taken to produce an object is much faster than using conventional methods.

▶ Costs of designing and producing an object are cheaper because less turnaround time is required.

▶ Can print onto a variety of surfaces; plastic, metal, ceramic.

Disadvantages of 3D printers

▶ Limited form of printing as it can only print a prototype (not full scale).

▶ Not yet economical for large-scale manufacturing.

Hard disc drive

A hard disc drive consists of a number of rigid discs stacked on a spindle and enclosed in a sealed unit. The sealed unit helps to protect the discs against damage from dirt and dust. For data to be stored on a hard disc, the disc must be formatted first. This involves dividing each disc surface into a number of tracks (or concentric circular paths). Each track is then divided into smaller areas, called sectors, which allow data to be stored as blocks. Each disc has two surfaces. To allow data to be read or written onto the disc, read/write heads are allocated to each surface. As the discs rotate at high speeds the read/write heads move back and forth across the surface.

Advantages of hard disc drives

▶ The cost per gigabyte is cheaper than other forms of external storage.

▶ Storage capacity is much greater compared to solid state storage devices.

Disadvantages of hard disc drives

▶ Due to moving parts such as read/write heads they are prone to breaking down.

▶ Access speeds are slower than the speed of 'flash' memory devices.

High-definition (HD) storage media

High-definition storage media use laser technology to store and retrieve data at high data transfer speeds to and from optical discs such as Blu-ray™ discs. Although they are similar in size to a DVD they have a larger storage capacity; they can store over 50 GB of data (more than ten times the amount that can be stored on a DVD). Instead of a red laser (used on a DVD) they use a blue laser which burns much smaller pits onto the surface. This increases the density and therefore the storage capacity. They are used to store high-definition data such as films without any loss of quality.

Solid-state storage devices

A solid-state storage device does not contain any moving parts (such as rotating discs). The storage components are embedded as part of an electronic circuit board. They are referred to as 'flash memory' and are described as **non-volatile** as they can retain the contents of memory when the power to the device is turned off. USB memory sticks are a type of solid-state storage and are attractive to users as they are compact, portable and contain a large storage capacity. As they do not require a software driver to be installed they are often described as 'plug and play' devices.

Memory cards

These are electronic flash memory storage devices used in a range of digital devices including mobile phones, digital cameras and MP4 players. For example, in mobile phones a SIM (subscriber identity module) card is used to store data. An additional memory card can be added to the phone to store music, photos and videos. These are compact and non-volatile storage devices. Memory cards come in a variety of shapes and sizes such as SD cards and mini-SD cards. Using a USB connection, data from these cards can be downloaded to a computer.

Smart cards

Bank cards use a form of flash memory known as 'chip and PIN'. These cards contain a small embedded integrated circuit (IC) which allows data to be written to and read from the card using a smart-card reader. They are small in capacity and are reliable. They are also used in other applications including satellite TV cards and hotel and office door entry systems.

Internal memory

Internal memory is divided into categories:

1 RAM (random access memory)

2 ROM (read only memory)

3 Cache memory.

RAM (random access memory)

This type of memory can be read from or written to. It is **volatile** which means the contents of the memory are lost when the machine is switched off. It is used to hold programs and data that are currently being used such as parts of the operating system, applications software, for example, word processing software, and documents being edited. The contents of RAM change as the user switches to a different application program. All programs and data including those which are currently in RAM are also stored permanently using a storage device such as a hard disc. Typical RAM size in a home computer is 64 GB. The size of RAM can also influence the speed of the processor (the larger the RAM capacity the faster the processor).

Tasks

Research a range of storage devices and compare prices with storage capacity.

ROM (read only memory)

This type of memory can be read from but not written to. Programs stored on ROM are permanent which means the contents cannot be altered. Therefore if we describe RAM as volatile then ROM is non-volatile. ROM is used to store programs that are frequently required by the computer such as the boot program for Windows that runs automatically when the computer is switched on.

Cache memory

Cache memory is a type of memory used by the CPU and is similar to RAM in that instructions can be read or written.

Cache memory is discussed further on page 34 of this chapter.

Checkpoint ✓

▷ The CPU has three main components: control unit, arithmetic and logic unit (ALU), and immediate access store (IAS).

▷ A register in the CPU is a high-speed memory location used for a specific purpose; for example, the MAR stores the current address of the current instruction being executed.

▷ Speed of a processor depends on clock speed, cache memory and the processor core.

▷ There are a range of dedicated input devices available to a computer system such as microphones, mice and touchscreens.

▷ There are a range of dedicated output devices available to a computer system such as speakers and printers.

▷ Solid-state storage devices include memory cards and smart cards.

▷ Internal memory of a computer system includes RAM, ROM and cache.

Practice questions

1 Name and describe the role of the main components of the CPU. [9 marks]

2 Explain the difference between the MAR and the MDR. [4 marks]

3 Describe how clock speed influences the performance of a computer's processor. [4 marks]

4 State two advantages of using a touchscreen as an input device. [4 marks]

5 State two disadvantages of using a microphone to input data to a computer system. [4 marks]

6 Briefly describe the main features of a 3D printer. [5 marks]

7 Name and describe two types of solid-state storage devices. [6 marks]

8 Explain the difference between ROM and RAM. [4 marks]

9 State a use for ROM. [2 marks]

10 Explain the purpose of cache memory. [3 marks]

Chapter 6 Network technologies

What this chapter covers

▶ Computer networks – LAN and WAN

▶ World Wide Web, internet and intranet

▶ Network communications technology

▶ Network resources

▶ Network topologies

Computer networks – LAN and WAN

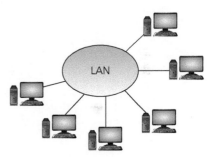

A **network** consists of a number of computers linked together either by cable or using wireless technology. This allows computers on a network to share resources including hardware and software. Computers on the network can also communicate with each other. A standalone computer is not connected to a network.

A computer network can be a **LAN** (local area network) or a **WAN** (wide area network). A LAN is spread over a small geographical area, such as a building or an office. A WAN is spread over a large geographical area on a global scale and requires a telecommunications link, such as a fibre optic cable or a satellite, to allow computers on the network to communicate.

Organisations view networking as an essential and reliable way of sharing information in the business by linking their computers together either by cable or wirelessly.

Advantages of using networks

▶ Users can save their work on the file server and retrieve it on any other computer within the network.

▶ Expensive hardware devices such as laser printers can be shared by all computers on the network.

▶ When files are stored on a file server it allows data to be shared throughout an organisation.

▶ Backing up data files can be done at the file server. This is more efficient than backing up data which is stored across an organisation on a number of individual computers.

▶ Security on a network can be managed centrally by controlling access to data and software amongst users.

▶ Installing software and updates once onto the file server will allow all computers to access software quickly.

Disadvantages of using networks

▶ When a software virus is installed onto a network, it can quickly spread, affecting all user data and the organisation's software.

▶ When a large number of users are logged onto the network using large data files and different software applications the network speed can slow down if there is a limit on the bandwidth.

▶ The set-up costs can be expensive as additional hardware such as file servers, network interface cards, switches and routers has to be purchased

▶ When a network is installed additional staff are required to ensure it is fully maintained. This increases staff costs.

World Wide Web, internet and intranet

Although the **internet** and the **World Wide Web** (WWW) are separate technologies, they work closely together. The internet is an example of a WAN, which allows information to pass between computers linked to a global network: it is a method of transporting data. The WWW is an application which uses the internet.

A website has a unique address, known as its **URL** (uniform resource locator), on the WWW. Each website consists of a number of webpages developed using a web authoring language such as **HTML** (hypertext markup language). Webpages are interconnected using **hyperlinks** and the first page is called the 'home page'. To allow websites to be accessed using the internet requires a **communications protocol** known as **http** (hypertext transfer protocol) (see p.52 Protocols used for data transfer section).

While the internet is accessible to any user who has a communications link, an **intranet** is a private network set up as a secure website, owned and managed by an organisation. An intranet uses the same communications protocol as the internet, but only authorised users, with a username and password, can access it. This allows people employed by an organisation to work remotely from home and access their documents securely. Like the internet, intranets are used to share information, communicate and facilitate discussion through bulletin boards and electronic messaging facilities.

Through developments within C2K, more and more schools have access to an intranet, which allows staff and students to access course resources and communicate more easily. A major advantage of having an intranet in schools is that once learning resources are uploaded they can be accessed and viewed by all students 24/7.

The 'internet of things' (IoT) is a phrase used to describe the future impact of the internet on how we live and work. Today, **broadband** internet access is available in more geographical locations and to more people than ever before. There is also a greater range

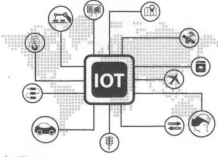

▲ The internet of things

of devices that can connect to the internet via built-in sensors using Wi-Fi technology. For example a fitness watch can collect biological data about a person such as heart rate and sleeping habits and, in turn, this can be communicated to a computer using Wi-Fi for further analysis by the user.

The scope of IoT is increasing as the cost of this technology decreases, as more Wi-Fi-enabled devices are developed, and as high-speed broadband becomes ever cheaper. The increased use of smartphones and apps allows people more control in their lives; for example people can now use an app to control the central heating in their house when they are away from home. Generally, any device that can be turned off or on can now be controlled by Wi-Fi technology.

Network communications technology

The development of wireless and optical fibre communications technology has led to an increase in the use of networks, such as mobile phone networks.

Wi-Fi (wireless fidelity)

Modern devices are manufactured with a built-in wireless adapter which allows the user to connect to a **Wi-Fi** network. Wi-Fi connections are made possible through radio waves and a wireless router; this means there is no need for network cables. Wi-Fi networks are used in many places, such as libraries, schools, home, airports and coffee shops. A wireless router providing access to the internet at home makes use of Wi-Fi. These home networks need to be protected by requiring the user to log on using a password.

Using Wi-Fi, data can be transmitted at speeds of up to 54 Mbps depending on the standard of Wi-Fi being used.

Advantage of using Wi-Fi

▶ Being able to set up networks without the need for cabling.

Disadvantage of using Wi-Fi

▶ Signal strength varies depending on how far you are from the wireless router.

Bluetooth

Bluetooth uses short-range wireless technology (in the form of radio signals) to connect two devices together allowing data to be transferred between them. This means the devices need to be in close proximity. For the devices to begin transferring data they have to be synchronised. Since the devices communicate directly with each other there is no need to have a router or a third-party provider, which makes this technology cheaper to use. Bluetooth also uses less power than other wireless technologies.

Typical uses of Bluetooth technology include the ability to make hands-free phone calls, using a wireless mouse with a computer or connecting a digital camera to a printer.

Tasks

Use a search engine to research how the 'internet of things' impacts our lifestyles.

▲ Optical fibre

Optical fibre

Optical fibre is a technology that uses very thin glass strands to send data at very fast transmission speeds. Data is transmitted as pulses of light. A fibre-optic cable consists of a bundle of glass strands. Each strand carries one data signal which means many data signals can be sent at one time in the bundle. The advantage of using glass rather than copper is that signals (or data) cannot be interfered with by hackers, meaning security of data is very good. Due to the greater **bandwidth**, a larger capacity of data can be sent over a period of time. Drawbacks of using optical-fibre technology are that it is very expensive to install and it requires the use of **repeaters** for data to travel over longer distances.

Mobile communications technology

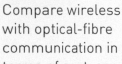

Tasks

Compare wireless with optical-fibre communication in terms of cost, speed and reliability.

4G (generation technology) mobile-phone technology is capable of high-speed data access and high-quality video streaming using wireless technology on a global scale. It has allowed mobile-phone providers to expand access to multimedia applications at higher speeds on their networks and at the same time lower the cost per bit for downloading data. Due to the expensive hardware required, its coverage is focused on areas where population is greater. One of the drawbacks for a mobile-phone 4G user is that it uses more battery life. 5G mobile-phone technology is more reliable and works across a greater range with greater speeds than 4G.

Network resources

Network interface card (NIC)

Ethernet port

▲ A network interface card (NIC)

A **network interface card** (NIC) is an electronic circuit board that needs to be installed in a computer to enable it to be connected to a network. Each computer on the network must have its own dedicated NIC so that it can communicate with the file server and the other computers on the network. The NIC also provides a 'port' on the computer to allow a network cable (such as Ethernet) to be attached to the network interface card.

Portable computers such as laptops are supplied with a standard wireless network interface card (WNIC) provided by the manufacturer.

Network cables

A network cable physically connects a computer to a network. These cables are plugged directly into the NIC within the computer and then connected to another device, such as a switch. Generally, cables are made of copper and the data travels along the cables to and from the file server. Network cables are classified into categories depending on speed of transmission, for example, CAT6 cabling generally has increased transmission performance compared to CAT5 cabling.

Switch

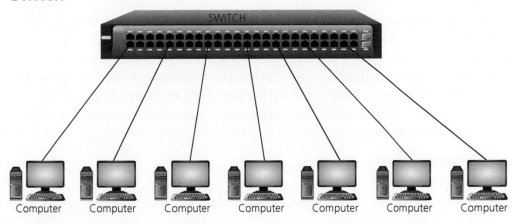

▲ A switch checks the destination of data received and forwards it to the intended computer.

A **switch** is a hardware device which is a single connection point for computers on a network. It allows a large number of computers to be connected to it directly using network cables. A switch checks the destination of data it receives and ensures it is forwarded to the intended computer.

Router

A **router** is a hardware device which connects a number of networks together either by cable or wireless. Routers are situated at gateways, where two or more networks connect. The router examines data as it passes, and forwards the data using the most appropriate route to its destination. IP addresses are used to determine the route the data travels on. A router would be used at home to connect your laptop to the internet. Some routers can filter incoming and outgoing data using a firewall feature.

Network topologies

Bus network

In this network, all computers are connected to a main cable known as a 'backbone'. Data can travel in both directions along the backbone. Terminators are placed at each end of the backbone to stop signals bouncing back onto the backbone. To add a new computer to a bus network, its cable is attached to the backbone. If a cable attached to the backbone fails, only that computer will fail to operate. If the backbone cable fails then the whole network will not operate.

Star network

In this network, all computers are connected by their own cable to a central powerful computer known as a file server. All data on the network must pass through the file server. If a cable fails it will only affect the computer it is connected to and the rest of the network will operate as normal. An additional computer can be added by attaching it (using its own cable) to the file server.

Tasks ✎

Use the internet to investigate the costs of different network resources.

▲ A bus network

▲ A star network

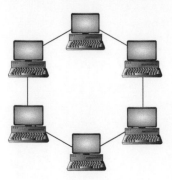

▲ A ring network

Ring network

In this network there is no central or controlling computer. Each computer is directly connected to two other adjacent computers to form a ring. All data travels in one direction by visiting each computer in turn until it reaches its intended destination. If the cable fails then the whole network is affected. To add a new computer to the network it is more difficult than a bus or a star network as the cable between two existing computers has to be broken and each part of the broken cable attached to the new computer.

Checkpoint ✓

▷ A network consists of a number of computers linked together by cable or wireless technology.

▷ Organisations view networking as an essential way of sharing information by linking their computers together either by cable or wirelessly.

▷ A LAN is spread over a small geographical area, such as a building or an office, whereas a WAN is spread over a large geographical area on a global scale and requires a telecommunications link.

▷ The internet is accessible to any user who has a communications link whereas an intranet is a private network set up as a secure website that requires users to login.

▷ Wi-Fi, Bluetooth and optical fibre are ways in which computers on a network can communicate.

▷ NICs, network cables, switches and routers are examples of network resources.

▷ Bus, star and ring are methods used to design a local area network.

Practice questions

1 Distinguish between a LAN and a WAN. [2 marks]

2 Distinguish between the internet and an intranet. [4 marks]

3 Describe three ways you can make use of the 'internet of things' in your everyday life. [6 marks]

4 State two features of Wi-Fi technology. [2 marks]

5 State one advantage and one disadvantage of using fibre optic as a communications medium. [2 marks]

6 Name and describe three network resources. [9 marks]

7 Describe the main features of a bus network. [6 marks]

8 State two advantages and two disadvantages of using networks. [4 marks]

Chapter 7 Cyberspace, network security and data transfer

What this chapter covers

▶ Cyber crime and threats to cyber security

▶ Malware

▶ Network protection

▶ Protocols used for data transfer

Cyber crime and threats to cyber security

Cyber crime is defined as using a computer to commit a crime. Apart from planting viruses, cyber crime also includes theft of personal information, stealing money from credit cards and theft of company data that could be sold to competitors. People involved in cyber crime are known as 'cyber criminals'.

Threat	Example of threat to cyber security
Hacking	A **hacker** is a person who gains unauthorised access to a computer with the intention of corrupting data stored on a hard drive/file server or to steal data.
Pornography	Pornography is often used as a means of hiding malware. When an employee downloads adult content they are increasing the risk of organisation data being corrupted by a virus or stolen by an unauthorised user.
Cyber stalking	Where individuals use technology to harass others, for example by sending inappropriate emails or making inappropriate comments on **social media**.
Data theft	The theft of customer records to obtain personal details which are then used to commit identify fraud such as credit card or passport applications.
Denial of service	A malicious attack on a network, for example disrupting connections to a web server, preventing users from logging on to access their data or email accounts because access to the internet is denied.
Digital forgery	Intentionally and falsely altering digital content, such as pictures and documents. For example, changing a passport photograph and/or names to sell on to a criminal who wishes to enter a country.
Cyber defamation	Using the internet with the intention to damage the reputation of a person or organisation by posting slanderous messages using mediums such as electronic forums or bulletin boards.
Spamming	Sending bulk junk emails such as adverts for products. As a result, the user's email inbox becomes overloaded, as the spam emails take up a large proportion of the bandwidth. Time is wasted opening and reading such emails.
Phishing	Sending emails that appear to be from a reliable source. These emails often ask the user to update their personal information by clicking a hyperlink to a webpage. This information will then be used by hackers for the purpose of identity theft.

Malware

Malware is malicious software that is downloaded onto a computer unintentionally via the internet or from email attachments, or even by connecting a portable storage device such as a USB storage device. Malware can be annoying and can also threaten the security of computers. Computer systems are under constant threat from malware such as viruses, Trojans horses, worms, key loggers and spyware.

Virus

A **virus** is a computer program which is designed to deliberately damage or make a computer system unreliable by slowing down the processor. A virus can store itself automatically on a computer hard drive as a hidden file but can be activated when a certain program is opened or when a predetermined condition is met, for example a certain date. It can spread without any intervention from one computer to another.

Virus protection software can be installed on computers to prevent potential attacks. The anti-virus software is designed to scan a computer regularly, searching for potential threats. The software is automatically updated, at least daily, to take account of any new viruses.

Trojan horse

A Trojan horse gains entry to a user's computer 'in disguise'. The user is tricked into thinking that it is a useful piece of software, such as an anti-virus program and, as such, the instructions encourage the user to open and download the software. Once installed, some Trojans can do serious damage, such as deleting data files, while others can be more annoying by continually changing your desktop layout. Other Trojans known as 'backdoor Trojans' provide hackers with an entry point into a computer without the need to enter a password, allowing access to personal data such as bank details.

Worm

A worm is designed to spread from computer to computer around a network without the need to be attached to any document or program. A worm spreads around a computer system by replicating itself. For example, it could copy itself on to every contact in an email address book and then travel to each recipient when an email is sent. It can then do the same to all email addresses in the recipient's address book as it continues to replicate. This can cause problems on a network as the worm requires bandwidth which results in slower data transmission speeds.

Key logger

A key logger is a piece of software that is designed to record a user's keystrokes, for example the content keyed in to emails or to the web address bar of a browser. The user is unaware that this is happening. The keystrokes are saved as a log file and then sent to the person who created the software at a later stage. Key-logger software is used to steal personal information from users but also is used by employers to monitor employees' computer activities.

Spyware

Spyware is malicious software which is secretly installed on a user's computer. It uses an internet connection to collect information about user activity, such as the websites they visit. Without the user knowing, spyware can sometimes be bundled with 'shareware' software that is downloaded from the internet. After spyware software has been installed, it tracks a user's activities, gathering useful information such as credit card and password details. Spyware uses valuable computer memory, which can cause applications to crash due to lack of memory available. In some cases, user information is collected and then sold on to third-party advertisers to allow them to market products to a number of users.

Network protection

Data encryption

Data which is transmitted on a network is at risk of being intercepted by unauthorised users. To prevent this happening, organisations use **data-encryption** techniques. Encryption uses special software to encode or 'scramble' data before it is transmitted to make the data unreadable or meaningless if intercepted. Only a user with the encryption-key software can unscramble the data when it arrives at its destination.

Sender		Recipient
Clear text		Clear text
Hello	Encrypted text	Hello
	%fd$jh	
Encryption		Decryption
Recipient's public key		Recipient's private key

▲ The process of data encryption

Usernames and passwords

The network manager allocates each user on a network with a unique user ID and a randomly generated password made up of a series of letters and digits. When a user logs on for the first time, they are given the option to create a new password, which normally needs to be entered twice for verification purposes. Generally passwords should be eight characters long, be a mix of letters and digits and include at least one upper-case character. This guidance helps the security of the network. Users are usually 'forced' to change their passwords regularly by the network software thus reducing the chances of password theft.

The user details are stored by the system in a secure database. Each time a user logs on, the system checks their user ID and password against a database of user details stored on the file server and because each user has a unique user ID and password, a network manager can maintain a log of who has been on the network, when and the location of the computer.

> **Tasks** 🖊
>
> Evaluate this statement: 'Anti-virus software is important to an organisation that sells goods on the World Wide Web'.

At the login stage the user ID can be seen but the password usually appears as asterisks (***). This means other users cannot see the actual password, reducing the risk of unauthorised access to a user's account. User IDs and passwords are checked against those stored on the file server: if the password and user ID entered are not valid the user will not be allowed to access the network. Some networks only allow users a limited number of attempts at logging on and disable the user ID for a period of time after too many unsuccessful login attempts.

Access levels

Another way of keeping the network secure is to limit the activities different users can perform by allocating different levels of access to different users. For example, students in a school may have controlled access to data files, such as 'read only' access. This means the user can see the contents of the files but cannot modify any data in those files.

Access rights can be classified as 'read only', 'read and copy' and 'read and write' and are stored in a table linked to the user ID and password database. Each time a user attempts to access a data file the computer can check what level of access has been allocated. If they do not have the appropriate access right they will be denied access.

Backup

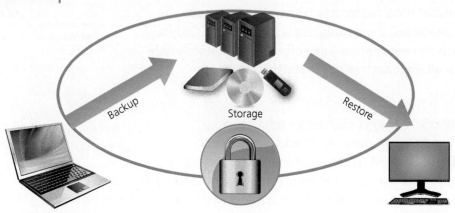

▲ Backup of data

If data stored on a network is lost, or becomes corrupted, the system must have a method of recovering it to allow the network to function again. The user's data needs to be protected and stored securely. Network systems use a backup process to make sure there is a copy of the data that can be loaded on to the system if the original data is lost or corrupted. Backup copies of data are stored on a variety of storage media in a safe location away from the network server(s), such as an external hard drive. Network backups are usually automatically scheduled to run at certain times, such as the end of each day. When the backup is used, the system software runs a 'restore' program which will transfer the data back on to the network server(s).

Firewall

A **firewall** can be a hardware device or a software program. It monitors and filters data entering or leaving a network. It uses security settings or rules that block data which does not comply with the organisation's security policy from entering or leaving. At the same time it allows data that *does* comply with the security policy to enter or leave.

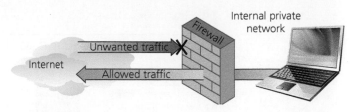

▲ A firewall monitors and filters data

A firewall can prevent activities that may affect the network's performance, for example:

▶ hackers from entering the network via the internet

▶ viruses and spam from entering or leaving the network via the internet

▶ users/computers within the network from uploading or downloading undesirable data to and from the internet.

Firewall software can produce reports detailing unauthorised access attempts and web addresses that do not comply with the organisation's security policy.

Tasks

Research how C2K uses network security to protect user accounts from unauthorised access.

Protocols used for data transfer

Computers on a network need to be able to communicate with each other to allow data to be sent and received. In simple terms they must be able to 'speak the same language'. A communications protocol is an agreed standard or set of rules for sending or receiving data on a network. Therefore if a computer receives data on a network, it must support the communications protocol of the sending computer. There are many different types of agreed communications protocols which are defined by organisations who manufacture network hardware and develop software.

The **protocol** used on the internet is **TCP/IP** (transmission control protocol/internet protocol). The use of a router ensures that data travels on the correct network path and arrives at the correct computer.

FTP (file transport protocol)

FTP (file transport protocol) is a widely used protocol that allows users to send and receive files over the internet. Users access a file server to download or upload files. This protocol can also be used to send software updates to network devices such as routers and switches. To ensure that data is sent in a secure way, data is encrypted and usernames and passwords are used to prevent unauthorised access to the file server.

Http (hypertext transfer protocol)

Http (hypertext transfer protocol) is a protocol used by the WWW to identify and transfer webpages using the internet. When a user enters a URL into the address bar of the browser, this protocol sends a command to the web server to request the required webpage. If a webpage cannot be located (because

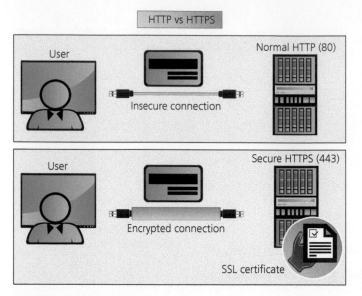

HTTP vs HTTPS

User — Insecure connection — Normal HTTP (80)

User — Encrypted connection — Secure HTTPS (443) — SSL certificate

 Http versus https

it has been deleted or the user keyed in the incorrect web address) the http will report an error back to the user from the web server. These error messages are referred to as 'status codes', for example '404 File Not Found'.

Https (hypertext transfer protocol secure)

Https (hypertext transfer protocol secure) is similar to http but uses a **secure socket layer** (SSL) to ensure data is transmitted securely. It is designed to allow access to a secure web server for secure data communication. It uses encryption for sending data and decryption for receiving data. The main use of this protocol is in financial applications, such as banking and **e-commerce** where credit card or PayPal payment transactions are managed on the WWW.

Tasks

Investigate the types of applications that would require the use of the https protocol.

When using http it is possible to intercept data; an individual could gain access to a customer's personal bank details such as their credit card number. When using https, an individual could still gain access to personal data but it would be scrambled and therefore would be meaningless. **Web browsers** display a padlock icon on screen to indicate that the webpage currently in use is secure.

Checkpoint ✓

▷ Threats to cyber security include hacking, pornography, cyber stalking, data theft, denial of service, digital forgery, cyber defamation, spamming and phishing.

▷ Malware comes in different forms that include viruses, Trojan horses, worms, key loggers and spyware.

▷ Organisations use encryption, usernames and passwords, levels of access, backup and firewalls to protect data on a network.

▷ Protocols are used to allow different networks to communicate.

▷ Networks use a range of protocols including FTP, http and https to communicate.

Practice questions ?

1 Name and describe three threats to cyber security. [9 marks]

2 Describe the difference between Trojan horse and spyware as forms of malware. [4 marks]

3 Identify and explain three different levels of access. [9 marks]

4 Explain how data encryption is used when transferring files across a network. [4 marks]

5 Compare these internet protocols: http and https. [6 marks]

Chapter 8 Cloud computing

What this chapter covers

▶ What is cloud computing?

▶ Impact of cloud computing on gaming

▶ Impact of cloud computing on file storage

▶ Impact of cloud computing on file sharing

What is cloud computing?

The term cloud computing refers to '**the cloud**' whereby a number of computing resources, including data storage and software applications, are offered and delivered on demand to an organisation using the internet. In cloud computing, organisations access their data and programs over the internet instead of accessing their own hard drive(s) locally.

Cloud computing is growing quickly, attracting both small and large organisations to subscribe on a global scale.

▲ Devices that can use the internet can access data stored in the cloud.

Advantages of cloud computing

▶ Cost effective: the cost of providing software, maintenance and upgrades for cloud computing is cheaper than buying software licences for multiple users. Cloud computing providers also offer options such as 'pay as you go'. An organisation can take advantage of the flexibility offered by the cloud by increasing or decreasing their demand for bandwidth.

▶ Unlimited storage: if an organisation is using their own hardware resources there is a limit to the storage capacity of the hard drives. In the cloud, unlimited storage capacity is available.

▶ Software updates: the cloud provides organisations with software and automatic software updates. This removes the need for an organisation to spend time manually scheduling and installing it themselves.

▶ Backup and recovery: the responsibility for this sits with the cloud provider and therefore there is no need to have additional storage devices available for backup files or procedures for **data recovery**. In the cloud, data is backed up automatically at regular intervals.

▶ Greater accessibility to information: once signed up to a cloud provider, employees of an organisation can access their information anywhere, and from any device, as long as they have an internet connection. This allows greater flexibility for employees in choosing where they work from.

▶ Reduction in carbon footprint: since less technology is needed within an organisation using the cloud, demand for electricity is reduced which reduces the organisation's carbon footprint. This helps to promote an environmentally friendly workplace. Our carbon footprint is a measure of the impact of our activities on the environment.

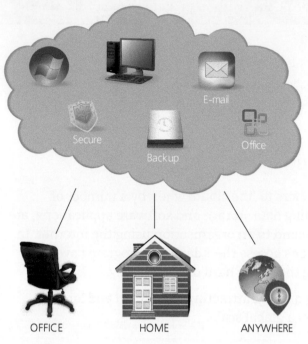

E-mail

Secure

Backup

Office

OFFICE   HOME   ANYWHERE

▲ Data is accessible anywhere at anytime.

Disadvantages of cloud computing

▶ Bandwidth limitations: some cloud providers only offer a limited bandwidth allowance. If an organisation uses more than their allowance, the additional charges can be very expensive.

▶ Potential downtime: cloud computing is reliant on communications technology as it is internet-based. If the internet connection or a communications hardware device, such as a router, fails then there is no access to the cloud. Additionally, if the speed of connection slows down due to heavy internet traffic this will impact an organisation. If the cloud servers require maintenance, an organisation's information and data may not be accessible until this is completed.

▶ Security: security and privacy are always compromised when using the internet to send and receive sensitive data. A cloud provider will manage hardware and software resources but they cannot guarantee that all data will be totally secure. For example, in recent times credit card companies have reported the hacking of customer databases, resulting in the theft of customer account details.

▶ Customer support: organisations who use cloud computing require customer support services to help resolve technical issues. This can be time-consuming if the response of the cloud provider is slow. It can also be expensive as the organisation may have to pay an additional fee to ensure they receive the help required.

Tasks ✎

Investigate advantages to a school in using the cloud.

Impact of cloud computing on gaming

Cloud computing is a major influence in the gaming industry. Privacy is an ongoing issue; games are normally produced and sold to customers in disc format, but these can be illegally copied and then sold on to others. Although there are laws in place to protect the game suppliers against this content theft, they are difficult to enforce. The selling of pirated games can lead to a loss of sales, which can have implications when funding is required to develop new games.

By using the cloud, game producers are able to reduce their costs as they don't need to pay high street shops to sell their games. They can pass these savings to customers by reducing the price of the game. The customer who buys the computer game can download the game immediately when it becomes available, as opposed to waiting until it is released and distributed into physical shops.

With developments in hardware and software, the customer can also benefit from the cloud. Modern games are produced with higher resolution graphics which require faster and more powerful gaming hardware. Using the cloud means that gamers do not need to keep purchasing more up-to-date hardware. They have access to powerful game servers and game streaming, which can support more complex visual effects, and are able to access additional storage without the need to expand their computer's processing power and hard-drive capacity. The drawback for the user is that they need to ensure their broadband capacity is capable of streaming high-quality graphics.

Since the internet is global, game producers have the advantage of access to a much larger global customer base. This could lead to increased sales resulting in higher profits. To ensure customers are happy with the game products, software updates and software patches can be applied via the game servers and made available to gamers immediately. Game suppliers can also release demo versions of new games to attract customers.

> **Tasks**
>
> Research the following statement: 'Gaming is better on the cloud than buying discs from a game shop.'

Impact of cloud computing on file storage

One of the major impacts of cloud-based systems is the facility to store data files on very powerful high-capacity cloud servers. When users are working with their data files, automatic saving to the cloud takes place every few seconds. This reduces the chances of losing data considerably.

Cloud providers also ensure that user files are stored permanently online without the need for a local hard drive. Unless the user removes the file it will not disappear from the cloud. The cloud providers are also able recover lost files if their server(s) crash and return them to their original state. This can all take place without the user needing to understand the technical processes involved in file recovery.

Impact of cloud computing on file sharing

Cloud technology allows employees from an organisation to collaborate and share folders and files from anywhere in the world. A user can upload files to the cloud and share these with other users who can then edit the files themselves. This way of working enables employees from different parts of the world to collaborate as a team on the same project.

Collaborative working, where each user can make changes to files and documents stored on the cloud, means that there needs to be a process of synchronisation (or sync). This ensures that when one user makes a change to a file, this change will appear in the versions used by others. It is also possible to maintain a history of any changes made to the documents online and send automated email alerts to employees when changes are made to documents.

Google Docs is an example of a cloud-based application that allows users to create online documents, presentations and spreadsheets and share these with others who can all access these files at the same time. Similarly, Microsoft Office 365 provides online versions of Word, Excel and PowerPoint which can be used from the cloud to allow employees to create files for sharing.

Tasks

Using the internet, investigate collaborative tools available for file sharing from different cloud providers.

Checkpoint ✓

▷ The cloud allows resources to be accessed on demand through the internet.

▷ Cloud computing provides unlimited storage and backup facilities to organisations.

▷ Cloud computing relies on communications technology, so if the internet connection fails it does not work.

▷ Using the cloud for gaming allows the user to access powerful game servers and make use of game streaming.

▷ Organisations use collaborative tools available in the cloud for file sharing.

Practice questions ?

1 Define the term 'cloud computing'. [2 marks]

2 State three advantages to an organisation of using cloud computing. [3 marks]

3 Describe two disadvantages of cloud computing to an organisation. [4 marks]

4 Evaluate the impact of cloud computing on gaming. [6 marks]

5 Describe how files are stored on the cloud. [4 marks]

6 Discuss the benefits of using the cloud for a group of employees working on a project. [6 marks]

Chapter 9 Ethical, legal and environmental impact of digital technology on wider society

What this chapter covers

▶ Legislation relevant to digital technology

▶ Ethical impact of technology on society

▶ Impact of digital technology on employment

▶ Digital-technology-related health and safety issues

Legislation relevant to digital technology

Consumer Contracts Regulations 2013

The Consumer Contracts Regulations 2013 specify the rights of customers when shopping online. They require online traders to provide customers with a full description of the products available, product prices, delivery charges, methods of payment accepted and information on how products can be returned. A customer has the right to cancel an order, and be given a full refund, for physical products (up to 14 days from the date received); if they download digital content they will not be entitled to cancel their order.

If a customer purchases DVDs or Blu-rays (high definition video or games discs) and breaks the security seal, they lose the right to cancel their order. This also applies to digital goods that are tailor-made by a company, such as a digital wedding album. Companies are also not allowed to charge for items customers place in electronic shopping baskets until the customer goes to the 'checkout' and agrees to purchase items. For products sold online that include digital content, the supplier must provide details on hardware and software compatibility.

Data Protection Act 1998

Personal data is data about an individual. The Data Protection Act 1998 controls how this personal information can be used by organisations. The legislation protects the rights of individuals whose data is being held. The Act has strict rules that must be obeyed when using and storing personal data and these are known as the 'data protection principles'. The main principles of the Data Protection Act 1998 are that personal data should:

▶ be processed fairly and lawfully with the consent of the data subject.

▶ be used for the specified purpose only.

- ▶ be adequate and relevant for its intended purpose.
- ▶ be accurate and up to date.
- ▶ not be kept for longer than necessary.
- ▶ be processed in accordance with the rights of the data subject.
- ▶ be held safely and securely.
- ▶ not be transferred outside the European Union without adequate protection.

Organisations which do not comply with the terms of the Data Protection Act 1998 can be prosecuted. It is therefore critical that organisations have procedures in place to ensure that data is held securely, that it is accurately maintained and that it is used appropriately.

Organisations are encouraged to have policies in place to ensure that any such data they hold is both accurate and up to date. Ensuring that data is up to date may involve regular contact with **data subjects**, asking them to verify currently held details. There should also be measures in place to protect the integrity and physical security of personal data held, such as access rights, firewalls and backup procedures.

Organisations should also provide regular staff training to raise awareness of data protection issues and their responsibility for ensuring the terms of the Act are complied with. Data subjects should also be made aware of their rights under the terms of the Act.

Organisations must employ a **data controller** who is responsible for controlling the way in which personal data is processed.

The government employs an **information commissioner** who is responsible for enforcing the Act and promoting good practice to organisations responsible for processing personal data, as well as making the general public aware of their rights under the Act.

Copyright Designs and Patents Act 1988

This Act is designed to protect the property rights of those individuals and organisations that create and produce material based on original ideas. Material of this kind is referred to as 'intellectual property' and this includes computer software. The Act helps to deter piracy – the illegal copying (or downloading) and distribution of software without permission.

Many organisations use computer networks to carry out their business activities. When they purchase a software package to install on their network, they must also purchase a **software licence** to cover the number of users (or computers) using the software. If the organisation wants more users to access the software package at a later date, then they have to purchase more licences. Any organisation distributing software without a proper licence is breaking the Copyright Designs and Patents Act 1988. Software producers can subscribe to organisations such as FACT (Federation Against Copyright Theft) to protect against illegal use of their software.

Enforcing and controlling the Copyright Designs and Patents Act 1988 requires an organisation to have policies ensuring employees are aware of the terms of the Act and the consequences of being in breach of it. The organisation is responsible for monitoring which employees have access to licensed software. Employees are only allowed to have authorised programs on their computers. Unauthorised software downloaded from the internet is not permitted.

Computer Misuse Act 1990

This Act is designed to protect users against computer misuse, including unauthorised access to computer systems and the deliberate hacking of computers to plant viruses or install malicious software such as spyware.

Tasks

Use the internet to research examples of when these laws have been enforced.

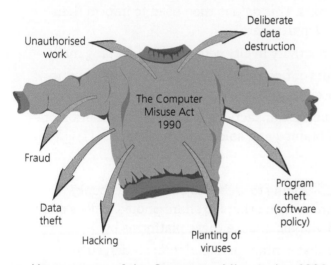

▲ Key aspects of the Computer Misuse Act 1990

The Act states that it is illegal to gain unauthorised access to change passwords and computer settings (to prevent users from accessing their accounts), or to modify software and data stored in a computer system.

Ethical impact of technology on society

Internet misuse can be seen across society:

▶ The theft of usernames and passwords, which are then used to access websites and make transactions, such as the purchasing of games or music.

▶ Piracy, where users illegally download copyrighted materials from the internet

▶ Phishing, where hackers use official-looking online adverts or emails to trick users into providing personal details.

▶ Websites created to promote violence and negative behaviour in society.

▶ Plagiarism, where students copy and paste materials for coursework assignments and sign it off as their own work.

▶ The misuse of the internet in the workplace, when employees spend too much time using the internet for personal use such as booking holidays.

This has resulted in the creation of 'acceptable use of the internet' policies that employees must agree to in their employment terms and conditions.

▶ Sharing of personal data between companies without prior permission, which is then open to misuse.

▶ Use of the 'dark web', which is a collection of websites that exist on an encrypted network and cannot be found by using traditional search engines. The searches may contain links to illegal material including terrorist activity.

▶ Use of pornography.

Our personal data can often be collected without us being fully aware of it:

▶ Loyalty cards used by supermarkets allow organisations to collect data about our shopping habits. This data is then used to inform their marketing and advertising departments.

▶ CCTV cameras monitor our activity in city centres and shopping malls.

▶ Mobile phones can transmit your geographical location at any point in time when you make or receive a phone call.

▶ By analysing credit or debit card transactions, customer information on shopping patterns can be obtained and sold on to third parties.

Social networking

Social networking involves subscribing to websites such as Facebook, Instagram and Twitter, to connect with others to share photos, videos and personal messages. Some individuals misuse these platforms by:

▶ searching for profile pages that contain personal information such as addresses or phone numbers. Problems can occur when users fail to manage their accounts to ensure no personal information is publicly available.

▶ posting racial and religious hatred (even though social networking sites discourage this use in their terms and conditions).

▶ stealing identities. Criminals can create an account to impersonate someone's identity with the intention of committing a crime. It can result in the victim being held responsible for the consequences of the crime.

GPS (global positioning system)

GPS (global positioning system) uses a number of satellites orbiting around the Earth that provide real-time information such as the geographical location of an individual. When a user makes a mobile call or is driving a car with a GPS enabled, data about their location can be tracked. If this is done without consent, this can infringe on an individual's right to privacy.

GPS systems can also be used in a positive way by:

▶ helping to track individuals who need to be monitored through the use of a tracking device. This could be offenders who are on 'home arrest' or vulnerable patients such as dementia sufferers who could wander off and get lost.

▶ the tracking of buses, taxis and company vans to help monitor and inform customers of arrival and departure times of services and goods.

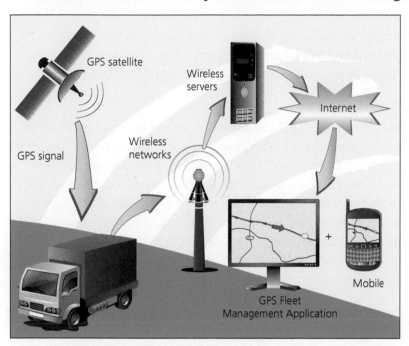

▲ Data available anywhere at any time

The increasing uptake of cloud-based services, with cloud servers situated in different countries, has implications for the security and privacy of personal data. Privacy laws vary in different countries, for example EU (European Union) laws differ from those in non-EU countries. If personal data is processed in a country with less strict laws, this could adversely impact the security of such data.

Impact of digital technology on employment

Increased job opportunities

Digital technology is changing the world of work and is a major influence on increasing job opportunities. There are now more opportunities for employment in information technology (IT) with specialist jobs in hardware and software technologies:

▶ Software engineers are required to develop and maintain programming code for new software. Larger organisations often employ their own in-house team(s) of software engineers. A typical software engineer will design, write and test programming code and is usually an integral part of a project development team.

▶ Digital media and design jobs include app and web designers, computer game designers and developers, computer-generated imagery (CGI) producers for the film industry and positions in audio and visual (AV) communication.

▶ There is a greater demand to protect people from hackers, online scams and fraud. This has led to more employment opportunities for forensic

> **Tasks** 🖉
>
> Research how different social media apps protect users' personal data.

computer analysts. These jobs focus on analysing business data ensuring that computer systems owned by organisations are secure from malicious attacks.

▶ Organisations such as banks and hospitals use database systems to store, manipulate, retrieve and backup information using database software which provides job opportunities for database administrators.

Job displacement

Modern countries have encouraged the development of technology skills in their workforces to help generate higher levels of economic growth. Therefore digital technologies have been introduced to many aspects of employment. This has changed the way some jobs are carried out. In manufacturing, for example, robots now carry out the work of a number of manual workers. Jobs that are highly repetitive and tedious for humans are often carried out by robots as in the car manufacturing industry, which uses robots for assembling and painting cars. In warehouses, heavy stock is moved from one place to another using computer-controlled forklift trucks.

▲ An automated car assembly plant

Office clerical jobs now require greater use of generic software, such as databases and spreadsheets to store and manage data, and multimedia software to produce more professional documents and websites. These advances have led to organisations reducing specialised office staff and encouraging existing staff to learn new skills.

Changes in work patterns

The development in technology has led to changing work patterns for employees and their employers. The development of 'smart' technology such

Tasks 🖉

Produce a list of new jobs created due to the developments in digital technology.

as smartphones and the development of 'smart techniques', such as cloud computing, have been major influences on our work patterns.

As cities become more congested, the environmental pressure to reduce our carbon footprint has encouraged many employees to work from home rather than using transport to travel to and from their workplace. This also helps employers reduce their overhead costs as large offices do not require renting.

Teleworking is the use of ICT to work from home. Portable wireless technology such as tablets and other mobile devices, the internet and video conferencing allow more people to carry out their work at home. Employees can log on to a company's intranet from home and still be contacted at any time using instant messaging or email.

Because of the ease of contact between office and home for the home worker, the boundaries between home and work have become less defined and employees can find this difficult to manage. There is no clear cut-off point for the end of the working day if you are always contactable, especially if you work for a global company with workers in different time zones. Businesses who want to operate in the global marketplace must be available 24 hours a day, seven days a week because of the time difference between countries. This and the upsurge in 24-hour call centres has meant that employers are now using a 'global' work base where employees from other countries carry out tasks within the business. Local employees also have to work in shifts to cover daytime and night-time hours.

Need for upskilling

In a fast-changing technological work environment people require continuous training to enable them to carry out their job. For example, office workers have to be continually trained in new software and hardware.

For the employer to ensure that staff are fully motivated in the workplace, they need to offer relevant training courses. This helps to boost morale and improve retention levels. In digital technological workplaces it is also important to ensure employees receive training for the most up-to-date software so productivity levels can continue to increase.

Digital-technology-related health and safety issues

In today's society, computers are fully integrated into the workplace. This has resulted in a great number of employees working at computers for long periods each day. There are a number of health problems and injuries that can arise because of the prolonged use of computer technology.

The Health and Safety at Work etc. Act 1974 ensures that employers have obligations to provide a safe working environment for employees who carry out their work while using a computer. The law states that organisations should have a company policy on health and safety and that employees should be aware of the contents of this policy.

There are various health problems associated with the regular use of computers.

Health problem	Description	How can it be reduced?
Repetitive strain injury (RSI)	A range of conditions affecting the neck, shoulders, arms and hands. Caused when an employee is using the same muscle groups to perform the same actions over and over again, such as working at a keyboard all day. Can result in a condition of the wrists known as carpal tunnel syndrome.	Take regular breaks. Use **ergonomically** designed keyboards and mouse. Use appropriate furniture, such as adjustable swivel chairs. Use a wrist rest underneath the keyboard to avoid carpal tunnel syndrome. Use a foot rest.
Eyestrain	A common problem caused by over-exposure to computer screens. Can lead to headaches, blurred vision and an overall deterioration in a user's eyesight. This condition can cause discomfort resulting in less work being done.	Use anti-glare screens. Use swivel bases on screens to deflect light away from the user's eyes. Use screens that have adjustable brightness and contrast. Have good lighting in the office. Provide regular free eye tests.
Back pain	Can be related to the poor posture while sitting at the computer for prolonged periods. Could lead to mobility problems.	Use adjustable chairs that allow height adjustment and backrest tilting. Take regular breaks and regularly exercise muscles. Provide training for improving desk posture.

Other safety issues that should be given priority in the workplace include:

▶ regularly carrying out portable appliance testing (PAT testing) on hardware devices.

▶ using proper cable management for cables to and from computers.

▶ providing controlled air conditioning for a more comfortable working environment.

▶ correctly locating appropriate fire extinguishers (such as CO_2 that are suitable for electrical fires).

▶ not eating or drinking near computers.

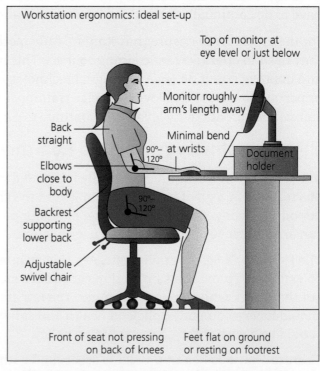

▲ Workstation ergonomics: the ideal set-up

Checkpoint ✓

▷ Consumer Contracts Regulations 2013 specify customer rights when shopping online.

▷ Data Protection Act 1998 controls how personal information can be used by organisations.

▷ Copyright Designs and Patents Act 1988 makes it illegal to copy and distribute software without permission.

▷ Computer Misuse Act 1990 protects computer users against crimes.

▷ GPS (global positioning system) uses a number of satellites orbiting the Earth to provide real-time information such as the geographical location of a person.

▷ Digital technology is changing the world of work, increasing new job opportunities.

▷ Teleworking is using ICT to work from home.

▷ Health problems associated with the regular use of computers include repetitive strain injury (RSI), back strain and eye strain.

Practice questions

1 a) State four principles of the Data Protection Act 1998.   [4 marks]

   b) Name and describe two other laws associated with ICT.   [6 marks]

2 Briefly explain the roles of the information commissioner and the data controller.   [4 marks]

3 Describe three ways in which the internet can be misused.   [6 marks]

4 Describe two ways in which social networking can be misused.   [4 marks]

5 Identify four jobs that have been created due to developments in digital technology.   [4 marks]

6 What is meant by 'teleworking'?   [2 marks]

7 Describe three advantages of teleworking to an employee.   [6 marks]

8 State three health problems associated with ICT and explain how each can be minimised.   [6 marks]

9 Identify three ways in which an organisation can assist in making the workplace safer.   [3 marks]

Chapter 10 Digital applications

What this chapter covers

▶ Gaming applications

▶ Simulation applications

▶ Mobile phone applications

▶ Online banking

▶ Online training

▶ E-commerce

Gaming applications

▲ User wearing a virtual reality headset and data gloves

Gaming applications are electronic games played on devices including game consoles, mobile phones or computers. The concept of gaming has developed from the installation of discs on games consoles and playing alone, to the use of the cloud and online multi-player games.

Educational gaming applications allow users to apply their knowledge and support their learning within a virtual world. Features such as leaderboards motivate individuals to improve their scores. Users can also take on different roles within the game and reflect on what happened in certain situations, enhancing learning. From a teacher's viewpoint the range of multimedia assets used within gaming applications can increase the motivation and communication skills of the learner.

Gaming applications can also be used to support training in the workplace. Games are designed with rules and increasing levels of difficulty; the user must comply with the rules and cannot move to the next level before completing the previous level. Each level provides new challenges to the user which makes games attractive for training purposes. Games also provide immediate feedback, helping users to evaluate what has been achieved and make decisions on what activity to do next.

From a social interaction viewpoint, gaming allows users to join online gaming groups where they can compete against each other on a global scale using the internet. Some gaming applications encourage collaboration where groups of users work together to solve a problem. Microphones and headsets allow users to communicate with each other in real time.

Tasks

Research the impact of gaming applications on education.

Simulation applications

A simulation uses a computer model to represent a 'real life' object. Models are created from large volumes of data, along with mathematical equations, to produce 3D graphics to represent the object. These models are then used to simulate the actions and reactions of the real life object. Car manufacturers use simulations to test cars during the design stage to see what happens when they crash. Architects use simulations to create models of new buildings before they are built to test how they would be affected by physical disasters such as earthquakes and flooding.

Virtual reality uses simulations to recreate 'real' experiences (virtual world). They have great potential for training people in the workplace. Virtual reality immerses the user in a 3D world using specialist hardware. These devices can simulate a combination of human senses such as vision, hearing and touch to allow the user to feel that they are experiencing a real situation.

Simulators can be used successfully to train people for jobs with a high risk of endangering life. Training a pilot to fly an aeroplane can be both dangerous and expensive due to fuel costs and loss of airfares by taking a plane out of service. Using aircraft simulators, a pilot can be trained for a range of different 'real' experiences, such as turbulence, thunderstorms or flying a plane with only one engine working. The pilot's actions can be recorded by the computer system and used to provide feedback for both the pilot and the trainer.

In the medical world, body scanners are used to collect large amounts of data about a person's internal system. A computer can then be used to produce a 3D model of the whole, or part, of the body, creating a virtual patient. This can be used to brief and train surgeons before using 'real' surgery to deal with a medical problem. Surgeons can plan and practise (simulate) a particular operation on the virtual patient, before actually carrying it out for real.

Tasks

Research ways in which simulation is used in the workplace.

Mobile phone applications

Smartphones have grown from an accessory in life, to a necessity. People depend on these devices to access information and communicate with others at any time and from anywhere. Gradually, users are moving away from internet-enabled desktop computers and replacing them with mobile devices and apps to carry out daily activities.

In the past, organisations created a website targeted at desktop users and then developed a mobile-friendly version of this website. Now, organisations focus on developing apps that can run on mobile phones. Smartphones now come with a number of preloaded apps and users can download further applications from app stores. Popular app categories include games, music, movies and instant messaging.

▲ Mobile phones can access a range of apps.

Mobile applications have provided opportunities for teaching and learning. For example, iTunes U offers teachers opportunities to create, edit and manage online courses by including a range of resources in the form of audio, video and books. When combined with cloud technology, students can access these mobile apps from home and school to complete assignments. This concept can also be extended to providing training programs in the workplace. Through the use of instant messaging, groups of people can join together in a **user forum** or on an electronic bulletin board to communicate, share news and work together on projects. Employers can also use these apps to make announcements to particular groups of employees. The same technology can be used by schools to keep in contact with parents about forthcoming events.

App developers have also encouraged the use of their apps by allowing users to personalise and customise the settings and layout of the app on their mobile device. Apps also have features that allow intuitive ways for searching and filtering data. For mobile phone apps to continue to support education and training, loading speeds must be fast and security of users' private information is vital. App support and app updates must also be provided by app developers.

Tasks

Compare and contrast three mobile apps that you have used for social interaction

Online banking

Customers can use the internet to access their bank account via the bank's secure website. This is known as 'online banking'. To use online banking facilities customers must first register their details. Each subsequent time the customer will need to enter a username and password to log on to the website. The customer might also be asked a security question(s) before being allowed to view their account details. Once online, customers can carry out a range of activities including:

▶ viewing transactions and bank statements

▶ paying bills

▶ transferring money from one account to another

▶ setting up regular payments using direct debits/standing orders

▶ searching for particular transactions.

▲ Using a mobile device to access a bank account securely

This technology means the customer does not ever have to visit their local bank branch to carry out these transactions. Since the website is available 24/7 the customer is not limited to certain opening or closing times either. The customer can also access their bank account when abroad as it is available on a global scale. Customers can also make faster transactions using 'faster payments services' which allows money to be moved from one account to another almost immediately.

The main drawback of online banking is that customers may not have access to the necessary technology or have the necessary skills to carry out online transactions. Some customers prefer face-to-face transactions as they may not be confident of transactions taking place without human involvement. Some customers also worry about fraud, resulting in loss of money or their personal details being stolen.

The main advantage of this technology for the bank is that they can save money, as fewer branches require fewer staff leading to a reduction in wage costs. Banks can provide online-only products such as e-statements, which can save on paper and postage costs. As banking is done through their website they can also attract a bigger customer base as customers do not have to live near a banking branch.

The main disadvantage of this technology for the bank is that online banking requires the storage of large volumes of personal data which calls for complex security systems to be implemented and maintained. As technology develops, security procedures must be reviewed and updated. The bank will also have to employ specialist technical staff such as staff who can maintain their website.

> **Tasks**
>
> 'Customers who use online banking are afraid of fraud.' Research ways in which banks use security for online transactions.

Online training

Due to rapid developments in digital technology and changes in the workplace, employers often use online training (or web-based) programs to train their employees in a more hands-on **interactive** environment. Advances in internet and broadband communications have made online training much more accessible. It is also more economical in both time and costs than conventional training.

Advantages of online training

▶ Employees can learn at a time that is convenient and they can work at their own pace. Employers also gain here because travelling to training venues can take up valuable staff time.

▶ Employees in different office locations can easily access the training at the same time.

▶ Employers can monitor employee progress through automatic tracking systems which record progress made, including training modules completed and end-of-module assessment scores.

▶ Multimedia assets such as animations, graphics, sound files and video files help make the training content attractive to employees.

▶ Training platforms which are compatible with mobile phones give the employee more options on when and where the materials can be used.

▶ Virtual reality customised training programs in the form of work-related simulations offer a highly interactive and realistic form of training. For example, airline companies have been using flight simulators successfully for many years to develop a pilot's range-flying skills.

Disadvantages of online training

▶ Traditional training allows opportunities for employees to ask questions face-to-face but with online training support is often limited to an FAQ section. This can lead to the employee feeling isolated and unsupported. Even if an employee can email an instructor there can still be a delay in getting a response.

▶ Online training does not suit all learning styles, for example some employees may prefer learning through graphical images while others prefer materials in a text-based format.

▶ An organisation may feel that they are not in full control of the training even though they can track progress of the employees.

▶ Creating deadlines for the completion of training modules is difficult since each employee may be working at a different pace or even on a different module.

▶ Over reliance on the technology needed for online training can also cause problems. For example, a poor internet connection could interrupt learning, or an employee may have to update their web browser to access online materials.

Tasks

Research how virtual reality is used to help students learn at school.

E-commerce

E-commerce is the buying and selling of products and services over the internet. E-commerce has a major impact on the shopping experience.

Advantages of e-commerce

▶ One big benefit of shopping online is that it is more convenient for customers. Ordering goods online takes less time than travelling to local shops. It is particularly attractive to those with disabilities, and those who have young children or who live outside town centres as they would find it difficult to make regular trips to a shopping centre.

▶ Using the internet and search engines, customers can access more information about products they wish to purchase, such as reviews and price comparisons. Customers also have a greater choice and availability of products compared to visiting their local shop(s) which may not stock the full range of products or may not have products in stock.

▲ Customers pay for goods using credit cards before they are dispatched.

▶ The main benefit to an organisation of using e-commerce is that they do not need to rent or buy expensive retail outlets; they can use out-of-town warehouses. Since they do not need to employ checkout operators, they require fewer employees. The organisation can pass on the savings made from rent and staff costs to customers by providing cheaper goods and services. To ensure success, the organisation needs to have a website capable of selling products and services, including a secure method of accepting payments.

▶ Since an e-commerce website can be accessed on a global scale this increases the chances of securing more customers, making the organisation more profitable. E-commerce websites include review forums that allow customers to read what others thought about their products and services. Some products, such as games, become very popular even before they are released. Using e-commerce, customers can pre-order and pay for goods before they are delivered on the release date.

Disadvantages of e-commerce

▶ A major concern for customers using an e-commerce website is that it may not be authentic and has been set up solely to scam customers into entering personal details including their credit card details, which can then be used for fraud. PayPal is a safe, online payment system that keeps customers' details secure; credit card details are not shared with the e-commerce organisation.

▶ When customers shop for goods online they use images and descriptions to make purchasing decisions; they do not have a hands-on experience. Sometimes these images or descriptions are misleading and when the goods arrive they do not meet the expectations of the customer, meaning they need to be returned. The customer will then have to go through the inconvenience of posting goods back and ensuring they receive a refund, which can lead to a negative experience of using e-commerce.

▶ When goods are ordered online there is also a time delay in waiting for the delivery. Customers are usually offered a range of delivery options such as a standard delivery or a next day delivery. The cost of these options is usually met by the customer and this can make the goods more expensive than the initial selling price. Other issues, such as goods not arriving on time particularly around Christmas, can give customers a negative experience of using e-commerce.

> **Tasks**
>
> Use the internet to compare different ways and costs used to deliver goods from online retailers.

Checkpoint ✓

▷ Gaming applications can now be accessed using the cloud, allowing users to play with and against others online.

▷ Virtual reality uses simulations to recreate real life experiences, providing great potential for training people in the workplace.

▷ Advances in internet and broadband communications have made online training more accessible.

▷ Organisations have moved from creating mobile-friendly versions of their website to developing mobile applications (apps) that can run on mobile phones.

▷ Customers do not have to visit their local bank to carry out transactions as this can be done from home or their mobile phone.

▷ Shopping online is more convenient as customers can stay at home and use the internet to purchase goods.

Practice questions (?)

1 Describe three features of gaming applications that would support training programmes. [9 marks]

2 State three advantages of using simulation for training airline pilots. [6 marks]

3 Describe two advantages for the bank in providing online banking facilities. [4 marks]

4 Describe two concerns a customer might have in using online banking. [4 marks]

5 Evaluate the following statement: 'Developments in broadband technology have made it attractive for companies to provide online training for their employees.' [6 marks]

6 Briefly describe how virtual reality can assist in developing online training programmes. [5 marks]

7 Describe three benefits for customers of using e-commerce. [6 marks]

Chapter 11 Designing solutions

What this chapter covers

▶ End user involvement in prototyping

▶ Multimedia design elements

▶ Database design elements

End user involvement in prototyping

System developers can employ a wide range of methods when developing digital systems. All development approaches involve some form of interaction with the **end user**. How the end user is involved will vary depending on the approach used. Here we will look at the development approach known as prototyping.

Who is the end user?

The term 'end user' is used to describe the person the system is ultimately being designed for. This term helps to distinguish the person for whom the system is being designed from any other individuals involved in the design and development stages (for example multimedia developers, programmers or systems analysts).

Before a development team starts to produce a new system they investigate the end user's needs and produce a set of **user requirements** based on what the end user has said they would like the new system to do. During the design process the design and development team must always consider the requirements of the end user.

What is prototyping?

Prototyping refers to the method of producing incomplete versions of a digital technology system. Often the **prototype** will show the layout of the system interface to help the end user understand how the system will operate. The prototype may simulate some operations but it will not usually accept any real input data, process data or output results. In this form the prototype can be used to support discussion between the end user and the developer as they try to determine the requirements for the system or any changes that may be needed. This process where the prototype is discussed, updated and presented to the user for feedback can continue for as long as is necessary. Prototyping does not provide a full working solution, but instead opportunities for the solution to improve through feedback and suggested improvement. This process is iterative.

Two of the most common types of methods of prototyping are evolutionary and throwaway prototyping.

> This chapter can be reviewed in conjunction with Chapter 18 Designing solutions using appropriate tools (Unit 3) where additional examples of design tools are studied.

Evolutionary prototyping is where an incomplete version of the final system (as described above) is developed and presented to the end user. This review, feedback and **refinement** process continues until the end user is presented with a fully operational system which meets all of their user requirements. A **throwaway prototype** is one that will not be part of the final solution. A model of the system or a part of the system is developed to help support discussion between the end user and the developer. It might be used to answer questions about the user requirements, or in instances when the end user is not fully able to express their needs to the developer. The prototype can then be discarded and the system developed using an alternative development method.

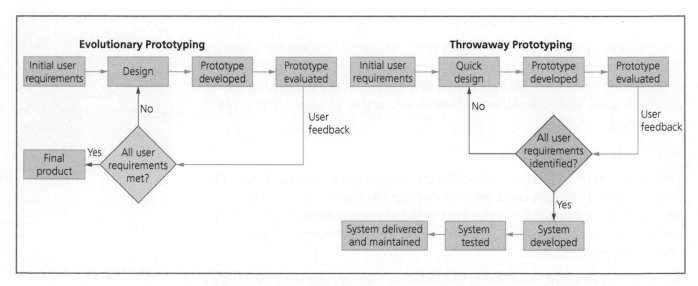

▲ Evolutionary prototyping vs throwaway prototyping

Advantages of prototyping

▶ Increased end user involvement means less chance of misunderstanding between the developer and the end user. Any changes that are needed can be detected early in the process and therefore money can be saved.

▶ Final digital system more likely to meet end user's needs. Errors can be detected early and the end user can see from an early stage how the system will operate.

▶ Very useful where there is a high degree of end user interaction, such as with online systems. This enables users to interact with a prototype providing thorough feedback.

Disadvantages of prototyping

▶ End users may confuse the prototype with the final system and therefore expect to see all elements shown to them during experimentation with the prototype as part of the final system.

▶ Continued end user involvement can lead to the system growing as they add on more and more features, which can lead to an increase in development time, increased project size and therefore development costs.

▶ Not suitable for systems which use batch processing. These systems generally involve a lot of processing and coding and can be too expensive to develop using prototyping.

Tasks

1 Carry out additional research into the advantages and disadvantages of prototyping. How many additional advantages and disadvantages can you find? Produce a short report on your findings.

2 Consider the advantages of using prototyping as a means of developing a website for an online store where the customer has no technical experience. Explain how using a prototype might support the developer and the end user in this instance. Would the prototype take the form of an evolutionary or a throwaway prototype? Give a reason for your answer.

End user role in prototyping

Prototyping allows the end user to take an active role throughout the development process, especially where evolutionary prototyping is being used. The end user provides feedback after every refinement or **iteration** of the system and the system will be updated based on their feedback. The end user's continued involvement gives them increased ownership of the final system and helps to ensure the end product meets the user's needs.

Multimedia design elements

The development of interactive multimedia applications is one of the biggest areas in digital technology. To be successful in this area, it is important that a developer can design, present and create successful multimedia applications. Some of the elements contained in multimedia design documents are outlined below.

Target audience and user requirements

When designing any multimedia application, it is important to always consider the **target audience** at the initial design stages. The target audience is the demographic group who will be the primary users of the application. For example, in the development of a website or a mobile phone application, the target audience will be the group for whom the application is being marketed at. When considering the target audience as a designer and developer, it is important that you examine many features including their age, gender, interests and reasons why they will use the application. These details will inform many decisions you make regarding the presentation of the app and its general **user interface**, such as colour scheme, level of language used, functionality, type of graphics or animations included and so on. For example, in designing a multimedia application to teach primary school children simple algebra you might consider using basic language and content, presenting minimal content on screen and use of colourful graphics.

A user requirements document for a multimedia application will explain why a system is being developed, and will include a section which identifies the end user requirements. In addition it will include details relating to what the system should look like and what it should do (rather than how it will do it!). It often forms part of the contract between the developer and the end user.

A good user requirements document will include requirements which:

▶ are necessary for effective operation of the system

▶ can be easily measured or tested (for example, the page should load in x seconds)

▶ are easily understood by the end user/customer (who may have no technical experience)

▶ are numbered or coded requirements so they can be referred to in testing

▶ can be easily met within the given budget and/or technology available.

Tasks 🖉

Examine a website of your choice.

1 Discuss the target audience for the website and how the target audience may influence any design decisions made by the website developers.

2 As a class, or in small groups, produce a list of items you think would have been incorporated into the user requirements document for the website you have chosen when the end user first met with the development team.

Navigation structure diagram

A **navigation structure diagram** identifies the various pathways along which the end user can move through a multimedia application. This helps the developer visualise the overall structure of the application. Some standard conventions used in navigation structure diagrams include:

1) Page 1 ——— Page 2

2) | page name |

3) ..... | www.external_page.com |

1 the use of arrows or lines to show links between pages. Here the diagram shows that page 1 is linked to page 2

2 page names are normally presented inside a rectangular shape

3 external links (sites or pages or applications outside the context of your own application) can be shown.

The hierarchical structure of the multimedia application can be illustrated using a navigational structure diagram. Such diagrams take on a tree diagram form which can help illustrate the various pathways through the application and show the links between various multimedia elements.

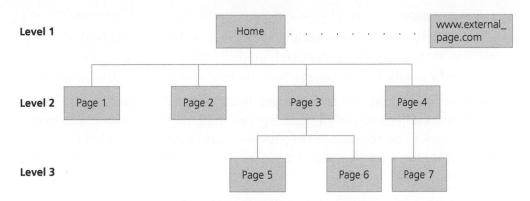

▲ A navigational structure diagram

This navigational structure diagram illustrates that the external page with the address, www.external_page.com can only be accessed from the home page (as they are presented at the same level, level 1, on the navigation structure diagram). It also shows that:

▶ page 1, page 2, page 3 and page 4 can only be accessed from the home page

▶ pages 5 and 6 can only be accessed from page 3

▶ page 7 can only be accessed from page 4.

Tasks

Examine the structure of your school website (or any alternative if your school website is too complex) and construct a navigation structure diagram to show how the pages are linked. Your diagram should consider levels of page presentation, external web links and how the user can navigate from one page to the other.

Storyboard and image sources

Good planning is key to the successful development of any multimedia application. Having discussed requirements with the end user and defined the navigational structure of the multimedia application, the next step is the development of a **storyboard**. A storyboard helps the designers, developers and end user visualise the end product. A good storyboard will help reduce development time and therefore keep the cost of development down.

A good storyboard should have enough detail to allow **third-party implementation** and should contain details on the following:

▶ background colour/images

▶ navigational elements

▶ locations of page banners and any other such identifying graphics, for example company logos

▶ any headings and subheadings

▶ details of any text to be incorporated into the webpage (only an outline of the content is needed at this stage – a full script is not required)

▶ **image sources**, so the developer will be able to create or access any images required for the multimedia product

▶ movie timeline

▶ details of any interactive or **scripted elements** to be included in the website. **Interactive elements** can include audio, video, roll over buttons, hyperlinks to other websites, documents downloads and form completion.

The storyboard should also incorporate details regarding font, text style, text size and text colour for all headings, subheadings and main body text. Since this should be consistent throughout, this could be included in the storyboard for the home page and used as a reference for all other pages on the website.

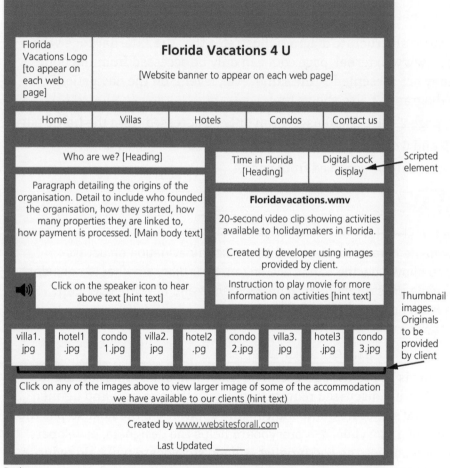

Design notes
• Page background: light blue block colour with watermarked Florida Villas logo embossed in middle.
• Florida Vacations Logo and Banner to be designed by development team.
• Headings – Font: **nonserif**, size 14, style: bold, colour: dark blue.
• Main body text – Font: nonserif, Size 12, colour: dark blue.
• Hint text – Font: nonserif, Size 10, colour: dark blue.
• Scripted element – local time script, displays time in selected location available from www.dynamicdrive.com.
• Navigation Buttons – roll over images: colour change from blue to white, font: nonserif, font size: 11, style: bold.

⌃ A detailed storyboard will contain enough detail to support third-party implementation.

Movie timeline

A **movie timeline** provides the end user with a series of images which show how a movie will be broken down. It contains the detail of each scene/frame in the movie, timings, information on the duration of each frame and a description of any special features to be applied or presented on each scene (for example any special effects to be applied or, if it is a title or credit screen, how this information appears). Descriptions of frame content can be text- or graphic-based, and you would expect to see around one frame in the movie timeline for every two seconds of content. A movie timeline should be detailed enough to support third-party implementation.

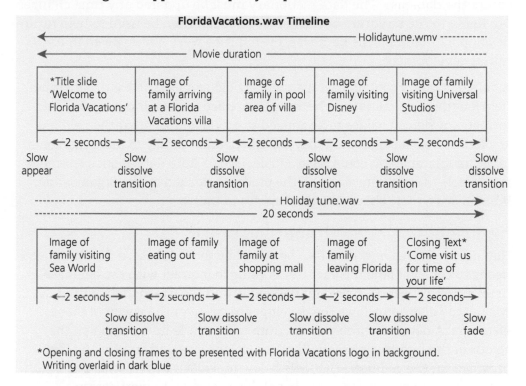

▲ A movie timeline

Scripted elements

Many multimedia applications are now created using authoring packages. These software applications allow the end user to create an application using drag and drop tools in a **WYSIWYG** (what you see is what you get) environment. These packages then create any code needed to support the presentation of the application on various platforms. For example, a website authoring package allows the user to create their webpage using a range of appropriate tools. It will then generate the HTML code necessary to allow that page or site to be uploaded to the internet.

Some authors may wish to add more complicated features to their website. Often it is possible to download script/code which has already been developed by someone else to do a specific task and you can then incorporate this into the HTML created by the **multimedia authoring** package. These scripted elements are often in the form of dynamic HTML or JavaScript and once downloaded they can be used to help increase the interactivity of a website, without the developer needing to be too familiar with HTML or Java code.

Database design elements

Databases are powerful applications used by many organisations to store, organise, retrieve and present data to end users in a useful and timely manner. Some of the elements considered when designing databases for use by organisations are outlined below.

Data dictionary

A **data dictionary** is a file which contains details relating to the structure of data held in a database. It is produced at the design stage during database development and contains enough information for a database developer to create the database. The data dictionary must be updated any time changes are made to the structure of the database. It can then be used to help future developers maintain the database, even if they were not involved in its initial development.

A data dictionary contains details such as field names (**attribute**), data types, field lengths, any validation checks to be applied to data, input masks, field format, any default values to be applied to a field and whether the field is a key field. The data dictionary may contain details relating to more than one table, for example you could have a table used to store data about customers and a table to store data about all the products stocked by the organisation. We will learn more about data dictionaries in Unit 3.

Form and report wireframe diagrams

Having considered how data is to be stored by the database, a developer also needs to consider how the end user is going to interact with the database in terms of navigation, forms for data input and reports for data output. A **wireframe diagram** allows the developer to consider the layout of these elements. A detailed wireframe diagram will include information on the colour of the interface element, the font, colour, size and style of any text provided for the end user. The table below provides a key to some of the important elements represented in database form and report design.

Element Being Represented	Example	Description
Label	Customer Num	e.g. text label which could be used beside data entry field in database form design
Graphic place holder	Company Logo	e.g. showing the location of graphics on a database form or report design
Data entry area	dd/mm/yyyy	e.g. data entry areas on database form design. This e.g. shows how input masks are being used to control data entry
Navigation button	Main Menu	e.g. navigation button which could be used on reports or forms design
Dropdown menu	Mr Mrs Miss	e.g. of the use of a dropdown box in a database form design
Option buttons / Radio buttons	◉ Business ◉ Vacation	e.g. of the use of radio buttons to allow selection of options in a database form design
Output field in a report	=CustTBL(Surname)	e.g. representing an output field in a database report design (data source is identified)
Calculated output field	=SUM([Costs])	e.g. representing a calculated field in a database report design

▲ Elements that form part of a form or report wireframe diagram

Navigational structure diagram

We have already seen how a navigation structure diagram identifies the different pathways by which an end user can move through a multimedia application (see page 76). Navigational structure diagrams can also be used support database design. In database design documents, they can be used to illustrate the pathways the end user can take through a package using the menu system presented to them through the package interface.

Entity-relationship diagram (ERD)

We saw earlier that a database for one organisation may have more than one table. Each table will represent one type of item or thing represented in the database. These items, or things, are known as entities. Each **entity** will have a set of attributes and these are recorded under field headings.

Where multiple entities are represented in a database, a link or relationship generally must be established between those entities. At the design stage, the links between entities will be illustrated using an **entity-relationship diagram**. The most common types of relationships formed between database tables are shown in the table below.

Relationship Type	Description	Diagram
one-to-one ⎯⎯	e.g. adult 1 is married to adult 2	adult 1 ⎯ adult 2
one-to-many ⎯<	e.g. one parent can have many children	parent ⎯< children
many-to-many >⎯<	e.g. a grandparent can have more than one grandchild and each grandchild can have more than one grandparent	grand parent >⎯< grand child

▲ The different types of entity-relationships

In Unit 3, we will look at how each of the above elements of database design can be combined with other design elements and used to formally represent a working database.

Checkpoint ✓

▷ The end user is the person/organisation for whom a digital system is being developed.

▷ Prototyping is a method of developing a system from a basic model through to the final system by reviewing and updating the system (evolutionary prototyping) or it can be used to help determine end user needs before being discarded (throwaway prototyping).

▷ End users are involved at all stages during prototype development.

▷ Multimedia design documents incorporate a range of elements including target audience and user requirements, navigation structure diagrams, storyboards and image sources, movie timelines and details on scripted elements.

▷ Database design documents incorporate a range of elements including data dictionaries, form and report wireframe diagrams, navigational structure diagrams and entity-relationship diagrams.

Practice questions ❓

1 Define the term 'prototyping'. [2 marks]

2 Identify the role played by the end user during prototyping. [2 marks]

3 Explain the key difference between evolutionary and throwaway prototyping. [2 marks]

4 Describe two advantages of prototyping. [4 marks]

5 Identify three features of a good user requirements document when developing a multimedia application. [3 marks]

6 Explain what is meant by a 'storyboard' in multimedia application development and list four items you would expect to see detailed in a website storyboard. [6 marks]

7 Describe the main features of an ERD (entity-relationship diagram). [3 marks]

8 Describe two types of relationships which can exist between data in a database and give an example to illustrate each. [4 marks]

Chapter 12 Digital development considerations

Human–computer interfaces

Digital technology systems process binary data, i.e. 1s and 0s, but human beings communicate in written or spoken language known as natural language. **Human–computer interfaces** are therefore needed to support the issuing of commands and the presentation of output to the end user in forms that both the end user and the digital technology system can understand.

The user interface can be in the form of software or may incorporate a combination of hardware and software elements. A range of interface types are available to support interaction between the end user and digital applications.

Graphical user interfaces

Graphical user interfaces (GUI) are interfaces which allow user interaction through the selection of on-screen options. Actions are carried out through a GUI via direct interaction with the on-screen options presented to the end user. GUIs are said to provide the end user with a **WIMP** (Windows Icons Menus Pointers) environment.

Windows

A **window** is an area on a computer desktop which is presented to the end user. It shows the actions being performed by an application at that moment in time. Most operating systems support the display of multiple windows at any time but only one window can be active at any one time, i.e. the window the user is interacting with. The user can change the active window by selecting another window on the desktop and clicking on it.

Icon

An **icon** is a small picture presented to the user on screen. It represents a shortcut to a task or an application, normally the program executable file (.exe). The icon image should be familiar to the user; for example the icon which represents 'open' is generally shown as an open folder.

The user can select an icon by using cursor keys, using their finger on a touchscreen device or by double clicking on a left mouse button. Some interfaces support navigation between icons through the use of the keyboard.

Menu

Menus provide a way of grouping similar or related tasks together. By grouping similar options together, the menu system allows the end user to locate related tasks in an intuitive way.

Pointer

A pointer is an on-screen icon which moves around on screen in response to the user's movements of a mouse, tracker pad or other similar input device. By placing the pointer over a shortcut or any other on-screen option, the user can activate that option using further keystrokes or clicks. Generally the end user will know when an on-screen option is available for selection as the option will be highlighted in some form to show it is now an active option on screen, e.g. it may change colour or shape.

Most desktop computers now support user interaction through the use of a GUI such as MS Windows.

Advantages of GUIs

▶ Intuitive and user-friendly. Icons use familiar images so the task they represent can be recognised by the user.

▶ User does not need to understand how the computer operates in order to complete a task.

▶ Normally supported by shortcuts in the form of keystrokes to help increase speed of operation for more experienced users.

Disadvantages of GUIs

▶ Increased processing power, storage space and RAM are often required to support a GUI.

▶ More powerful graphics card needed to present a GUI than some other interface types.

▶ Can be restrictive and slow for experienced users to use.

Natural language interfaces

Natural language interfaces provide users with a means of interacting with digital technology using their normal everyday language to speak or type instructions into the computer using regular sentence structures.

Natural language interfaces can be used for a range of applications, for example, computer games where the end user can communicate in conversational mode with other characters in the gaming scenario. Many search engines now support natural language interaction. The user can enter in full sentences, and the search engine can successfully extract the key terms from the user's input sentence and return a reasonably precise index of results.

Advantages of natural language interfaces

▶ Suitable for users with limited technical experience as they are not expected to remember specialised commands.

▶ Suitable for users with limited movement to interact with digital devices.

▶ Supports hands-free interaction with digital technology.

Disadvantages of natural language interfaces

▶ Where interaction is voice input, significant time must be spent 'training' the interface to recognise a voice.

▶ The system will only respond to those voices it has been 'trained to recognise'.

▶ Technical demands of such a system may be high in terms of RAM, processing power and storage.

▶ The interface will often only recognise limited commands, especially where voice input is used.

▶ Natural language can at times be ambiguous and this can lead to instructions being misinterpreted by the interface.

Tasks 🖊

Research examples of digital applications which make use of natural language interfaces (spoken or typed). Produce a short report on your findings. In your report you should detail additional hardware needed in a digital technology system to support voice entry in a natural language interface.

Motion tracking interfaces

Motion tracking interfaces are implemented using devices which convert movement in a 3D space into digital signals for use as input into a computer game. They can use either specific imaging devices (such as the ones described below) or sensors to track movement.

Motion tracking methods that use imaging systems are known as 'optical methods' and normally involve the use of a camera and reflective markers, sensors or LEDs on a specialised body suit. These can then be used to record any movements made.

▲ Using sensors to support motion tracking

Some gaming systems have integrated camera-based motion tracking successfully into their interfaces. No markers are required in these cases. Instead, provided the subject remains within the view of a specialised infrared camera (which has depth-sensing capabilities), their movements can be tracked and used to support interaction with the digital application.

▲ Head-mounted devices can support the integration of limited movement into virtual reality applications.

Advantages of motion tracking interfaces

▶ Can help make interaction with digital applications more realistic for the user.

▶ Allows inexperienced users to interact with applications in a natural way.

▶ Supports interaction with users who have limited fine motor control.

Disadvantages of motion tracking interfaces

▶ Because the technology is still fairly new it is limited.

▶ High-end motion tracking technology is still expensive.

Touchscreen

Many digital applications and hardware devices now support touchscreen interaction through the use of a stylus or by touching the screen with the fingers. Many applications now also provide users with an on-screen keyboard to support text entry via a touchscreen interface. Here, we will focus on the advantages and disadvantages of touchscreen interfaces as a means of supporting interaction with digital applications.

The features of touchscreen technology are examined in Chapter 5 Computer hardware (Unit 1).

Advantages of touchscreen interfaces

▶ The integration of a keyboard into the touchscreen display reduces the need for additional hardware and increases the portability of the device.

▶ Uses intuitive actions such as swiping or tapping the screen to interact with the device.

▶ Easily wiped clean.

Disadvantages of touchscreen interfaces

▶ If touchscreen is damaged, interaction with the technology is affected.

▶ Small screens/on-screen shortcuts and buttons can make interaction difficult.

▶ Options can be limited due to the small screen size.

▶ Technology is still relatively expensive.

▶ Difficult to operate if visually impaired.

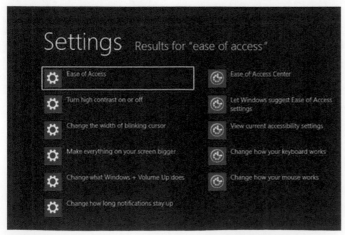

▲ Personalisation of settings on a PC to support accessibility

Developing accessible digital applications

Most hardware devices and digital applications come available with specialised settings which can enhance the **accessibility** of the product. For example, many digital devices now support interaction via narrators and touch-enabled devices and allow the use of an on-screen magnifier.

W3C (the World Wide Web Consortium) is an international standards organisation whose aim is to put standards in place to ensure that internet and mobile phone applications are accessible for all users. The guidelines developed by W3C were initially designed to cover webpages and web applications, but are now being expanded to include how such content can be displayed on mobile devices. Some of the recommendations presented by W3C for the development of internet-based applications include the inclusion of 'alt' text for graphics, no reliance on mouse input for interaction and the provision of transcripts for podcasts.

Tasks

1 Visit these webpages and investigate how the W3C propose to increase accessibility of websites and mobile phone apps.
   ▶ www.w3.org/WAI/mobile
   ▶ www.w3.org/standards/webdesign/accessibility

2 Examine the accessibility options available on your mobile phone and desktop computer. Produce a list of the accessibility elements available on each device and describe how each can enhance the accessibility of the device for a user with a special need.

Developing cross-platform digital applications

In computing, a **platform** is defined as the hardware and/or software which allows an application to run. Developers now want to be able to share their developments on a range of platforms to take into consideration the fact that not all of their target audience will use the same technology.

Platforms today are no longer limited to personal computers and their supporting operating systems; instead they can refer to any piece of digital technology, for example tablets, mobile telephones and gaming consoles, among others. **Cross-platform applications** are applications which are designed to run on different hardware and software platforms (although the characteristics of each platform may mean slight variations are introduced into the different interfaces associated with each platform).

The successful development of a cross-platform digital application is dependent upon a number of factors.

▶ Remember that what looks good on one platform may not look good on another. Interfaces should be tailored to suit each platform.

▶ Platform-specific applications should be developed. An app which is designed for a specific platform will work better on that platform. When versioning apps for different platforms it is important to consider if there are any parts of your app which can be reused. You can also design apps which are web-based that may work on most platforms but may not link in with hardware on a certain platform, such as the camera on a mobile phone.

▶ Regular updates should be provided. As the platform operating systems update over time, you will need to consider how this might affect how well your application works.

▶ Applications should be fully tested on all target platforms.

Improving cross-platform compatibility

Plugin software

Plugin software can add additional functionality to an existing application.

Common examples of plugin software include QuickTime player, which supports video play and Java applets. These allow the end user to implement more completed elements into their digital application, such as interactive calendars or small gaming applications.

Developers should take into consideration the capabilities of the various platforms they are targeting when developing their applications. Where generic versions of applications are developed, the user can be presented with a prompt to install any additional plugins needed to support the operation of the package on that particular platform.

Portable document format (PDF)

PDF files can contain a combination of text, graphics and hyperlinks in a file format which is accessible via any platform which has the appropriate supporting software installed. By converting a document to PDF it can be viewed on any supporting platform regardless of operating system version, application or even hardware. PDF files offer the sender the security of knowing that the content is not easily edited and that that content is saved in a compressed file format so the file is more easily transferred electronically. Where electronic sharing prompts the opening of a PDF file through a web browser however it should be noted that this may often prompt the installation of supporting plugins as explained above.

Optimised file formats

The aim of **optimisation** is to minimise the time taken to load the digital application and for this reason, it is important to ensure **optimised** file formats are used during the development process.

Compression is the process by which files are reduced in size through the removal of unnecessary data. These files are known as 'compressed file formats'. The reduction of file sizes in this manner is known as 'optimisation'. This is to facilitate storage or electronic transmission.

When developing digital applications, it is important to consider how well supported your chosen file format will be on your target platform. Having a thorough understanding of your platform, including for example the target browser being used to display your application, allows you to select appropriate file formats to ensure that any additional multimedia elements can be displayed effectively through the application. Ideally the end user should be able to run your application without having to install too many plugin applications to support it. The table on the next page lists some optimised file formats which are supported by most web browsers and platforms.

Further information on optimised file formats including jpg, gif and mp4 can be found in Chapter 1 Digital data, *Data portability* (Unit 1).

Video file formats	Image file formats	Sound file formats
Flash video format (.flv) AVI format (.avi) Quicktime format (.mov) MP4 format (.mp4)	Jpeg format (.jpg) GIF format (.gif) TIFF format (.tiff) PNG format (.png)	MP3 format (.mp3) WAV format (.wav) is supported by most browsers although it is not a compressed file format

Tasks

Select a platform you are familiar with, for example your mobile phone or tablet computer. Research the file formats supported by this platform and complete a table similar to the one above to show which file formats your platform supports. How many of these file formats would require the user to download a plugin if they were to be used by an app running on Internet Explorer?

Checkpoint ✓

▷ A wide range of interface types are available to support interaction between users and digital applications and these include GUIs, natural language interfaces, motion tracking interfaces and touchscreen interfaces.

▷ W3C (the World Wide Web Consortium) have put standards in place to ensure that internet and mobile phone applications are accessible for all users.

▷ File compression and optimisation can help improve the load time and run time of digital applications.

▷ When designing digital applications it is important that you take into consideration your target platform.

▷ Plugins are often needed to support cross-platform compatibility of applications.

Practice questions

1 Expand the following acronyms.
   a) GUI [1 mark]
   b) WIMP [1 mark]

2 Describe the main features of a WIMP interface. [8 marks]

3 Identify two features of a GUI and explain how each improve the user-friendliness of a digital application. [4 marks]

4 A user interacts with their mobile phone using voice recognition on a natural language interface. Identify two hardware items the phone must have to support this type of interaction. [2 marks]

5 Describe the advantages and disadvantages to a user of being able to interact with their mobile phone using a natural language interface. [6 marks]

6 A mobile phone incorporates a touch-sensitive screen to support user input. What problems might a user have trying to enter text using a keyboard on a touch-sensitive screen. [2 marks]

7 How can the use of a natural language interface help improve the experience for a user when playing a game on their mobile device? [2 marks]

8 Jamie wishes to develop an application to be delivered using a number of platforms. Provide two pieces of advice Jamie should consider when developing cross-platform applications. [2 marks]

Chapter 13 Multimedia applications

What this chapter covers

▶ Multimedia features

▶ Interactive features

▶ Multimedia and interactivity in e-commerce

▶ Multimedia and interactivity in social media

▶ Multimedia and interactivity in gaming

▶ Multimedia and interactivity in generic applications

Multimedia features

Multimedia refers to the use of a combination of images, sound, animation, video and text to present information to users in a digital application.

Applications such as MS PowerPoint, Windows MovieMaker or online tools such as Prezi can be used to support the creation of multimedia applications.

Multimedia on the internet has progressed from the presentation of websites incorporating text and images to applications that can now support the streaming of:

▶ stored video or sound files, such as podcasts

▶ live audio and video presentations as now used on some social media websites

▶ video and sound in an interactive environment, for example VoIP and video conferencing applications.

> **More information on streaming can be found in Chapter 1 Digital data (Unit 1).**

Tasks

1 Revise the term 'streaming' from Unit 1. Explain the term and how streaming can help the user download and play large audio/video files without experiencing a delay.

2 Search the internet for examples of multimedia applications which present multimedia by streaming:
   ▶ stored files
   ▶ live video and or sound files
   ▶ interactive/realtime video and sound.

Interactive features

Many multimedia applications also incorporate interactive elements. Interaction (with a digital device) is the way a user uses hardware and software to view output, and generate input in response to that output, to help them complete a task. Application software will convert user input into commands which the computer can understand. This then leads to the production of **feedback** to the user, for example sound playing or an image moving on screen.

Interactive elements can be supported by a range of data entry types, including text entry, item selection (using mouse or touchscreen), voice data entry or video capture (generally in a real-time environment).

Basic interactive features of multimedia applications include the use of playing video or sound files, thumbnail images or roll over images. More advanced interactive features now include:

▶ virtual tours or 3D interactive displays

▶ memes (video or images normally with funny text explanations)

▶ live interactive video and chats

▶ links to other pages or websites

▶ Twitter feeds.

Multimedia and interactivity in e-commerce

Many e-commerce websites employ a combination of interactive and multimedia features to support the sales of their products. The table below shows how Amazon and ebay, two popular e-commerce sites, make use of these features.

Tasks

Produce a list of interactive features found in digital applications you use in school and at home. The applications can be internet-based, computer-based or delivered on a portable device.

The impact of digital applications on e-commerce is discussed in Chapter 10 Digital applications (Unit 1).

Interactive/multimedia feature	Amazon	ebay	Advantages	Disadvantages
Posting of reviews	Y	Y	Customer can see what other people thought of the end product.	Word length may be limited.
Tracking/watch lists	Y	Y	Customers can check stock levels of product/check if product has already been posted.	Not all sellers provide tracking information.
Product or seller ratings	Y	Y	Allows customers to gain insight into other customers' thoughts on the product.	Reviews are subjective and not all users operate to the same standards.
Search facility	Y	Y	Allows customers to use key words to narrow down search.	Customer and seller must use the same key words to describe the item.
Secure online payment	Y	Y	Purchasers and sellers do not have to share their bank details.	Not all customers have access to electronic payment.
Live bidding system and alert system	N	Y	Customer can monitor items they are bidding on or be alerted to the fact that they have been outbid even if they are not using the application.	Messages relating to bidding can lead to a lot of alerts appearing.
Push technology	Y	Y	Used to send alerts to customers as emails or pop-ups on digital devices.	May lead to a lot of alerts appearing.

Interactive/multimedia feature	Amazon	ebay	Advantages	Disadvantages
Sharing of product information via other media	Y	Y	Customers can send a link to an item on the e-commerce site to someone else via social media or email.	
Help systems and dispute resolutions	Y	N	Customer has security of knowing that if product is unsatisfactory they can return it (ebay offers resolutions to users through PayPal).	
Image display tools, for example video descriptions, 360° photos and photo collage	Y	Y	Allows sellers to illustrate products. Purchaser can see product before purchasing.	Images may not show on all devices.
Shopping carts	Y	Y	Customer can save items and purchase them later.	Items reserved in the shopping cart indefinitely may not be available for others to purchase.

Multimedia and interactivity in social media

Social media is the use of digital technology to support the creation and sharing of multimedia content which represents our thoughts, ideas (and sometimes even products) on an online interactive platform. The increase in sharing of user-generated content has led to the development of **virtual communities** where content can be submitted from all around the world.

Social media applications are **Web 2.0**-based and are generally delivered to the end user via web-based and mobile telephone technologies. Content is shared in an interactive forum and members are encouraged to view content posted by others, discuss content and share their own ideas. Common examples of social media include YouTube, Facebook, Twitter, WhatsApp, Viber and Instagram. While each application offers its own specific features, some features are common to all social media applications.

Multimedia/interactive feature	Advantages	Disadvantages
User-generated content can be posted at any time and be viewed and commented on by other users.	Creates a feeling of increased connectivity, especially where family or friends are in another country.	Can be open to abuse (for example online bullying/trolling/spam). Can be intrusive and distracting if posts and updates are frequent, especially if alerts are set up to notify the user of each new posting.
Live streaming	Generates a new medium for sharing thoughts and ideas.	If users are viewing social media sites using data packages from their mobile phone provider, the auto-play feature of some live streams and video content can become expensive.

➡

Multimedia/interactive feature	Advantages	Disadvantages
User profiles and personalised settings can be maintained by the user.	The end user has control over who views their content and how much detail they include in their public profiles (privacy settings). Users can link their profiles to other users through the sending and accepting of friend requests.	Users with limited experience may not be aware of the dangers of revealing too much information about themselves or they may not be able to navigate the interface to allow settings to be adjusted.
Free **web space**	Users do not have to pay to host their content.	Some users may not realise that the social media site retains the rights to posted content.
Conversational tools/chat clients	Messages posted can be read at a later date. **Chat clients** support instant messaging where communication is interactive. Posts can be scheduled to disappear from the recipient's screen after a period of time but messages can be recorded by other means and are always stored on the host's server.	Can lead to isolation as virtual conversations take over from social interactions in the real world.
Create pages: users can create pages to inform others of events they are organising or they can use the page to post details relating to a given topic.	Organisations can use this feature to promote their products or to organise events.	Not all members of a target audience may have access to social media.
Call-to-action buttons: navigational buttons which prompt the user to complete some form of action, for example a thumbs up to like a post.	Allows users to quickly indicate how they feel about a particular post without having to initiate a text-based conversation.	The icons presented to the user by the site may sometimes be limited and not representative of the user's response to the post.
Search facility	Users can search for other members and connect to them or the facility can be used to search for old postings.	
Check-in facilities	Users can use this space locator to let connected friends know where they are or perhaps to post a review of the location.	The posting of your location online can be subject to abuse if undesirable individuals are made aware of your location.
Web link and content sharing: users are able to link posts from other sites and applications to their postings to share with other users.	The range of content available to members can increase with minimum effort as the user is not expected to recreate the content, simply post a hyperlink to it on the social media site.	Some users may not have the plugins necessary to view the posted content.

> **Tasks** 🖊
>
> Investigate two social media sites and produce a list of the interactive features available to the users on each site.
>
> 1 How many of the features identified are available on both applications?
>
> 2 How have these features helped to make the social media site you are investigating a success?

Multimedia and interactivity in gaming

The way users interact with gaming applications has evolved rapidly over the years. Where previously interactions were limited to mouse clicks and moving characters on-screen using a joystick, we have now moved into the realms of **3D** interactions with and without hand-held peripheral devices. The high level of interactivity end users now expect from their gaming experiences is a key factor in the increasing popularity of gaming applications. Now, end user interaction with gaming applications often begins before the game has even started; many gaming applications will allow the end user to tailor **game settings** and characters before, as well as during, the gaming process.

Some examples of multimedia and interactivity in gaming applications:

▶ high-quality graphics and sound to support the gaming experience of the user
  - User can be presented with feedback in the form of on-screen movement of characters in response to input from a generic or specialised highly responsive peripheral device.
  - Feedback can be presented to the user in the form of sound generated in response to an on-screen action.
  - Feedback can be presented in a visual format through the increase/decrease of scores, lives or health bars.
  - Text and voice interactions are supported by some gaming applications, for example the user can type instructions to the on-screen characters.
  - Video elements are implemented in some gaming applications to support user interactions, with some games being supported by almost video quality images throughout game play.
▶ 3D interaction methods now allow end users to perform a range of tasks, for example walking around their living room as though they are moving through the game environment at the same time
▶ customisation of settings and characters: users can alter game personas (the character they are playing in the game) and levels of difficulty to suit their own preferences. This can also help the user identify with the game, especially in **role-play game** applications
▶ the creation of personas or soundtracks to further personalise the game play experience
▶ adjustment of visual elements of the game display, for example camera angles during game play to support game play from a different angle.

Instructions can be added using text.

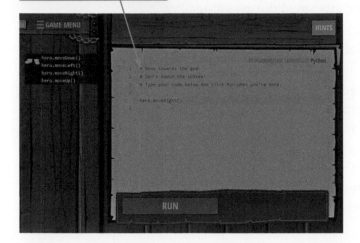

▲ Users can interact with the gaming environment using text.

▲ Users can personalise their game environment.

Tasks ✎

1 Produce a screenshot of a gaming application you have access to (or search for an image of a gaming application online).

2 Label all the interactive elements available to the end user.

3 Produce a list of all the multimedia elements available to the user during game play.

4 Produce a list of all of the ways the end user can interact with the gaming application. You should consider the type of interaction and the hardware used to support the interaction.

Advantages of multimedia and interactivity in gaming

▶ Increased interactivity during game play can help to increase enjoyment and motivation to continue playing.

▶ The availability of immediate feedback in a variety of forms encourages the user to remain alert at all times as they are expected to modify their behaviour and interactions with the game in response to feedback given.

▶ Settings and characters can be adjusted to suit the preferences of the user before and during the game; this helps personalise the game for each individual.

▶ High-quality graphics and sound output can help enhance the gaming experience and encourage the end user to feel fully immersed in the game.

▶ The use of specialised hardware devices (for example steering wheels used with driving games) for gaming interaction can help make the game feel more realistic to the end user.

Tasks

Produce a mind map (or an alternative diagrammatic illustration) of the contents of this chapter. Your key strands should focus on the types of interaction and multimedia used in the following areas:
- ▶ e-commerce
- ▶ social media
- ▶ gaming.

Make sure you include the advantages and disadvantages of the use of multimedia and interactivity in each application area.

Disadvantages of multimedia and interactivity in gaming

▶ Increased use of high-quality multimedia demands increased storage for games that are not being streamed during game play.

▶ Where multimedia games are being streamed during game play, the end user is reliant upon reliable broadband links to ensure game play is not interrupted.

▶ Complex code is required to support high-speed, realistic interactions with multimedia gaming elements. Large programs are expensive to develop and distribute to end users.

▶ Hardware demands are increased if high-quality multimedia elements are to be supported. If the game is to run smoothly then increased processing power, increased RAM and high-quality graphics and sound cards are needed. High-resolution displays and sound output are also needed.

▶ Specialised input devices are often required to support high-speed or realistic interactions. These can be expensive to develop and purchase.

▶ High-speed interactions in response to feedback require complex programming and high-speed processors to ensure real-time interaction is supported during the gaming experience.

▶ Inexperienced users may feel overwhelmed by high levels of interactivity and multimedia and may not find the experience as enjoyable.

Multimedia and interactivity in generic applications

The use of multimedia and interactive content is now expected and commonplace in most of our interactions with digital technology. We will therefore now consider the advantages and disadvantages of multimedia and interactivity in generic applications.

Advantages of multimedia and interactivity in generic applications

▶ Interactive media keeps users engaged and interested; this helps them to retain information.

▶ Communication between users can now be supported via messaging tool.

▶ The widespread availability of digital devices means interactive messages can be made available to users anywhere and at any time, for example using **push technology** to send alerts to users. In this way, a message can reach a wider client-base.

▶ Content on interactive multimedia applications can be updated quickly where necessary.

▶ Most interactive multimedia applications are designed to be intuitive and can be used with limited technical knowledge.

Disadvantages of multimedia and interactivity in generic applications

▶ To access interactive multimedia systems, access to specialised hardware and software is needed.

▶ There is no guarantee that all members of your target audience will choose to access the information you are presenting to them.

▶ Messages presented to the user by interactive multimedia applications can sometimes be intrusive, for example pop-ups and alerts.

▶ Some interactive multimedia applications require a high level of maintenance, for example e-commerce sites must be regularly updated to show new products and popular social media pages must provide regular updates to keep the target audience engaged.

▶ Some technical skill is needed to support the creation of and the maintenance of an interactive multimedia application.

▶ Interactive applications are often designed to be used with specialised hardware devices which can be delicate and expensive to replace, for example touchscreens.

▶ Code needed to support such high levels of interaction can be complex.

▶ Applications which are media-rich can demand increased processing power, memory and storage requirements.

Checkpoint ✓

▷ A wide range of features are used in e-commerce, social media and gaming applications to support user interaction with multimedia elements. These include but are not limited to:
   - e-commerce: posting of reviews, tracking facilities, secure online payment, search facilities, live bidding and alerts, sharing of content, help systems and dispute resolution, image display tools, shopping carts
   - social media: user-generated multimedia content, live streaming, profile maintenance and settings adjustment, free web space, chat clients and other conversational tools, page creation, **call-to-action buttons**, search facilities
   - gaming applications: feedback elements, voice- and text-based interactions, 3D, visual interactions in **virtual space**, customisation, adjustment of visual elements.

Practice questions

1 Describe how the use of multimedia and interactive features in a digital application can make the application more appealing to the end user. [4 marks]

2 Describe four main interactive or multimedia features of a specific social media website and identify the advantages and disadvantages of each feature. [6 marks]

3 Describe three ways an end user can interact with the multimedia content of a gaming application. Your answer should consider the interactive actions the user has to take and the hardware used to support the interaction. [6 marks]

Chapter 14 Multimedia authoring

Multimedia authoring

This chapter should be reviewed in conjunction with Chapter 19, Building and testing a solution (Unit 3). In Chapter 19, additional features of the authoring tool used in this chapter are addressed, in addition to further examples of the use of scripted solutions to add interactivity to multimedia applications.

Multimedia authoring refers to the development of an application which integrates a range of media in a way that it can usefully present information to a target audience. By presenting information using a range of media, for example video, text, graphics and sound, an application can appeal to a wider target audience through the integration of continued interaction and provision of constant feedback.

Multimedia applications rely on the use of **hypertext** and **hypermedia** to support the user's movement through the material presented to them. Where hypermedia links are used, end users can move through the content of an application in a non-linear manner by following links, branching off into different trains of thought; similar to the way the human brain works (for example surfing the internet). Scripted elements in multimedia applications can help support this type of non-linear movement. We will see later in this chapter how scripting can be used to dynamically change the content of a document based on a decision made or an action taken by the end user.

Creating multimedia elements

Before embarking on the development of a multimedia application it is important that the content is carefully planned and, where possible, created in advance. Chapter 11 outlined the methods employed in planning multimedia applications and content elements. Creating multimedia content need not be a difficult task as there are many applications available which can support the development of graphical, video and sound files. The software used by the developer in the creation of supporting media is a matter of personal choice and may be dependent upon the supporting platform. Some examples of the resources available for the creation of multimedia content are listed on the next page.

Multimedia resource	Resources available for creation
Sound	Record via microphone and store in appropriate format. Online applications such as www.text2speech.org can be used to enter text content which can be converted to spoken text for download.
Video	Windows Live MovieMaker biteable.com Record using mobile phone and then upload to computer .
Animation	www.animatron.com cooltext.com
Graphics	Photoshop pixlr.com

Any supporting multimedia file should be saved in an optimised file format regardless of the application used to create it (see Chapter 12).

Multimedia authoring software

A multimedia authoring application contains a set of pre-defined elements which can be used to support the creation of a multimedia package, for example, a website. Many authoring applications provide the end user with a WYSIWYG environment. This provides a series of tools and elements that can be amended visually without the end user needing to understand any of the intricacies of the underlying programming language. The application creates all of the code in the background.

We will look here at the main features of a multimedia authoring application called Microsoft Expression Web 4. We will consider how this application can be used to create a multimedia package which can be displayed using a web browser.

Creating a new website

1 In the menu bar of the application, click on **Site** and select **New Site**.

2 Browse to the location where you would like to store your site and click **OK**.

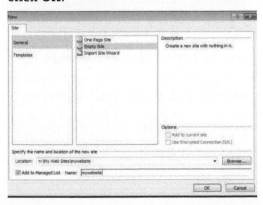

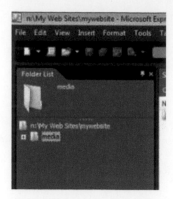

3 The folder containing your blank website will appear in the window on the left-hand side.

4 At this stage it is a good idea to consider how you would like to organise the content for your website. For example, should you have separate folders to store images and other multimedia content?

5 To create a folder for your multimedia content, right click on the pathway shown for your website and select **New** and then **Folder**. We will create a folder called 'Media' and any image or other multimedia elements will be stored here.

Creating a template

A good web developer will plan the content of their website before starting the development process. This allows them to create a document template which contains any elements which will be repeated on all the website pages.

In this example we will use a table to organise the content of the document template.

1 Select **New** and then **HTML** to create a blank page.

2 Add any content which will appear on all other pages in your website. This could include: a table to help you manage layout, a company banner, company logo, or navigation buttons.

a) Use the **Table** menu to insert a 1 column 3 row table.

b) Use the **Format** and then **Background** menu options to select an appropriate background colour and text for your website.

c) If you don't already have one, create a logo or web banner using a graphics package of your choice (save in an optimised file format) and insert this into the first row of the table.

d) Press enter to create a blank row underneath the banner.

e) Use the **Insert** and then **Interactive Buttons** menu options to add appropriate navigation buttons to your website. In this example we shall add only two: **Home** and **Contact Us**. Add the text you wish to see on your navigation button here.

f) In the third row you should add details about who created the webpage and when it was last updated. Your page should look similar to the example.

g) Once you have added all of the repeating elements needed, you should identify the areas which are to be made available for future editing. In this case this will be the second row.

i) Right click on the second row of the table and select **Manage Editable Regions**.

ii) Name this area 'body', click **Add** and then **Close**. Your display on the page will change as shown.

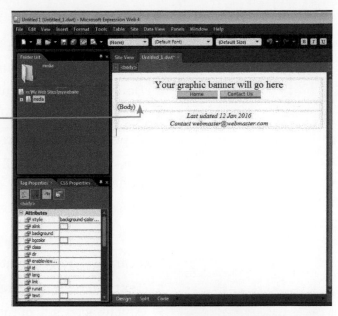

You will see the editable region now included in your template. Once you save your template this will be the only area available for future editing.

h) Once you are satisfied with the layout of this page click **File**, **Save As**. Under **Save as type**, select **Dynamic Web Template**. Give the template an appropriate name (for example pagetemplate) and click **Save As**.

i) You will be asked if you wish to **Save Embedded Files**. Click **OK**.

j) You will now see a series of images for your buttons and you will see pagetemplate.dwt appear in the folder list window. How might you use a folder to help you organise this content? Try creating a folder called buttons and drag and drop all of the button images into the folder. What happens?

Creating pages from a template

1 Close the page now named pagetemplate.dwt.

2 Click **File**, **New** and select **Create From Dynamic Web Template**. Select pagetemplate.dwt from the dialogue box and click **Open**. Your page will appear as shown, with any areas available for editing shown in white. All other content will be in grey.

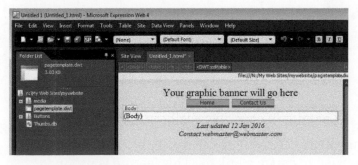

3 Save your page now as index.html.

4 Repeat steps 1 and 2 to create your second page called contact.html.

5 Close both pages.

Editing a template

We can now add our hyperlinks to our dynamic web template.

1 Open the file **pagetemplate.dwt**.

2 Double click on the button labelled **Home**.

3 Browse to the page called **home**, Click **OK**.

4 Repeat steps 1–3 to create a similar link to the page called **contact**.

5 Click **File** and **Save All**. All links within your document will now be updated.

6 Close pagetemplate.dwt.

Adding content to your webpages

You can now add content to the main body of your website.

1 Text can be added straight into the area by clicking and typing.

2 Any images (still or moving) stored in website folder structure can be dragged and dropped from the Folder List onto your webpage.

3 Sound and video files can also be added in the same way, although they will be presented as a text-based hyperlink.

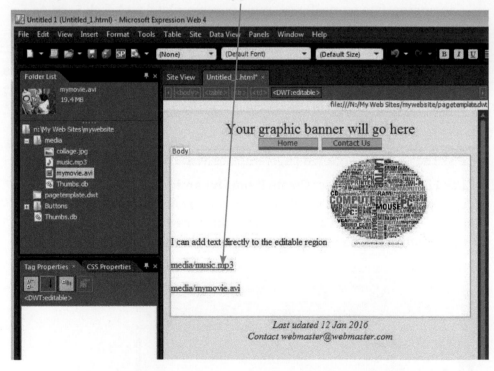

4 You can add hyperlinks to images by right clicking on the image, selecting **Hyperlink** and then entering the web address or by browsing to another file or webpage you wish to create a link to. (This feature is useful for adding links to external websites, using images as prompts, for example a microphone image to play sound files.) You can also use the Hyperlink tool to create a link to an email address.

5   If images are too large when displayed on the page, you can reduce their size, and load time, by right clicking on the image and selecting **Auto Thumbnail.**

6   Email links can also be added to text or other images.

7   You can preview your pages at any time by clicking on the **Preview** icon.

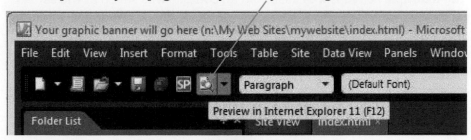

8   You can view the code created by the application at any time by clicking on the Code tab at the bottom of the page window. (You will see how this can be useful to advanced developers later when we consider how HTML and scripting can be applied to webpages.)

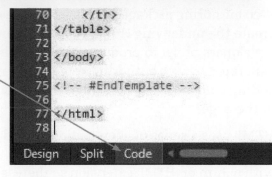

Tasks ✏️

Use the features of the web authoring application referenced above to design a basic template and then create a two-page website containing a range of multimedia elements. The pages can be on a topic of your choice and both pages should be linked using hyperlinks.

Advantages of using a web authoring application

▶ Little technical knowledge needed: developers can create professional applications with little programming knowledge.

▶ Intuitive interface: leads to faster development of final package, elements can easily be placed on-screen by selecting appropriate tools and developer sees immediately how the screen layout has changed.

▶ Updated links: authoring applications will often update hyperlinks for the developer when they move content around using the correct folder management tool.

Disadvantages of using a web authoring application

▶ Limited options: often the developer will have to revert to coding if complex interactions are required in the multimedia application they are developing.

▶ Use of templates: while templates provide consistency and improve development speed they can lead to the production of unoriginal interfaces as other developers may use the same template.

Using folders to manage content

In the example above it was assumed all content was saved at the same level in the folder structures. On page 100 the importance of using folders to organise web content was examined and this also applies when creating webpages using HTML. It is however important to consider how this will affect the pathways when referring to images in HTML code; remember to always include the full pathway!

Using HTML to create websites

Web authoring packages, such as the one described above, automatically create the underlying HTML code as the user adds objects to the page. Some developers prefer to produce websites using HTML as, on occasion, code generated by web authoring applications may not always be optimised. Plus, coding your website yourself gives greater opportunity to tweak the layout of the pages.

HTML uses a series of abbreviations called 'tags' to describe the main elements of a webpage. HTML documents are basic text documents saved with a .htm or .HTML extension so there is no need to purchase complex software to create a webpage using HTML.

Before we look at creating a webpage using HTML we must first look at the structure of a HTML document and the tags used to define layout in a webpage.

Here you are identifying the version of HTML being used – in this case HTML5.

<HTML> tag opens the document – you will see a matching </tag> at the end of the page to indicate the document is being closed.

The <head> tag can contain information about the document. It currently holds the document title but it can hold other elements of **metadata** such as any scripts or styles or the character set used in the document. We are only concerned with the title tag at this stage.

The <title> tag allows us to provide the user with additional information about the page they are viewing.

The body section is used to define any multimedia elements which will appear in the browser window.

Basic structure of a HTML document

```
<!doctype HTML>
<HTML>
  <head>
    <title>
    </title>
  </head>
<body>
<!--Add HTML here for webpage content-->
</body>
</HTML>
```

HTML tags to change browser and text display

There are a range of tags available to developers to enable them to alter the way text appears in a HTML document.

<title> </title> tag displays the webpage title in the browser window.

<h1> </h1>is a predefined heading tag. There are six heading tags in total (h1–h6). <h1> represents the largest text size.

The <div> </div> tag is used here to define a section (or division) in the HTML document and apply CSS formatting to that section. In this case any text enclosed within the div tag would be centre aligned.

The <p></p> tag defines a paragraph. Most browsers will add a space before and after a <p> element to separate it from the rest of the text.

In this paragraph, the <b></b>, <i></i> and <u></u> tags were used to format the text.

In this paragraph, the </br> tag was added after the word *line* to create a line break.

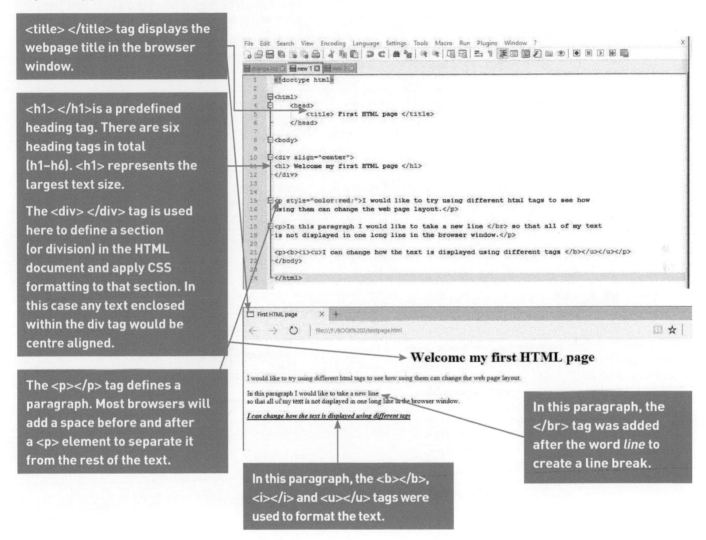

HTML tags for displaying graphics, video and inserting sound files

Multimedia documents must support the presentation of images (still and animated), video and sound files.

Tag	Example	How it affects display
<img>	<img src="buildings.png" alt="city skyline" height="200" width="200"> src identifies where the image is located alt will display alternate text for the image if the viewer places the cursor over the image <img> can also be used to integrate animations into the body of a HTML document.	Displays an image called buildings.png. Image width is 200 pixels and image height 200 pixels. If the user of the multimedia application places a cursor over the image, the text 'city skyline' will appear.

<audio> </audio>	<audio src="music.mp3" autoplay> This file type is not supported by your browser. </audio>	Supports automatic playback of the sound file music.mp3. The audio tag allows you to insert **fallback text** (an error message in the event that the file cannot be played by the browser).
	<audio controls> <source src="music.mp3" type="audio/mpeg"> This file type is not supported by your browser. </audio>	Inserts audio controls with the sound file so the user can select to play the music file or not.
<video> </video>	<video width="200" height="200" controls> <source src="mymovie.mp4" type="video/mp4"> This file type is not supported by your browser. </video>	Embeds an external video called mymovie.mp4 into a HTML5 document. MP4 file formats are supported by Google Chrome.
	<img dynsrc="mymovie.avi" start="fileopen">	Inserts videos for automatic playback to be viewed in Internet Explorer. If you prefer your user to have control over the playback of movie files you can add a hyperlink to the original movie file.

HTML tags for displaying tables and lists

Tag	Example	How it affects display

<table> </table>
<tr> </tr>
<th> </th>
<td> </td>
	<table bgcolor="blue" border="1" bordercolor="black">
	   <tr>
	      <th>Student</th>
	      <th>Score</th>
	   </tr>
	   <tr>
	      <td>Jack</td>
	      <td>90</td>
	   </tr>
	   <tr>
	      <td>Jane</td>
	      <td>91</td>
	   </tr>
	</table>
		Creates the following table of information.
		
		| **Student**
			Score |
			|---|---|
			| Jack | 90 |
			| Jane | 91 |

<ol> </ol>	<ol type="1">
	   <li>Alexander</li>
	   <li>Max</li>
	   <li>Emma</li>
	</ol>
		Displays an ordered list. In this case the ol tag has the '1' type (or style) assigned to it so items in the list will be numbered. Here, the list displayed would be
		1 Alexander
		2 Max
		3 Emma
		Other styles include 'a', 'A', 'i', 'I' representing list styles labelled in lower case, upper case, lower case Roman numerals and upper case Roman numerals.

<ul> </ul>	<ul style="list-style-type:disc">
	   <li>Alexander</li>
	   <li>Max</li>
	   <li>Emma</li>
	</ul>
		Displays an unordered list.
		• Alexander
		• Max
		• Emma
		Other styles include circle, square or none.

HTML tags for commenting and adding hyperlinks

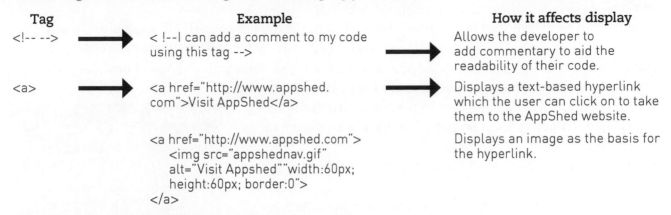

Tag	Example	How it affects display
<!-- -->	< !--I can add a comment to my code using this tag -->	Allows the developer to add commentary to aid the readability of their code.
<a>	<a href="http://www.appshed. com">Visit AppShed</a>	Displays a text-based hyperlink which the user can click on to take them to the AppShed website.
	<a href="http://www.appshed.com"> <img src="appshednav.gif" alt="Visit Appshed""width:60px; height:60px; border:0"> </a>	Displays an image as the basis for the hyperlink.

NB All above examples worked with IE11 (unless otherwise specified) at time of print. Where multimedia elements such as graphical, sound or video files have been referenced, similar resources should be created before trying these practical exercises.

Advantages of using HTML to create a multimedia solution

▶ HTML is easy to understand and use: most developers are familiar with HTML so if you need to use a different developer to update your application they will understand the code.

▶ All browsers support HTML: this means your application will display on all browsers.

▶ HTML is free: no additional software is needed to support development, you only need access to a web development tool and most development tools also support HTML.

Disadvantages of using HTML to create a multimedia solution

▶ Updating links: if images or other elements are moved between folders after the content has been referenced in a hyperlink, the developer must update the hyperlink in the code otherwise a dead link will be reported back to the user and the content cannot be displayed.

▶ It can only create **static pages**, if a **dynamic page** is needed, then additional script is needed. Static web pages tend to end with the extensions .htm or .html. An example might be a web page advertising a local historical attraction. Dynamic web pages may end with the extensions .php, .asp or .jsp. An example might be a web page displaying up-to-date bids on an online auction site.

▶ It can take a lot of HTML to produce a basic webpage.

Using CSS

CSS (cascading style sheets) is a language that describes the styles within a HTML document. It allows you to set the colour, font and text size of the document, headings and paragraphs of text within a webpage.

Tasks

1 Colours can be referenced by name as shown in some of the previous HTML examples. Research the list of colours you can specify in HTML and create a list of names for future reference.

2 Not all web browsers support all video and audio file types. Research a range of browsers and produce a list of audio and video file types they support.

   a) Open a text editor file and type in the basic structure of a HTML document shown on page 104. Save your document as a HTML file.

   b) Double click on the saved HTML document and view it in your default browser.

   c) Practise using the HTML examples listed in the tables on pages 105 to 107 to add additional content of your choice to the body of the HTML document. This will help you understand the **syntax** of HTML tags.

3 Open a Notepad document and type in the following.

```
<!DOCTYPE HTML>
<HTML>
  <head>
  <style>
  body{
    background-color:yellow;
    }
    h1, h2 {
    color:red;
    font-family:ariel;
    }
    p{
    font-family:ariel;
    font-size :12px
    }
  </style>
    <title>My HTML Example</title>
  </head>
<body>
    <!--Add the code to display the heading and table shown below-->
    <!--Use h1 style to display your heading-->
    <!--Your table should display the information shown below -->
    <!--Add borders, background colour and text colour to your table -->
</body>
</HTML>
```

We have created three different CSS styles in this example, one for the background colour, one for h1 and h2 (heading 1 and heading 2 text) and another for p (paragraph text).

Practical tip

Remember: If you need to edit the HTML for the page you must open Notepad again, select All Files and then browse to your HTML document.

Practical tip

It is always a good idea to keep your text editor and your browser window opened on the screen at the same time. That way each time you make a change to the HTML code you have saved you can refresh the browser window and preview the impact of the change.

Using scripting in multimedia authoring software

JavaScript can be added to multimedia applications to support more dynamic interactions which would not normally be supported by HTML. For example, changing the on-screen display in some way, hiding or displaying additional information on-screen or, in more advanced examples, validating the contents of a HTML-based form before it is submitted online. There are many examples of JavaScript available online and once you are familiar with how JavaScript can be incorporated into a HTML document it can be fun to experiment with.

JavaScript can be incorporated into HTML-based applications in several ways:

▶ incorporating into the body of the HTML code between an opening and closing script tag <script> </script>

▶ linking to external files which have a .js file extension

▶ placing in the <head> section of a HTML document and then calling/ activating this Java script by another element in the <body> section.

We will focus on the first and last approaches.

All programming languages such as JavaScript use a range of constructs to determine the order in which code is to be executed. We will look here at how **sequencing**, **selection** and **repetition** constructs can affect how code is executed using JavaScript examples. We will also look at how JavaScript can also use event-driven programming to determine how the application will respond to input from the end user.

Sequencing

Sequencing refers to a situation where lines of code are designed to run one after another from the beginning to the end. All lines of code are executed and the order of execution of the script will never change.

In this example, the JavaScript is contained between the <script> </script> tags.

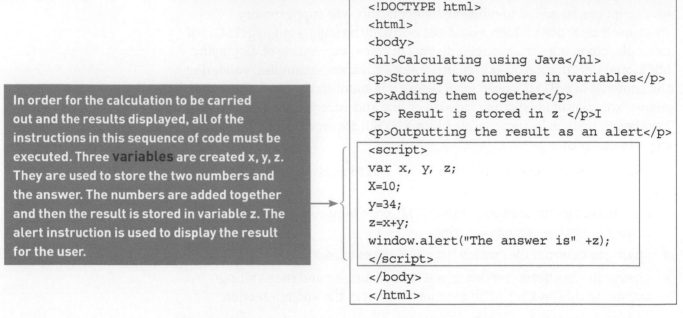

```
<!DOCTYPE html>
<html>
<body>
<h1>Calculating using Java</h1>
<p>Storing two numbers in variables</p>
<p>Adding them together</p>
<p> Result is stored in z </p>I
<p>Outputting the result as an alert</p>
<script>
var x, y, z;
X=10;
y=34;
z=x+y;
window.alert("The answer is" +z);
</script>
</body>
</html>
```

In order for the calculation to be carried out and the results displayed, all of the instructions in this sequence of code must be executed. Three **variables** are created x, y, z. They are used to store the two numbers and the answer. The numbers are added together and then the result is stored in variable z. The alert instruction is used to display the result for the user.

Repetition

Repetitive code structures cause specified lines of code to be executed again and again. Repetition in JavaScript can be implemented using FOR or WHILE loops. The 'FOR' loop allows the developer to decide how many times a code inside the loop needs to run for (this is called a fixed count loop). The 'WHILE' loop will allow the code inside the loop to repeat until a particular condition is met (for example while there are names in a list). (This is called a variable count loop.)

We will look here at the FOR loop. In this example the FOR loop is used to print out a list of names stored in a variable called 'members'.

This HTML document has created a list of members of a quiz team.

```
<!DOCTYPE html>
<html>
<body>
<h1>JavaScript For Loops</h1>
<p>The members of the team are</p>
<p id="testloop"></p>
<script>
var membersdisplay = "";
var member s = ["Sharon", "John", "Martha", "Ernie"]
var i;
for (i = 0; i < 4; i++) {
  membersdisplay += members[i] + ", ";
}
document.getElementByld("testloop").innerHTML = membersdisplay;
</script>
</body>
</html>
```

The script in this HTML document contains a loop which will run four times. It will take the list of names from the members list and add them one by one to the members display list (membersdisplay += members [i]). Each name will be separated by ", ".

You can see the FOR loop has three main statements in the syntax of its first line; all separated by semicolons. The lines of code to be repeated are surrounded by curly brackets {}.

The first statement (i=0) is carried out before the block of code is executed. "i" is the counter, so the loop will start at 0. This means the first item on the list "Sharon" which is members[0], can be accessed (lists are numbered from 0) and read into "membersdisplay".

The next statement (i<4) is the condition which helps determine how long the loop needs to run for.

The nest statement ensures the counter will be increased by 1 so that, for example members[1] which is "John" can then be read into membersdisplay.

Tasks

1 Enter the code above into a Notepad document and run the HTML document you have created. Print out your code and annotate it to explain how the FOR loop controls the repetition of the code to ensure you understand the syntax of the FOR statement.

2 Amend your code to replace the FOR loop with the WHILE loop shown below. The output should remain unchanged.

```
while (members[i])
{
  text += members[i] + ",  ";
  i++;
}
```

3 Print out your code and annotate it with a friend to explain how the WHILE loop controls the repetition of the code to ensure you understand the syntax of the WHILE statement.

4 JavaScript also uses the DO ... WHILE statement to implement repetition. Search for simple JavaScript examples which use the DO ... WHILE loop. Print out the code and annotate it to ensure you understand the syntax of the statement.

Selection

Selection programming structures are used in instances where only some lines of code need to be run and only if a certain condition is met. The example given below uses an IF ... ELSE statement to display a message for the end user when they load this webpage.

```
<!DOCTYPE html>
<html>
<body onload="myFunction()">
<p>Display alert on page load to tell a student to study
   or relax</p>
```

JavaScript is called/activated here using the onload event (see the event-driven programming example on page 112).

The JavaScript used to check the data and issue an alert is defined here within the <script> </script> tags in this example.

The date/time is collected using the Date().getHours command, which returns the time according to the 24-hour clock.

The date/time is stored in a variable called hour.

The IF ... ELSE statement checks if time is less than 9 p.m. (21:00) then display an alert message which says "You still have time to study" else return an alert saying "Perhaps you should relax for the evening".

```
<p id="demo"></p>
<script>
function myFunction( ) {
  var hour = new Date().getHours()
  if(hour < 21) {
  alert("You still have time to study");
  } else {
  alert("Perhaps now you should relax for the evening");
  }
}
</script>
</body>
</html>
```

Tasks

Enter the code provided above into a blank notepad file and test the code.

JavaScript also uses IF, ELSE ... IF and SWITCH statements to implement selection. Search for simple JavaScript examples which use the IF, ELSE ... IF and SWITCH statements, print out the code and annotate it to ensure you understand the syntax of the statements.

Event-driven programming

In **event-driven programming**, the end user's interactions with the application (for example through mouse clicks or key presses, selection of an option from a dropdown box or entering data into a text box) will determine how the application is presented to the user. The application is designed to respond to user interactions.

The example given below uses JavaScript to change an image on screen when the user clicks a button.

JavaScript is included within the body tags and used to change the on-screen display following the execution of an event by the end user (button click).

```
<!DOCTYPE html>
<html>
<body>
<h1> Event Programming Example <h1>
<p><h6>Using the onclick handler <h6/></p>
<p>Other event handlers in java include.</p>
<p>onmouseover - the programmed event will occur when the
    cursor passes over a html element</p>
<p>onkeydown - the programmed event will occur when a
    particular key is pressed</p>
<p>onload - the programmed event will occur when the page has
    been loaded by the browser</p>
<button onclick "document .getElementByid ('myimage').
    src='building2 .jpg' ">Change the building</button>
<img id="my mage" src="building .jpg" style="width: 100px">
<button onclick="document .getElementByid ('myimage').
    src='building .jpg' ">Restore building</button>
</body>
</html>
```

Tasks

1   Create two versions of the same image (perhaps one with the image flipped). Save them as two different file names. Enter the code provided above into Notepad and amend it to reference your two images. Use the onclick handler to change the appearance of the images and back again.

2   Research the use of other event handlers and amend your code to change the image on a different event, for example onmouseover.

3   Open the two-page website you created using a multimedia authoring application. Access the script in each of the pages and add some of the JavaScript elements you have just practised. You might want to use an alert message to send your user a message, for example "good morning" or "good evening".

Remember you can access the script for each of the pages you created either through the web authoring application (see page 103), or you can open Notepad and browse to the webpage you wish to edit.

Checkpoint

▷ Multimedia authoring refers to the development of an application which integrates a range of media using hypertext, hypermedia and some scripting.

▷ Multimedia applications can be created using multimedia authoring applications or they can be created using programming languages such as HTML and JavaScript.

▷ Multimedia authoring applications generally provide the developer with a WYSIWYG interface which generates the underlying code for the developer. They are suitable for users with little programming experience.

▷ HTML uses tags to describe the main elements of a webpage.

▷ HTML can only be used to develop static page content; other scripted elements are needed if dynamic web content is required.

▷ Metadata is data that describes other data. In a HTML document metadata is defined inside the <head> </head> tag.

▷ CSS can be used to describe the style of a HTML document.

▷ JavaScript can be incorporated into HTML code using a variety of methods.

▷ Scripted elements can be coded sequentially, using repetition or selection.

▷ Most coding solutions now incorporate some element of event-driven programming.

Practice questions

1   Explain what is meant by the terms 'hypertext' and 'hypermedia'.   [2 marks]

2   Scripted elements are often used to include dynamic content in a webpage. Explain the term 'scripted elements'.   [1 mark]

3   Describe the difference between a static and a dynamic webpage.   [2 marks]

4   JavaScript uses repetition and selection when code is being executed. Explain the difference between repetition and selection.   [2 marks]

Chapter 15 Database development

What this chapter covers

- ▶ Relational databases
- ▶ Creating a database
- ▶ Using validation checks and data entry controls
- ▶ Creating relationships between tables
- ▶ Creating basic forms for data entry
- ▶ Creating complex queries
- ▶ Creating complex reports using calculations, groupings and sorting
- ▶ Using mail merge
- ▶ Using macros to automate tasks with forms

Tasks

This chapter should be reviewed in conjunction with Chapter 19 Building and testing a solution (Unit 3).

Relational databases

The concept of a single table or a flat file database and linking tables together in a database is discussed in Chapter 3 Database applications (Unit 1).

In this chapter, we shall look at the skills required to create a relational database which can support data input and information output to suit the needs of an organisation.

Using Microsoft Access, we shall produce a database system which will support the management of computer game loans for a small gaming library. On the next page you can see part of the table the organisation uses to record details about members and their loans.

You can see from the table that some data, such as name and address, must be recorded more than once, i.e. each time a game is rented out by a member of the gaming library. When data is repeated unnecessarily in this way, this is referred to as **data redundancy**.

You will also notice that an error has been entered into the data recorded for one member, Sarah Johnston. When data is being entered repeatedly into a system like this, mistakes can occur at the data entry stage. Such errors can have an impact on **data integrity**.

Relational databases can be used to help overcome some of the issues associated with storing data in a flat file database. A relational database is a database system which stores data in more than one table. Each table can represent entities which have data recorded about them in the database. In this case the main entities are members, loans and games. The tables representing each entity can then be linked in order to:

- ▶ reduce data redundancy (since data is not repeated unnecessarily)
- ▶ increase data integrity (since data is only recorded once it need only be updated once).

Member ID	Surname	First Name	House Number	Street	Town	Post Code	Game ID	Game Title	Platform	Game Rating	Date Out
1	Smith	James	3	Main Street	Newtown	BT19 7YT	1	FIFA 17	Xbox One S	3	21/11/2016
1	Smith	James	3	Main Street	Newtown	BT19 7YT	7	Minecraft	Xbox One S	7	21/11/2016
1	Smith	James	3	Main Street	Newtown	BT19 7YT	2	Football Manager	Xbox One S	3	21/11/2016
2	Jones	Amy	78	High street	Oldtown	BT18 6HY	5	NBA2K17	PS4	3	21/11/2016
2	Jones	Amy	78	High street	Oldtown	BT18 6HY	9	SIMS 4	PS4	12	21/11/2016
3	Brown	Jack	42	South Square	Oldtown	BT18 8PJ	6	Lego Jurassic World	PC	7	21/11/2016
3	Brown	Jack	42	South Square	Oldtown	BT18 8PJ	3	Ratchet Plant	PC	7	21/11/2016
4	Andrews	Sarah	6	Hill Street	Newtown	BT19 6GY	4	Marvel Pinball	Xbox One S	12	21/11/2016
4	Andrews	Sharon	6	Hill Street	Newtown	BT19 6GY	8	NHI17	Xbox One S	12	21/11/2016

Reduction in data integrity: errors have been introduced when entering data relating to member number 4.

Data redundancy: some data has been entered more than once (unnecessarily).

Using Microsoft Access, we will create three separate entities in a relational database to represent members, games and loans.

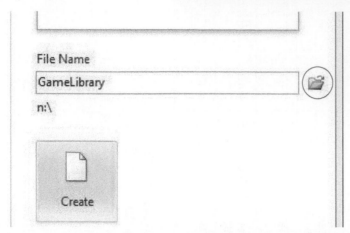

File Name

GameLibrary

n:\

Create

Creating a database

1 Open Microsoft Access and click on **Blank database**. Enter the name **GameLibrary** into the File Name data entry field.

2 Click on the yellow folder to browse to the location you wish to store your database.

3 Click **Create** to create a new database.

Structuring tables in a database

We shall now create a table which will store data on the member entities.

1 Click on the **Create** tab and click **Table** to create a blank table (if one does not already exist).

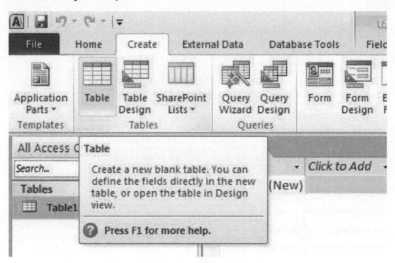

2 Right Click on **Table1** and select **Design View**.

3 You will be asked to assign a name to the table. Name the table **membersTBL** and then click **OK**.

4 Insert the following field headings and data types into the **table design** window.

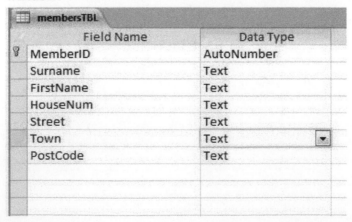

Field Name	Data Type
MemberID	AutoNumber
Surname	Text
FirstName	Text
HouseNum	Text
Street	Text
Town	Text
PostCode	Text

5 Notice that a small key has appeared beside the first field in the database table. This indicates that this field is the **key field** in the table. You can change this at any time by selecting any other field and clicking on the key icon visible in the File tab.

Key fields are discussed in Chapter 3 Database applications (Unit 1).

Setting field sizes

We shall now set appropriate field sizes and validation checks for each of the data types in the membersTBL table.

1 The MemberID data type default setting is Autonumber. This means that each time a new member entity is added to the table it will automatically be assigned a number. This feature helps ensure that no two members will be allocated the same number. Even if a member is deleted from the system their MemberID will not be reallocated to a new member.

2 Click on **Surname**. A list of field properties will appear at the bottom of the screen.

membersTBL

Field Name	Data Type	
MemberID	AutoNumber	
Surname	Text	
FirstName	Text	
HouseNum	Text	
Street	Text	
Town	Text	
PostCode	Text	

Field Properties

General | Lookup

Field Size	255
Format	
Input Mask	
Caption	
Default Value	
Validation Rule	
Validation Text	
Required	No
Allow Zero Length	Yes
Indexed	No
Unicode Compression	Yes
IME Mode	No Control
IME Sentence Mode	None
Smart Tags	

3   Change the **Field Size** property value from **255** to **35**.

4   Set the **Required** Property to **Yes**. This ensures this field cannot be left blank when an entity is being added to the database. This is an example of creating a **presence check** in Microsoft Access.

Tasks 🖉

1   With the rest of your class, discuss the advantages of reducing the Field Size value.

2   Set appropriate field sizes for each of the other attributes stored in the table.

   a) Repeat the steps above to create two additional tables. Name the first loanTBL and the second gameTBL. Assign the tables the following file headings and data types:

loanTBL	
LoanID	Autonumber
MemberID	Number/Integer
GameID	Number/Integer
DateOut	Date/Time
DateReturn	Date/Time

gameTBL	
GameID	Autonumber
GameTitle	Text
Platform	Text
Rating	Number/Integer
Fee (p/n)	Currency

   b) Select appropriate field lengths for each attribute.

Some fields, such as **MemberID** and **GameID**, exist (or are repeated) in **loanTBL**. Some level of repetition is needed if we are to successfully create links between each of the entities in a relational database.

You will be familiar with the concept of a key field from Chapter 3. **MemberID** and **GameID** can now be referred to as foreign key fields in **loanTBL**. You will see later in this chapter how foreign keys are used to create links between tables in a relational database.

The purpose of data validation is discussed in Chapter 3 Database applications (Unit 1).

Using validation checks and data entry controls

We will now look at how you can implement some basic validation checks using Microsoft Access.

The owner of the GameLibrary has realised most of their members are from Oldtown. They have decided they will only rent games to members from Oldtown or Newtown, and so would like to limit data entry in the town field so that only the values 'Oldtown' and 'Newtown' will be accepted.

1   Double click on the **membersTBL** table to open it. Go to the **Design View** window.

2   Click on the field heading **'Town'**.

3 Amend the field properties for Town, as shown below.
- By setting the Default Value to 'Oldtown' this value will automatically appear in the Town field when a new entity is added to membersTBL.
- By setting the Validation Rule to 'Oldtown Or Newtown', this ensures that only those two values can be entered as an attribute for a new entity.
- The Validation Text provides the user with feedback if data they are entering is not accepted by the database application.
- Another method of limiting entry for an attribute in a data table is through the use of a **look-up list**.

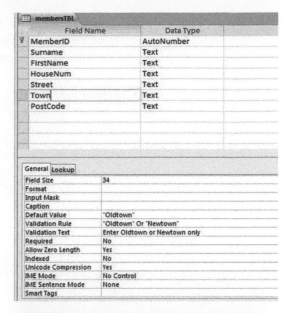

GameLibrary only provide games for the following platforms: PC, Xbox One S and PS4. We can use a look-up list to ensure these options are available for the user to select at the data entry point.

1 Double click on the table called **gameTBL** to open it. Go to the **Design View** window.

2 Click on the **Field Name** called **Platform**.

3 Select **Lookup Wizard** … under **Data Type**.

4 Select '**I will type in the values that I want**' and then click **Next**.

5 Enter **PC**, **Xbox OneS** and **PS4** into **Col1** in the dialogue box which appears. Then click **Next**.

6 In the next dialogue box leave the label unchanged and click **Finish**.

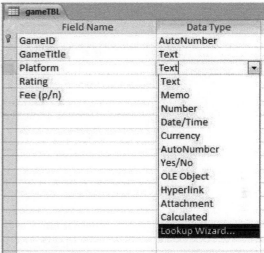

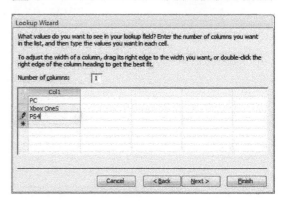

119

Some digital databases use **input masks** as a means of controlling data entry for attributes. Using an input mask ensures the user adheres to a particular format when data is entered.

0	0 to 9 only can be entered (+ or − NOT accepted). Data entry is required.
9	0 to 9 can be entered or SPACE (+ or − NOT accepted). Data entry is NOT required.
#	0 to 9 accepted, SPACE accepted, + or − accepted. Data entry NOT required.
L	A–Z accepted. Data entry required.
?	A–Z accepted. Data entry NOT required.
A	A–Z or 0–9 accepted. Data entry required.
a	A–Z or 0–9 accepted. Data entry NOT required.
&	Any character or space accepted. Data entry required.
C	Any character or space accepted. Data entry NOT required.
<	All characters following this symbol will be converted to lower case.
>	All characters following this symbol will be converted to upper case.

▲ Examples of input mask controls

To set an input mask to ensure that all surnames entered start with a capital letter:

1 Double click on the table called **membersTBL** to open it. Go to the **Design View window.**

2 Click on the **Field Name** called **Surname.**

3 In the Field Properties section click beside Input Mask and enter >L<???????? … (you should have 34 question marks in your input mask, can you think why this might be? (Look at the field size.)

When you click on the Input Mask field in Field Properties an ellipse symbol (...) appears.

Clicking on this will give you access to a set of predefined input masks. Use this feature to add an input mask for the PostCode field in your membersTBL (see Task below).

The owner of GameLibrary wants to ensure that DateOut cannot be set as a date in the future. In loanTBL set the field properties for DateOut as shown below.

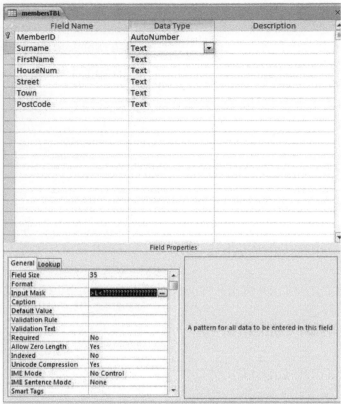

General	Lookup
Format	
Input Mask	
Caption	
Default Value	
Validation Rule	<=Date()
Validation Text	Date Out cannot be in the future
Required	No
Indexed	No
IME Mode	No Control
IME Sentence Mode	None
Smart Tags	
Text Align	General
Show Date Picker	For dates

Tasks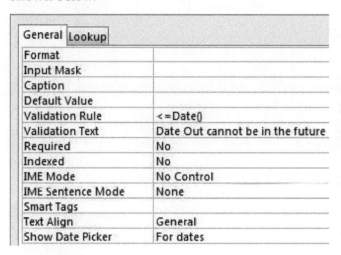

1 The rental fee for games is limited to between £2 and £5 per night. Refer back to Chapter 3 Database applications in Unit 1 for an example of how to set a range check for this field.

   The owner also feels it is important that all data in membersTBL be entered. Set the Required property to Yes for each field in the table.

2 You should now consider how each of the above examples of various types of validation and input control can be applied to each of the three tables you have created. Use the examples from this chapter and from Chapter 3 to help you add as many validation checks and input controls to your database as possible to help minimise data entry error.

Creating relationships between tables

We have already considered the fact that relational databases can help reduce data redundancy and improve data integrity.

Let us look at how this applies in our **GameLibrary** example.

1 Click on the **Database Tools** tab. Click on **Relationships.**

2 In the **Show Table** dialogue box click on **gameTBL** and then click **Add**. Repeat this process for the remaining two tables. Click **Close** when all three tables are displayed in the relationship window.

3 Rearrange the tables so your display is similar to here.

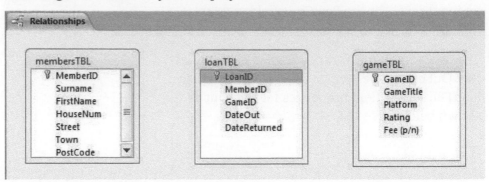

4 Click on **MemberID** in **membersTBL** and drag your mouse across to loanTBL. The following dialogue box will appear.

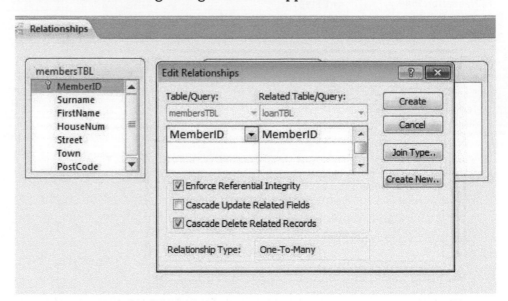

Tasks ✎

Repeat the steps detailed above to create a similar one-to-many relationship between gameTBL and loanTBL using GameID.

The use of the MemberID in loanTBL to establish a link with membersTBL is an example of a foreign key field. In some instances **composite key fields**, where two or more fields can be used in a table, can be used to establish links between tables in a database. You will see an example of how a composite key field can be used in this way in Chapter 19 Building and testing a solution (Unit 3).

5 Select **Enforce Referential Integrity** and **Cascade Delete** Related Records and then click **Create** in the dialogue box.

Creating basic forms for data entry

We will now create a form to allow us to input data into our database, using the Microsoft Access Wizard. This will allow us to enter details for customers and loans so we can complete the remainder of the practical tasks in this chapter.

Data can be added straight into the database tables but for less experienced users it is best to create a graphic user interface to support their interaction with the database application.

> Unit 3 will look in detail at creating forms and how to edit their layout.

Creating a form to add data to membersTBL

1   In the **Objects Window**, select **membersTBL**. Then click on the **Create** tab and select **Form Wizard**.

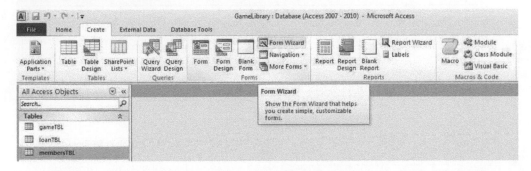

2   Click on the double arrow head (>>) in the **Form Wizard** to include all fields in the form you are creating, then click **Next**.

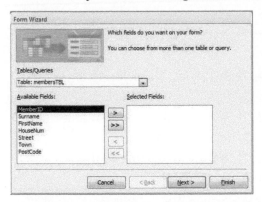 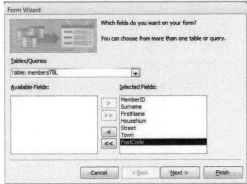

3   Choose **Columnar** layout and click **Next**.

4   Change the form title to **membersFRM**.

5   Choose **Modify the forms design** and click on **Finish**.

6   Spend some time customising your form and making it look more professional by editing the form title, adding a logo to the **FormHeader**, making the field names more readable, for example by adding spaces to **MemberID**, **HouseNum**, **FirstName** etc.

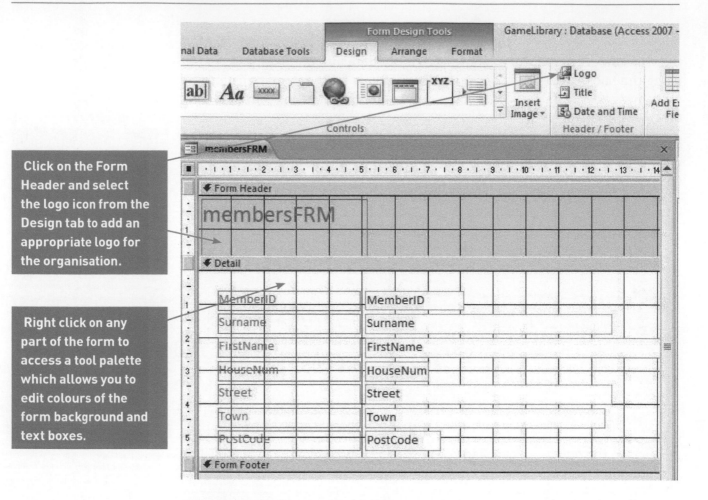

Click on the Form Header and select the logo icon from the Design tab to add an appropriate logo for the organisation.

Right click on any part of the form to access a tool palette which allows you to edit colours of the form background and text boxes.

Tasks

1   Repeat the above steps to create forms which allow you to enter data into **loanTBL** and **gameTBL.**

2   Use the Form Wizard to create a form which allows you to enter data into **membersTBL** and **loanTBL** at the same time.

3   Using the forms you have created add the data shown to the appropriate tables in your database.

MemberID	Surname	First Name	House Number	Street	Town	PostCode
1	Smith	James	3	Main Street	Newtown	BT19 7YT
2	Jones	Amy	78	High street	Oldtown	BT18 6HY
3	Brown	Jack	42	South Square	Oldtown	BT18 8PJ

▲ membersTBL

Game ID	GameTitle	Platform	Game Rating	Fee (p/n)
1	FIFA 17	Xbox OneS	3	£2.00
2	Football Manager	Xbox OneS	3	£2.00
3	Ratchet Plant	PC	7	£4.00
4	Marvel Pinball	Xbox OneS	12	£2.00
5	NBA2K17	PS4	3	£4.00
6	Lego Jurassic World	PC	7	£2.00
7	Minecraft	Xbox OneS	7	£4.00
8	NHl17	Xbox OneS	12	£3.00
9	SIMS 4	PS4	12	£3.00

▲ gameTBL

LoanID	MemberID	GameID	DateOut	Date Returned
1	1	1	21/11/2016	
2	1	7	21/11/2016	
3	1	2	21/11/2016	
4	2	5	21/11/2016	
5	2	9	21/11/2016	
6	3	6	21/11/2016	
7	3	3	21/11/2016	
8	4	4	21/11/2016	
9	4	8	21/11/2016	

▲ loanTBL

Practical tips

Make sure you input data to the tables in the following order: **membersTBL, gameTBL, loanTBL**. (Since you will have selected **Enforce referential integrity** when creating relationships between your tables, it is impossible to add a loan to **loanTBL** if the **memberID** or **gameID** do not already exist in the original table.)

You should find that you do not have to add **MemberID**, **GameID** or **LoanID** to your tables if you have selected **Autonumber** and that if you delete a record by mistake the ID cannot be used again!

It does not matter if your IDs vary from the examples shown.

> The use of simple database queries (using one criteria to extract data from a database) is discussed in Chapter 3 Database application (Unit 1).

Creating complex queries

We will now look at complex query structures, such as queries using more than one criteria, queries using data from more than one table or query, and queries which perform calculations.

Creating queries with more than one criteria

The owner of GameLibrary would like to find out how many games he has available which are for Xbox OneS *and* suitable for age seven or below.

1 Click on the **Create** tab and then Click **Query Wizard**.

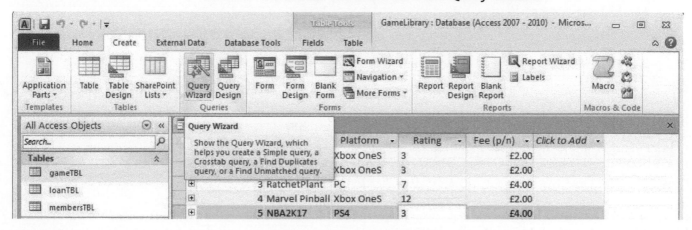

2 Choose **Simple Query Wizard** and then click **OK**.

3 From the dropdown list under **Tables/Queries**, choose **gameTBL**. Click the double arrow (>>) to select all fields and then click **Next** and then **Next** again.

4 Give the query an appropriate name, such as xbox_oneS_u7QRY. Select **Modify** the query design and click **Finish**.

5 Enter the following criteria into the query design window.

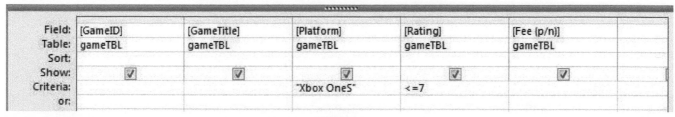

Field:	[GameID]	[GameTitle]	[Platform]	[Rating]	[Fee (p/n)]	
Table:	gameTBL	gameTBL	gameTBL	gameTBL	gameTBL	
Sort:						
Show:	✓	✓	✓	✓	✓	
Criteria:			"Xbox OneS"	<=7		
or:						

> ## Tasks
>
> Practise creating multi-criteria queries like this for the other two game platforms and various age ranges.

6 Click the Run icon.
Run

7 The query should generate the following results.

xbox_oneS_u7QRY

GameID	GameTitle	Platform	Rating	Fee (p/n)
1	FIFA 17	Xbox OneS	3	£2.00
2	Football Mana	Xbox OneS	3	£2.00
7	Minecraft	Xbox OneS	7	£3.00
* (New)				

Creating queries with calculated fields

Members of GameLibrary can rent games for seven days at a time. We can use a query to calculate the return date for a rental.

This query will be called due_backQRY.

1 Click on the **Create** tab, click on **Query Wizard**, choose **Simple Query Wizard** and then click **OK**.

2 Choose **loanTBL** from the dropdown list under **Tables/Queries**. Click the double arrow to select all fields and then click on **Next**.

3 Click **Next** again.

4 Give the query an appropriate name, such as due_backQRY. Select **Modify the query design** and click **Finish**.

5 Enter the following criteria into the field beside DateReturned.

Field:	[LoanID]	[MemberID]	[GameID]	[DateOut]	[DateReturned]	DueBack: [dateout]+7
Table:	loanTBL	loanTBL	loanTBL	loanTBL	loanTBL	
Sort:						
Show:	☑	☑	☑	☑	☑	☑
Criteria:						
or:						

6 Some of the results produced are shown below. You will notice how the **DueBack** date has now been calculated and added to the end of the results.

due_backQRY

LoanID	MemberID	GameID	DateOut	DateReturn	DueBack
1	1	1	21/11/2016		28/11/2016
2	1	7	21/11/2016		28/11/2016
3	1	2	21/11/2016		28/11/2016

> This creates a new output field within the query and then adds seven to that date to determine the date of return. We will use this query later when producing an invoice for a customer.

Creating queries using more than one table or query

The owner of GameLibrary would like to issue a receipt to each member each time they take out a loan. On the receipt he would like to include the member's details, details of the game they have rented, the date it is due back and the total fee for renting each game.

In order to do this we must first create a query which combines all of the data we require from **membersTBL**, **dueback_QRY** and **gameTBL** and which then calculates the fee due for each game.

1 Click on the **Create** tab, click on **Query Wizard**, choose **Simple Query Wizard** and then click **OK**.

2 Select **membersTBL** from the dropdown list under **Tables/Queries** and add the following fields to the right-hand panel in this order:

MemberID

FirstName

Surname

You can do this by selecting each field in turn and clicking on the single arrow.

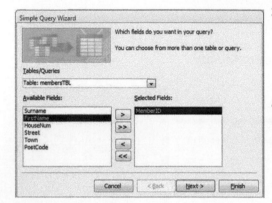

3 Select **due_backQRY** and add the following fields to the right-hand panel:

LoanID

GameID

4 Select **gameTBL** and add the following fields to the right-hand panel:

GameTitle

Platform

Fee (p/n)

5 Select **due_backQRY** again and add the following fields to the right-hand panel:

DateOut

DueBack

6 Click **Next**, select **Details** (shows every field of every record) and click **Next**.

7 Name the query **RentalFeeQRY**. Select **Modify the query design** and click **Finish**.

A query design window similar to the one shown should appear.

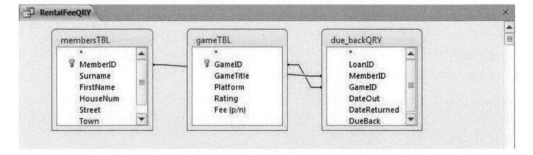

8 Under **MemberID** enter [Enter MemberID] as the criteria. This will prompt the user to enter a member ID each time the query is run so a report will only be produced for a specific member. This type of query is called a **parameter query**.

9 Enter the following criteria into the next available field in the design window:

GameRentalFee: [Fee (p/n)]*7

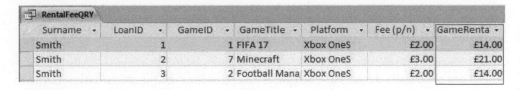

Field:	GameID	GameTitle	Platform	Fee (p/n)	GameRentalFee: [Fee (p/n)]*7
Table:	due_backQRY	gameTBL	gameTBL	gameTBL	
Sort:					
Show:	☑	☑	☑	☑	☑
Criteria:					
or:					

10 Click the **Run** button. When prompted to, 'enter memberID,' enter **1** and click **OK**.

The following results will be generated. Notice how the total rental fee for each game has now been calculated and added to the query results.

RentalFeeQRY

Surname	LoanID	GameID	GameTitle	Platform	Fee (p/n)	GameRenta
Smith	1	1	FIFA 17	Xbox OneS	£2.00	£14.00
Smith	2	7	Minecraft	Xbox OneS	£3.00	£21.00
Smith	3	2	Football Mana	Xbox OneS	£2.00	£14.00

Structured query language (SQL)

Some developers prefer to use **structured query language (SQL)** to retrieve data from a relational database.

SQL statements have three main components: select, from and where.

▶ Select will specify the data to be displayed.

▶ Where will identify the source of the data.

▶ From will identify the criteria to be used to select data from the source.

The following examples show how we could use SQL to extract data from our GameLibrary database.

To select all members in membersTBL who lived in Oldtown and only display their Surname, First Name and Town:

SQL query	Result
SELECT membersTBL.[Surname], membersTBL.[FirstName], membersTBL.[Town] FROM membersTBL WHERE (((membersTBL.[Town])="Oldtown"));	Jones, Amy, Oldtown Brown, Jack, Oldtown

To select all members in membersTBL who lived in High Street in Oldtown and only display their Surname, First Name, Street and Town:

SQL Query	Result
SELECT membersTBL.Surname, membersTBL.FirstName, membersTBL.Street, membersTBL.Town FROM membersTBL WHERE (((membersTBL.Street)="High Street") AND ((membersTBL.Town)="Oldtown"));	Jones, Amy, High street, Oldtown

Tasks ✎

You can examine the background SQL for any queries created in a relational database by viewing the query in Design View and then selecting View and SQL View.

Examine the structure of a range of queries, both complex and simple, that you have produced throughout the practical exercises in this chapter. Ensure you understand how SQL can be used to select data from a range of tables and using complex criteria.

Creating complex reports using calculations, groupings and sorting

We will now look at how we can use advanced report features to enhance how we display information to the end user.

The receipt the GameLibrary owner would like to issue should contain the member's details, details of the game and the loan but it should also contain an overall fee.

1   Select the **Report Wizard** from the **Create** tab.

2   Select **RentalFeeQRY** from the dropdown list in the dialogue box which appears.

3   Click the double arrow to add all fields to the right-hand window and click **Next.** The following dialogue box will appear.

Basic reports, and how they can be used to display information, are discussed in Chapter 3 Database applications (Unit 1).

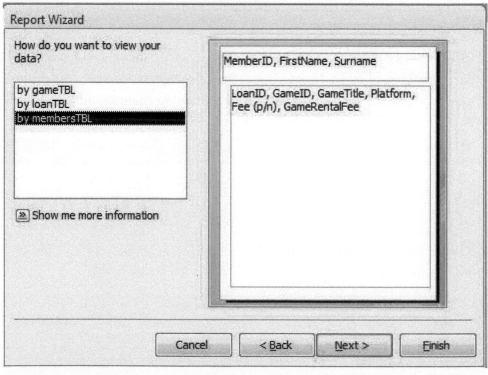

4 Click **Next** again.

5 You will be asked: '**Do you want to add any grouping levels?**' In this instance the answer is no, so click **Next** when the next dialogue box appears.

6 In the next screen you can choose how you would like to order the data in your report. Select **GameID** and **Ascending** and click **Next**.

7 Select **Stepped layout** and **Portrait orientation** in the next screen and click **Next**.

8 Give the report the title **receiptRPT**. Select **Modify the report's design** and click **Next**.

9 The report design will be similar to the one shown below.

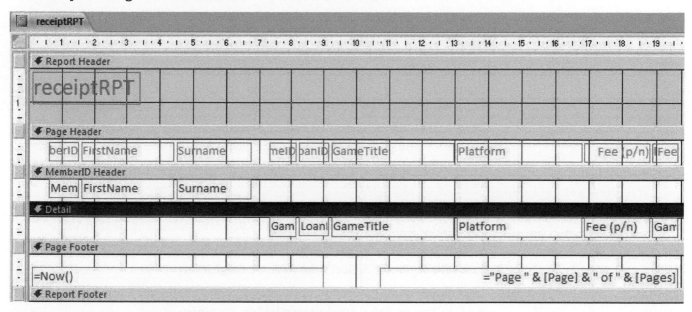

10 In the **File** tab, change Design View to **Report View**.

11 You will be prompted to **"Enter MemberID"**. (Remember this report was created using due_backQRY.) Enter **1** and click **OK**.

12 The following report layout will be displayed.

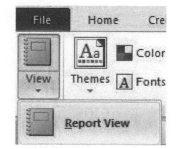

You will notice that many of the field headings and data cannot be read.

13 Select **Design View** and adjust the report layout so it is similar to the one shown here. You may also want to improve the design by adding a logo, or changing the colour, size or font of text.

You may find it helpful to switch between **Design View** and **Report View** as you make adjustments to the layout so you can preview how your changes in Design View work on the final report. You can also use layout view to change the look and feel of a report or form. It allows you to change the placement and size of fields etc. while still viewing the information to be displayed on the final report. Design View allows you to edit every area of the report or form, for example adding additional fields or changing the data sources of a field.

14 Once you are happy with the layout of your report select **Design View** again to add the overall rental total to the bottom of the report.

15 Click on the **Group & Sort** icon in the **Design** tab.

16 The following control panel will appear at the bottom of your report design window. Expand the display by clicking on **More**.

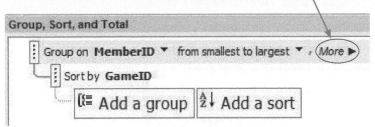

You will now see the following options. Ensure you have selected to display your report with a footer section.

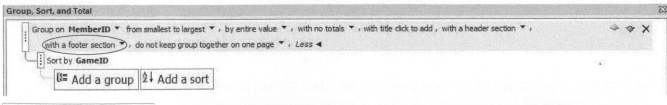

17 Click on the option which is currently set to '**with no totals**'.

18 Set the **Total On** value to GameRentalFee. Type should be set to **Sum** and place a tick beside **Show Grand Total** and Show subtotal in **group footer**.

19 Run your report for memberID 1 again to see how this affects the display.

You will notice an additional number appearing on the report display.

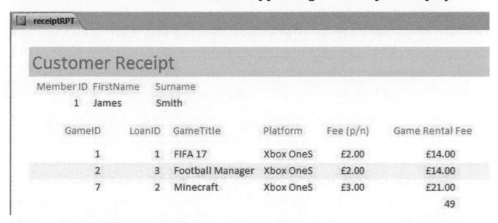

20 Return to **Design View** and right click on the new field which has appeared in the **MemberIDFooter**.

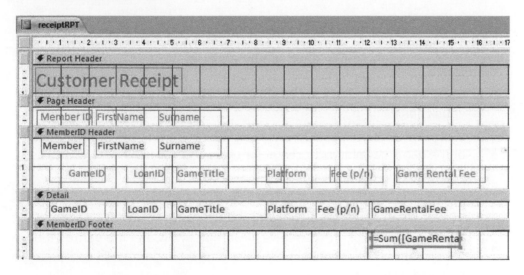

21 Select **Properties**; the following Property Sheet for that field will appear. Adjust the **Format** to **Currency**.

22 Select the **Label** tool from the **Design** tab.

23 Insert a label beside the field containing the Sum calculation. The label should read **Total Fee Due**.

24 Run the Report for memberID 1 one final time. The final report should be similar to the one shown here.

| receiptRPT | | |

Customer Receipt

Member ID	FirstName	Surname
1	James	Smith

GameID	LoanID	GameTitle	Platform	Fee (p/n)	Game Rental Fee
1	1	FIFA 17	Xbox OneS	£2.00	£14.00
2	3	Football Manager	Xbox OneS	£2.00	£14.00
7	2	Minecraft	Xbox OneS	£3.00	£21.00
				Total Fee Due:	£49.00

Tasks

1 Create a logo for the organisation using a graphics editing package of your choice.

2 Using the Report Wizard, create a report which will display a list of all of the games available for rental for the owner of GameLibrary. The list should be grouped by platform and then ordered by GameTitle.

3 Add your name to the report footer and add your logo for the organisation to the report header.

4 Create a report of all members of GameLibrary and the games they have rented. The report should be grouped by memberID and then ordered by GameTitle.

Your report should only include the MemberID, FirstName, Surname and then GameID, GameTitle, Platform and DueBack.

Practical tips (!)

Think carefully about the tables/reports/queries you might use to help you complete this task.

Using mail merge

The owner of GameLibrary would like to send a letter to all members from Oldtown to let them know he is reducing his rental fees.

1   Open MS Word and create the main letter as shown here.

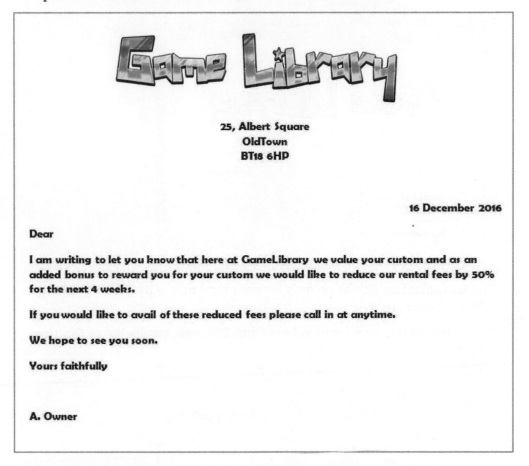

25, Albert Square
OldTown
BT18 6HP

16 December 2016

Dear

I am writing to let you know that here at GameLibrary we value your custom and as an added bonus to reward you for your custom we would like to reduce our rental fees by 50% for the next 4 weeks.

If you would like to avail of these reduced fees please call in at anytime.

We hope to see you soon.

Yours faithfully

A. Owner

2   From the **Mailings** tab, select **Start Mail Merge** and then **Letters**.

3   Click on the **Select Recipients** icon and select **Use Existing List** …

4   The **Select Data Source** window will appear. Browse to and select your **GameLibrary** database.

5   The **Select Table** window will appear. Select **membersTBL** and click **OK**.

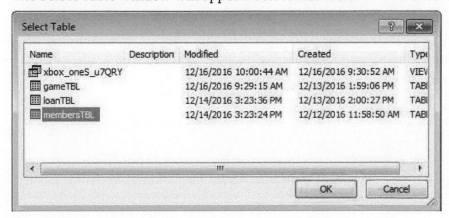

6   To add **merge fields** to the letter, click on the **Insert Merge Field icon**. Add each field in turn to the correct location in the letter. Remember to add spaces and any additional punctuation, such as commas.

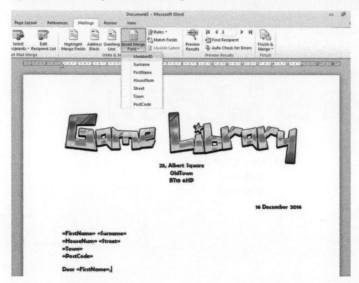

You will notice how the merge fields are shown inside << and >>.

7   You can select particular records for your mail merge by clicking on the **Edit Recipient List icon**.

8   Since this offer is only for members from Oldtown, untick James Smith as he is from Newtown. Click **OK**.

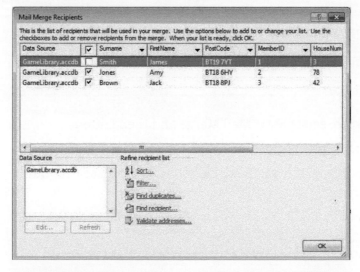

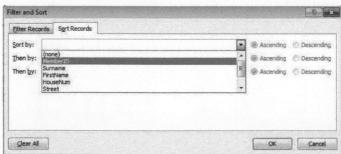

9 Complete the merge process by clicking **Finish & Merge** and selecting **Edit Individual Documents**...

10 Select **Merge All records** and then click **OK**. Your merged letters with data inserted will now be displayed.

11 It is important at this stage that you remember to save the merged letters and the copy of the letter with merge fields with different names so the letter template with the merge fields can be reused at a later stage.

Tasks

Rather than selecting mail merge recipients during the mail merge process as shown above, it is possible to base your mail merge on the results of a query.

1 Create a query in your GameLibrary database called newtownQRY. It should select only members from Newtown (you may want to add additional members from Newtown to your database before you complete this task).

2 Create another letter inviting customers from Newtown to the opening of a new shop in their town. You should use newtownQRY as the data source for this letter.

Using macros to automate tasks with forms

In Unit 1 we looked at how macros are created. We will look here at how we can use macros to improve the user friendliness of an application.

1 Create a new macro by clicking on the **Macro** icon in the **Create** tab.

2 Select **Open Form** from the list.

3 Select **membersFRM**.

Macros, and how they can be used to automate some tasks in a database, are discussed in Chapter 3 Database applications (Unit 1).

4   Click on **Add New Action** and select **Beep**. This could be used to provide some feedback to the user to let them know when the membersFRM is opened.

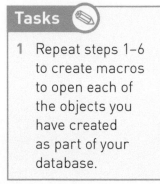

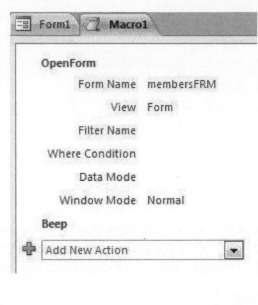

Tasks

1   Repeat steps 1–6 to create macros to open each of the objects you have created as part of your database.

Form Design

Create a new blank form in Design view.

In Design view, you can make advanced design changes to forms, such as adding custom control types and writing code.

5   Click the **Run** icon to test the macro. You will be asked to save the macro.

6   Enter **members_formMCR** as the name for the macro and click **OK**.

7   In the Create tab, click the **Form Design** tool to create a new blank form called **menuFRM**.

8   Add a logo to this form and a text label which reads Game Library Menu.

9   Click on the **Design Tab**.

10 Select the **Button** icon.

11 Draw a button on the menu form.

12 When the **Command Button Wizard** appears select **Miscellaneous** and then **Run Macro**.

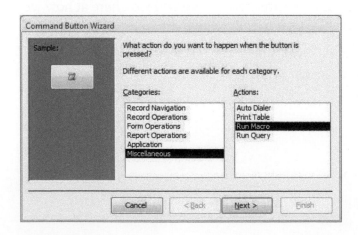

13 Click **Next**.

14 Choose **members_formMCR** and click **Next**.

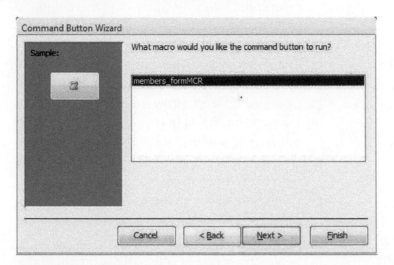

15 Select **Text** and enter **Open Members Form** as the text to appear on the button.

16 Click **Next**.

17 In the next dialogue box, name the button Open Members Form and then click **Finish**.

Tasks ✎

1 Repeat the process above to add buttons to open every form, report and query you have created for your database. You should name all macros and buttons appropriately.

2 Consider how you might add a macro button to your reports to allow the user to print the reports.

Checkpoint

▷ Data can be stored in a flat file or a relational database.

▷ Relational databases help reduce data redundancy and increase data integrity.

▷ Since data is not repeated unnecessarily this helps reduce the amount of storage required by the database

▷ Data validation methods, input masks and other controls such as look-up lists can be used to help minimise data entry errors in electronic databases.

▷ When creating relationships between tables in a relational database, the key field from the primary table must also exist in the second table.

▷ When the key field from one table exists in another table it is called a foreign key.

▷ When you create a relationship between tables in a database you can enforce referential integrity, apply cascade delete and **cascade update** to help maintain data integrity.

▷ A form wizard can be used to create forms for data input when developing a database.

▷ Complex queries allow us to prompt the user for search criteria (parameter queries) and allow us to perform calculations on data.

▷ Using complex queries we can also combine data from more than one table or query.

▷ Complex reports can be used to perform calculations, group data and sort data.

▷ Mail merge allows you to create a link between a word-processed document and a database so data can be extracted from the database and included in a word-processed document, for example a letter.

▷ Macros allow you to automate processes for the end user.

Practice questions

1 Relational databases help reduce data redundancy and improve data integrity. Explain the terms 'data redundancy' and 'data integrity'. [4 marks]

2 Identify three advantages of using a relational database over a flat file database. [3 marks]

3 Explain the term 'foreign key field'. [2 marks]

4 Database developers can use a wizard when creating some database elements. What is a wizard? [2 marks]

5 Identify two advantages of using a wizard when creating forms or reports in a database. [2 marks]

6 A store owner needs to create a query to allow him to search his product table for all the blue jumpers he has in small or medium size.

a) Complete the criteria row in the table below to show what criteria he would use to complete this query. [3 marks]

Field name	Product code	Product name	Colour	Size
Criteria				

b) Show how this query would be written using SQL. [3 marks]

Chapter 16 Significance of testing and developing of appropriate test plans

What this chapter covers

▶ The development process
▶ The role of testing during the development process
▶ Features of an effective test plan
▶ Testing approaches
▶ Multimedia testing

The development process

The systems development life cycle is the term used to describe the stages involved in the development of a new software application. A number of models for system development currently exist. The original model was known as the **waterfall model**. Other examples, some of which include the various types of prototyping examined previously (see Chapter 11 Designing solutions), represent a more **iterative development approach**.

Waterfall model

The waterfall model takes a sequential approach to system development. In the waterfall model a variety of stages must be completed in a particular order to develop or modify a digital application. Each stage in development leads on to the next one in sequential order; no one stage can begin until the one before it has been completed; for example, the entire system must be designed before development can begin. The diagram below outlines the key stages of the waterfall model. Over time, the changing needs and requirements of the organisation for whom the application has been developed will lead to further review, and the whole process will start again; hence the term 'system development life cycle'.

> This chapter can be reviewed in conjunction with Chapter 19 Building and testing a solution (Unit 3), where further examples are provided of a test plan being applied to a given solution.

▲ The waterfall model of system development

Iterative development process

The iterative development approach encourages the development team to break down the development of the application into smaller more manageable tasks. Unlike the more traditional waterfall model, each task, or part of the application, undergoes its own development life cycle. At the end of each life cycle, the developments or software builds will be reviewed, and changes required built into the next iteration. This allows the completed application to 'evolve' to a point at which the user requirements are fully met. The repeated application of the system life cycle following each iteration means errors are detected at the early stage of development.

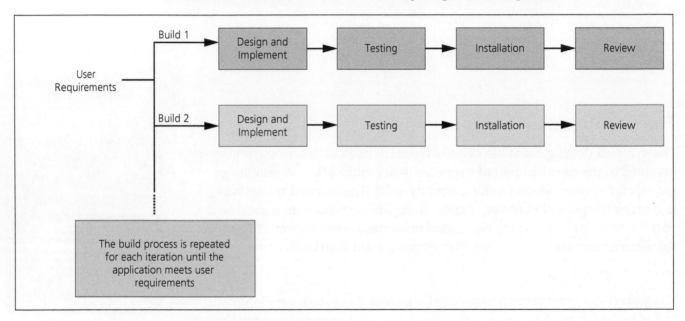

▲ Iterative approach to software development

Responsibilities of the system tester

Often the person, or team of people, responsible for testing an application will be different from those responsible for its development. Test plans should be well prepared and reviewed on an ongoing basis. It is important that the testing team take the user requirements into consideration when developing their test plans.

Any **bugs** detected during the testing process should be well documented and reported to the developer. In documenting a bug, the system tester should provide information such as the area of the application the bug relates to (for example, navigation, validation, processing), the steps that led to the error occuring, how many times the error occurred, and any error messages or actions noted. In order to help the developer resolve the error, screenshots could also be included.

The role of testing during the development process

Testing is an important part of the development process. Not only is it the process of identifying and correcting errors in the application being developed, it also helps the developer assess the reliability of the application and ensure it works in the way the user expects it to. A well-tested application will help to ensure the production of a high-quality application which meets user requirements or objectives, previously identified by the client.

User requirements for the system can be categorised as being qualitative or quantitative in nature and depending on the budgetary constraints may be prioritised in accordance with how important they are for the development of the application. In some instances the requirements may be deemed mandatory while others may be considered desirable (and therefore only applied if the budget allows for their inclusion).

Testing as part of the waterfall model

In the waterfall model, testing does not take place until after the system has been designed and implemented (see waterfall diagram on page 141). Once an application has been developed if an error is detected at the testing stage it can be very difficult to make any changes; especially if something has not been included in the earlier stages of design and development.

Testing during an iterative development approach

In the iterative development process tests are carried out at each stage of development of the application. This ensures bugs are corrected at an early stage in development. Errors detected early on are easier to correct. This in turn helps reduce the cost of correction and can in turn keep overall development costs down. It also means that it is less likely anything is left out of the development process.

Features of an effective test plan

An effective test plan will ensure any errors in the application are detected; this may involve debugging areas of the application or identifying omissions in the application in relation to user requirements. Testing can be conducted at any stage in development but in order for it to be carried out effectively it must be well planned and well documented.

The following list details the expected contents of a test plan.

▶ Introduction: this includes a summary of the application, or particular area of the application to be tested.

▶ Testing approach: we shall look at various approaches to testing later in this chapter.

▶ Test strategy: the testing strategy should include:
  − a number for each individual test so that each test can be identified separately in the **testing evidence**
  − a description of the area to be tested, for example a particular query or a navigational element of the application

- examples of the test data to be applied to a particular area of the application, i.e. what inputs are to be used. Test data should include a range of test items for each feature of the application being tested; these should include: valid data, invalid data, **null data** or **extreme data** items where appropriate
- expected outcomes from the completed test
- actual test outcomes
- comments about the outcome of the test or details of any corrections made to the application.

Test number	Area to be tested	Test data	Expected outcome	Test results	Corrections/ comments
1	Surname field	Invalid data – enter '3myth' Field is text only so 3 should not be accepted	Should not accept 3 at the beginning of the input data and should record Myth as the surname	3 not accepted at the beginning of the input data Myth recorded as the surname	Provide feedback to user explaining error which has occurred and how to correct it.
2	Surname field	Valid data – enter 'Smyth'	Smyth should be accepted as valid input	Smyth is accepted as valid input	n/a
3	Surname field	Null data – leave field blank	Field is a required data item – user should not be able to leave field blank	User cannot move on to add another record but no feedback provided to explain error	Provide feedback to user explaining error which has occurred and how to correct it.

▲ Part of an example test strategy based on membersTBL from the GameLibrary database created in Chapter 15 Database development.

Tasks 🖊

1 Part of a test plan for membersTBL is shown above. Add additional tests to the test plan for membersTBL. You should base your tests on the database completed as part of the tasks in Chapter 15 Database development. Carry out the tests you have included as part of your test strategy. You should provide evidence of the tests you carried out in the form of annotated screenshots. Annotations should highlight the test data, show the results of the test and show any corrections you made to this area of the application based on the tests you carried out.

2 With a partner, develop a test plan for other areas of your completed GameLibrary database from Chapter 15, for example, navigation, queries or reports. Document the results of your tests in the same way.

Testing approaches

A wide range of approaches to testing can be applied by the testing team and the methods chosen will depend on the type of application being developed. Some of the most common approaches to testing are detailed below.

Black box testing

Black box testing is a method where the design or structure of the application being tested is unknown to the person conducting the tests. The name comes from the fact that the tester approaches the system as a black box, which they cannot see into. During this approach the aim of the testing team is to identify errors which relate to, for example, the general interface or the operation of the application, such as missing or incorrect functions or incorrect data structures. Test data is developed based upon the user requirements document.

White box testing

White box testing allows the testing team to examine the underlying structure of the application. In order to carry out white box testing effectively a detailed knowledge of the development environment is needed. Specific inputs are selected to ensure all appropriate pathways through the application are examined and to ensure the appropriate output is produced. While tests are often applied to code that is being executed, the code may also be examined manually using a process called a **dry run**. **Trace tables** allow the testing team to examine the contents of any variables manipulated or outputs generated as the extract of code is executed.

Line number	Code	Num1	Num2	Result	Output	Comment
1	INPUT (Num1)	4				Get first value and store in Num1 variable
2	INPUT (Num2)	4	12			Get second value and store in Num2 variable
3	Result= Num1 + Num2	4	12	16		Add Num1 and Num2 together and store result in variable called RESULT
4	PRINT (Result)	4	12	16	16	Print contents of variable called Result

⌃ An example of a trace table for an extract of code which asks the user to input and add together two numbers and outputs the results

System testing

System testing is only carried out when all individual components or parts of an application have been developed and fully tested as standalone elements. System testing helps ensure that all individual components work together correctly to produce the correct outputs as identified in the user requirements document.

Alpha and beta testing

Alpha and **beta testing** are forms of developmental testing where the outcome of the testing process can be used to support the continued development of the application. They are most often carried out on versions of the application not yet completed but their key aim is to detect any bugs in the system which have so far gone undetected.

Alpha testing is normally carried out by a small number of users not previously involved in the development process. Alpha testing involves simulating the real world environment the application has been designed for.

Following the completion of the alpha testing process the application can be released to an extended user group who have been selected to take part in the beta testing process. This represents the final stage in testing and is carried out just before the final version of the application is released commercially. Often the application will be sent out in the form of a free-trial version for download across the internet in the hope that any minor errors will be detected, reported and corrected prior to commercial release of the application.

A/B testing

A/B testing is sometimes known as split testing and involves the release of more than one version of an application to see which one is preferred by the target audience. For example, two versions of a digital application are created and released to the general public. One half will be presented with the original version, the second with a modified version of the application. Statistical analysis will be carried out to help determine the impact any changes had on the success of the application.

Multimedia testing

Before any multimedia application is released for commercial viewing it is important that the application is fully tested and operational. Many companies now rely on their electronic presence through the internet or mobile phone applications to ensure they reach their target audience. We looked previously in Chapter 14 Multimedia authoring at how applications should be developed and tested to ensure they run efficiently on more than one platform. A webpage which returns dead links or which is slow to load will not promote return visits to the website and generate the impression that the organisation is unprofessional; both can lead to a loss of confidence in the organisation. Good testing of multimedia applications can lead to a more positive experience for the end user. Other organisations which might link to your site or application, for example search engines and online application stores, will view your site as being reliable and robust and provide increased referrals to your application. All of which can lead to increased use of your application and therefore increased profits for the organisation.

Navigation

Often applications are developed in a different location to the one where they will eventually be hosted and it is important to ensure that all hyperlinks (internal and external) remain live when the application is transferred across to its final destination. All links should be fully tested not only during development but also following the transfer of the application to its host location.

Multimedia asset operation

We saw in Chapter 14 how the inclusion of appropriate plugins to support the operation of multimedia assets is an important part of ensuring the cross-platform compatibility of the application. Application testers should ensure that the assets are in an optimised format, that they load correctly with the application and that the assets will display on all appropriate platforms. They should also ensure that appropriate links are provided to allow the end user to download any necessary plugins.

Consideration should also be given to the file size of individual multimedia assets as this can impact on load time for the application. For example, images should display correctly and without delay and, where appropriate, should display a text description if the end user hovers over the image.

Load times

Application testers should analyse the storage space required not only by the entire application but also individual pages or elements of the application. Where the application is to be displayed using a web browser it is important that the load time for each element is assessed on a range of hardware platforms and web browsers. A large number of multimedia elements can reduce the load time for a webpage so it is important that the tester takes this into consideration and considers the balance of distribution of such elements across the application. Where the inclusion of a large number of multimedia elements is unavoidable, the load time can be improved through the inclusion of optimised assets or, for example, the use of thumbnail versions of images as opposed to full-sized versions.

Scripted elements

Web developers often embed scripted elements into the HTML of their website. This allows them to add more complex functions to the website. Additional care must be taken here to ensure the scripted elements work and do not contain any errors before the application is launched. For example, most browsers will now display a notification about any script errors if the correct options are set in the browser tools. Not only will these advanced tools notify the developer or tester of the presence of an error in the scripted element, they will generally identify the location or line number of the error in the code also.

In some instances however, the fault with the operation of additional scripted elements may simply be due to the fact that plugins required to run the feature are blocked on the test computer, in which case the first stage in testing is to ensure these features are not blocked.

Checkpoint

▷ The waterfall model is a sequential model of system development; each stage must be completed before the next stage can be started.

▷ Iterative development supports the step-by-step development of an application with each iteration of the application undergoing its own life cycle.

▷ Testing helps ensure the quality of software applications, removes bugs and helps ensure user requirements are met.

▷ The user requirements document forms part of the contract between the developer and the client.

▷ User requirements can be qualitative or quantitative.

▷ Test plans should not be written or carried out by the person who originally developed the application.

▷ A range of approaches to testing applications exist. These include white box and black box testing, system testing, alpha and beta testing and A/B testing.

▷ Test plans should include a range of details, for example: a schedule for testing, details of area to be tested and not tested, details of staff responsible for testing and a testing strategy.

▷ Test strategies should incorporate the use of valid, invalid, null and extreme data elements where appropriate.

▷ Test strategies should be numbered and should include full descriptions of tests including expected and actual outcomes. Where appropriate they should also include details of any corrections made to the application.

▷ Testing of multimedia applications should at the very least incorporate tests on the following areas: navigation, operation of multimedia assets, load times and scripted elements.

Practice questions

1 Describe the difference between the waterfall model of system development and iterative development processes. [4 marks]

2 Identify the main stages involved in the waterfall development model and include a brief description of each stage. [6 marks]

3 Identify two advantages and two disadvantages of carrying out testing at the end of the development process, for example as in the waterfall model development model. [4 marks]

4 Identify two advantages and two disadvantages of carrying out testing throughout the testing process. [4 marks]

5 Explain the difference between qualitative and quantitative user requirements. Use the GameLibrary from Chapter 15 to give an example of each. [4 marks]

6 Explain the difference between black box and white box testing. [2 marks]

7 How can an organisation with an online store use A/B testing to improve the interface of a recently developed mobile phone app? [3 marks]

Chapter 17 Evaluation of digitally authored systems

What this chapter covers

▶ Purpose of an evaluation

▶ Evidencing an evaluation

▶ Points to consider

▶ Evaluating multimedia and database solutions to problems

▶ User requirements

Purpose of an evaluation

Evaluation is a continuous activity which should be carried out throughout the development of a system. The aim of evaluation is to improve the product being developed. Planning for an evaluation should start as early as the design stages in the development process.

Evaluation should be carried out:

▶ throughout the design process. The information gained enables changes to be made to the solution at an early stage, which is less costly than changes made at the testing stage

▶ when the product has been developed. The test data proposed in the test plan can be used at the different stages of testing. Unexpected results can be reviewed to identify problem components within the solution.

> This chapter can be reviewed in conjunction with Chapter 20 Evaluating a solution (Unit 3), where additional suggestions for evaluating can be viewed.

Evidencing an evaluation

An evaluation document should be structured approriately and include details of:

▶ the purpose of the evaluation

▶ the date and time the evaluation started and how long it is expected to take

▶ any previous evaluations of the product, such as when it occurred and what the main findings were

▶ who was involved in the evaluation process and their roles

▶ the stage in the development process the evaluation occurred, for example a final product evaluation or part-way through the development process.

The user requirements should form the basis for any evaluation, together with the time management and cost requirements of the project. If a project fulfils all the user requirements but is two years late, can it be considered a success?

Tables which include a list of the user requirements and successful testing could be used within an evaluation to evidence the statements being made.

When an evaluation is completed at the close of a project, the development team will consider their own performance in terms of time management and team contribution. The project manager will consider areas such as how close the final cost of the project was to the initial budget set out by the client organisation. The team may also review the solution and include a section on areas for improvement, based on feedback from the user. This will be used to improve the approach when undertaking future projects.

Reporting and recording the process of evaluation is important and the conclusions drawn in an evaluation must always be supported by evidence.

Evidence can be provided in the form of:
- the documented results from testing
- questionnaires, checklists or documented interviews to determine how well user requirements have been met
- observations of end users interacting with the application or end user entries into logs documenting their initial interactions with the application.

Points to consider

Evaluations will include feedback from the main stakeholders including members of the development team, management from the client organisation and end users from the client organisation. In Chapter 20 Evaluating a solution, we will look at methods we can use to collect feedback from others involved in the evaluation process.

The evaluation itself should be objective, meaning that it should not be biased in any way and should highlight both the strengths and weaknesses found at any point.

Aspects to be considered when evaluating a software product:
- identify areas of the solution which are unsatisfactory and therefore need to be modified
- decide whether or not it is a full and complete solution. This is done by checking to see if the user requirements have been met and if additional modules or sections of code need be added.

An evaluation should also take account of the outcome from user acceptance testing, when the product is tested using real data provided by the user.

Tasks

Some of the methods of gathering evidence as part of the evaluation process include interview, questionnaires and observations. In groups, discuss one of these methods. Produce a list of the advantages and disadvantages of this method and report back your findings to other groups.

Actions taken as a result of any of the above should be recorded for reporting purposes.

Evaluating multimedia and database solutions to problems

The evaluation process can involve the client themselves, members of the development team and end users. During the evaluation process, those involved review a number of areas, using the user requirements document. The key points to consider are:

▶ how robust the application is. A **robust system** is one which can handle valid and exceptional data

▶ how closely the application meets the original design specification

▶ whether the system is a complete solution to the problem identified

▶ whether the solution is efficient. An efficient solution is one which makes minimal use of resources during operation

▶ whether the solution operates on the specified platforms.

User requirements

The design criteria for any software system is driven by the user requirements. User requirements in database and multimedia solutions can be considered as being qualitative and quantitative.

Qualitative user requirements are those relating to the quality of the solution, for example the professional look of the application interface; two users may not view this equally.

Quantitative user requirements can be easily measured, for example the load time of a home screen of a website, or the time taken to run a query within a datbase application.

> The user requirements document is discussed in Chapter 11 Designing solutions. It is important that the success of the solution in meeting the user requirements is addressed during the evaluation process.

Presenting evidence based on user requirements

A well written set of user requirements should contain enough detail to support a full evaluation of the application being considered and the development team should use the user requirements document as a template for reporting back the success of the application.

User requirement number	Requirement	Evaluation findings	Actions taken/ required
1	Provide a form to allow the user to enter new member details.	This form was easy to set up. The development team created a form which linked to the company database. The end user thought the form would look better if the company logo was included.	Add company logo to the form.
……	……	……	……

User requirement number	Requirement	Evaluation findings	Actions taken/required
15	Results of a product search should be returned in 5 seconds.	The results were returned in less than 5 seconds for all searches carried out.	No action required
......	......	......	......
27	The application should work on android and iPhones as well as a range of internet web browsers on a PC.	All users reported the app worked well on all platforms.	No action required

▲ An extract of an evaluation report based on the end user requirements for a database and a multimedia solution

Tasks

Using an application (multimedia or database) which you have already created, prepare a structured evaluation report which contains examples of the evidence outlined in this chapter. Swap your evaluation report with another student and evaluate each other's program. Is the evaluation report accurate and objective?

Checkpoint ✓

▷ Evaluating a system involves ensuring that it meets the user requirements and is a full, robust and efficient solution.

▷ An evaluation can be undertaken throughout the design process, when the product has been developed, when handing the product over to the user, or by the development team at the close of a project.

▷ A range of personnel should be involved in the evaluation process including members of the development team, the client organisation and the end user.

▷ An evaluation report should be structured and should include details about the purpose of the evaluation, the timing and stage of development of the evaluation, the outcome of any previous evaluations of the product, the names and roles of those involved.

▷ An evaluation should contain evidence to support any statements made about the quality of the system.

▷ Sources of evidence include the outcome from testing, documented interviews and observations.

▷ The development team may undertake an evaluation which will include looking at their own performance, team contribution, management of budget, time management and user feedback.

▷ Areas for improvement will be used as learning points for future projects.

Practice questions

1 What is an evaluation? [2 marks]
2 How can evaluation be used to improve the quality of a software product? [2 marks]
3 List three items which should be included in the introduction to an evaluation report. [3 marks]
4 Give a reason why each item should be included in the introduction to the report. [3 marks]
5 List two individuals/groups of users who may be involved in the evaluation process. [2 marks]

(The publishers would like to make clear that this scenario is entirely fictional and is not based on any real-world person, company or organisation.)

Airtime is a new activity centre opening in the Boucher Road area in Belfast. The owner, Alexander Phillips, is planning to open the centre to the public in June 2017. Airtime will incorporate the largest trampoline park in Northern Ireland, an indoor play area, a Wi-Fi café and conference centre.

Airtime is aimed at individual and group use and for participants of all ages. The trampoline park is open to group bookings and the owner is hoping that the introduction of the conference centre will encourage corporate use of the facilities for team-building exercises by local organisations. Customers can book one-hour slots in the trampoline park or indoor play area for birthday parties or corporate events. Anyone who has booked into any area of the facility will have full access to Wi-Fi and the café area. The Airtime building is currently under construction.

Before opening Airtime, Alexander would like to have an interactive multimedia package available to potential customers and employees.

The package will be used to:

▶ advertise Airtime
▶ provide details of the facilities available
▶ provide booking costs for all facilities and parties
▶ provide information on jobs available (with a form to allow potential employees to request an application pack).

He would like the package to be unique to Airtime and has requested that original video and animations be incorporated into a professional interface.

Alexander must ensure that all equipment installed in Airtime complies with health and safety regulations. Staff will check all equipment at various stages throughout the day and detailed records of these checks are required. Where equipment is found to be damaged he would like ensure that this is logged in a database so that repairs are made and recorded immediately or, if necessary, replacements sourced and ordered by email or telephone at the end of each working day. The suppliers will then courier parts to the organisation overnight so repairs can take place before opening the next day.

Alexander has already started storing details of some parts, repairs and suppliers in tables as shown.

maintenanceTBL

ID	Repair description	Part required	Quantity	Date noted	Maintenance completed?	Date completed
1	Spring 2 repair Trampoline 2	1	2	06/02/2017	FALSE	
2	Spring 3 repair Trampoline 2	1	4	06/02/2017	FALSE	
3	Pole replacement Trampoline 4	18	2	06/02/2017	FALSE	
4	Stability Bar replacement Trampoline 33	10	1	06/02/2017	FALSE	
5	Spare Net Trampoline 29	16	1	06/02/2017	FALSE	
6	Fitness Trampoline replacement Trampoline 32	9	1	06/02/2017	FALSE	

partsTBL

Part ID	Description	Price	Supplier ID
1	5.5 inch Trampoline Spring	2.50	1
2	7 inch Trampoline Spring	3.00	1
3	8 ft Trampoline Mat Round	55.00	1
4	14 ft Trampoline Mat Round	70.00	1
5	8 ft Trampoline Mat Square	60.00	1
6	14 ft Trampoline Mat Square	80.00	1
7	Trampoline Basket Ball Hoop	75.00	2
8	Trampoline Dodge Balls	22.99	2
9	Fitness Trampoline	90.99	2
10	Trampoline Stability Bar	45.55	2
11	Trampoline Basket Ball Hoop	48.00	2
12	Trampoline Skis	70.00	2
13	Trampoline Spring Tool	25.99	3
14	Replacement Spring Foam	5.25	3
15	Replacement Tube Cap	4.99	3
16	8 ft Trampoline Net	45.75	3
17	14 ft Trampoline Net	65.99	3
18	Trampoline Pole	14.99	3

supplierTBL

Supplier ID	Supplier name	Street number	Street name	Town	County	Postcode	Telephone number	Email
1	Trampoline Parts and Supplies	3	George's Lane	Belfast	Co Down	BT5 7UJ	02890568985	info@ trampolineparts andsupplies.org. uk
2	Trampoline Spares	46	Main Street	Strabane	Co Tyrone	BT82 9OP	02871669656	trampolinespares @spareparts.com
3	Jumping Jack Spares	78a	Hill Street	Newry	Co Down	BT35 7YH	028302669875	orders@ jumpingjacks. com

parts_supplierTBL

Part ID	Supplier ID
1	1
2	1
3	1
4	1
5	1
6	1
7	2
8	2
9	2
10	2
11	2
12	2
13	3
14	3
15	3
16	3
17	3
18	3

Alexander would like to store these details in a database which should include:

▶ forms for data input

▶ data stored in appropriately linked database tables

▶ appropriate queries and reports which will allow him to search for and display data on repairs, equipment and suppliers

▶ reports which contain details of repairs and orders for parts from suppliers.

The database should also be easy to navigate and automated as far as possible.

Chapter 18 Designing solutions using appropriate tools

What this chapter covers

▶ Designing a database solution

▶ Designing a multimedia solution

Designing a multimedia solution

In this chapter, we are going to work through the Airtime scenario and provide solutions to its problems.

Defining user requirements

Defining user requirements is a key part of determining the success of any solution.

Before developing a multimedia solution to a problem, it is important to establish the target audience and the user requirements of the application.

Some of the user requirements for the Airtime multimedia solution could be:

▶ advertise the opening of the company; provide the Airtime location

▶ have one page for each of the main facilities available for booking

▶ there should be an animation on the home page

▶ there should be a page which introduces some of the staff and has a form which allows people to request information about jobs available

▶ each page should have the company logo

▶ each page should be accessible from the home page

▶ the home page should have some content which is accessible to people with visual impairment

▶ the owner would like the website to be interactive.

> The content of this chapter should be considered in conjunction with Chapter 11 Designing solutions (Unit 2).

Tasks

1 Review the Airtime scenario and Chapter 11 Designing solutions. Produce a detailed set of user requirements for a multimedia solution to the Airtime problem.

2 Identify the target audience for the Airtime website. Include details on their age range, characteristics, interests and any thoughts you might have on how these factors might influence your design decisions.

Tasks

Use what you have learnt about navigation structure diagrams in Chapter 11 Designing solutions to create a navigation structure diagram for your Airtime solution. Remember to show external links and any documents available for download throughout the application. You should include links to any websites required for the download of plugins required to run the application. Limit the number of pages for your solution to six.

Navigation structure diagrams

Once the user requirements are established, it is important that the developer considers how users will navigate around the application.

Storyboarding the solution

A storyboard allows the designer to consider the layout of each page in the application in terms of content, interactivity and the placement of digital assets.

Note that storyboards should also contain details of any interactive, scripted or accessibility elements throughout the package; some examples of how these elements can be detailed are shown in the storyboard extracts below.

We have previously considered the detail required in the production of multimedia storyboards, so we shall look now at how to detail the interactive elements in our multimedia storyboards. For example, below is part of the form completed by users requesting job application forms from Airtime.

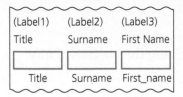

```
Outline of script used to validate
entry of data to Title text box
If title = " "
    Alert user "Please enter 'Mr', 'Miss',
        'Ms', 'Other'"
    Return cursor to title text box
End If
```

This example shows how the developer plans to use script to ensure the Title field is not left blank.

Practical tips

You will notice the names applied to each label and form text box are shown on the storyboard.

The following example represents an extract of a page with an interactive photo gallery the user can progress through using a next button.

```
If image being
displayed is not
last image in list
    increase
    imagenumber by 1
Else
    imagenumber =0
    (first image in
    list)
display
image(imagenumber)
```

All images are thumbnail images. When the user clicks on a thumbnail, a large version of the image is displayed.

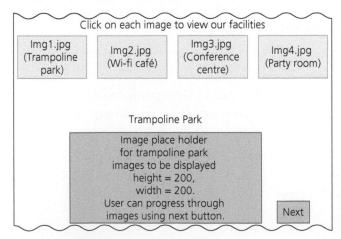

▲ Image gallery

Tasks

Refer to the examples of storyboarding provided above and in Chapter 11 Designing solutions.

Produce a detailed storyboard for your proposed solution to the Airtime problem.

You should include:

- interactivity on each page (this could be in the form of thumbnail images, image gallery, downloadable files, links to external webpages, forms for data entry, email hyperlinks, video assets)
- a script for any sound files to be included (this could support accessibility)
- details of any scripted elements to be included in your solution
- a storyboard for any animation or videos.

Make sure you consider accessibility as part of your solution. This could be in form of 'alt text' for image displays, the incorporation of sound files to play text content to users, or links to websites for the download of additional plugins required to support the display of your solution.

Think carefully about the range of assets you might require to support your solution to the Airtime multimedia problem.

If the assets are already available to you, list the names and file types for the assets (ensure the naming conventions are consistent and appropriate).

If they are to be organised in folders, identify the folder structure for the assets at this stage.

Evidence of prototyping

Multimedia packages are dynamic and interactive and support movement through the content in an order which suits the end user. For this reason it is important that working prototypes are used to present design ideas to the client at an early stage.

A couple of approaches to providing a working prototype are possible:

- presentation software or authoring packages could be used to provide clients with a basic mock-up of the content with clickable links using a presentation package
- A/B testing, where two versions of the same application are compared against each other to determine which one performs best. Each version of the prototype should be presented to members of the target audience and feedback sought.

Practical tips

Evidence of prototyping is a key element of the design process; remember to include evidence especially of A/B testing.

Evidence can be provided in the form of:
- ▶ screenshots of pages forming the A/B prototypes
- ▶ screenshots of any multimedia or grey-screen prototypes used
- ▶ feedback from end users and clients along with comments or design decisions made following feedback
- ▶ a scoring mechanism could allow you to determine the success of one prototype over another in A/B testing for example
- ▶ overall impression of the application and interface (score out of 10)
- ▶ thoughts on amount of, and type of, content on each page (score out of 10)
- ▶ ease of use of the application (score out of 10)
- ▶ thoughts on the suitability of digital assets (score out of 10).

Feedback from the prototyping process should be summarised at this stage along with any design decisions made based on user feedback. This can be referenced in more detail at the evaluation stage.

Tasks

Produce a more complete list of user requirements for the Airtime database problem. Consider the interface layout, naming conventions for field names, form layout and controls, the queries to provide the user with the output they require, the additional processing to provide the owner with output they require, the automation of tasks and navigational structures to allow the user to access the main features of the system.

Designing a database solution

Defining user requirements

Review the Airtime scenario and examine the data structures Alexander already has in place to create a set of user requirements for the database solution to this problem.

Some user requirements could be:
- ▶ data should be stored in linked tables to help reduce data redundancy and improve data integrity
- ▶ data should be validated upon entry
- ▶ forms should be available to allow users to enter data on each entity stored in the database
- ▶ all tasks should be available to the user via macro buttons
- ▶ all screens and reports should be consistent and contain the company logo
- ▶ reports should be available to allow the owner to see what repairs are outstanding.

It is important to consider factors which are important to the user but don't overlook the technical elements of your solution as this will aid the evaluation process at a later stage. Chapter 20 Evaluating a solution discusses some additional points for evaluation; these points should be among those considered when writing the user requirements.

Using ERDs to illustrate relationships between database tables

Alexander is already considering the use of a relational database to record details of maintenance and parts ordering.

The ERD (entity-relationship diagram) for Alexander's database solution is shown below.

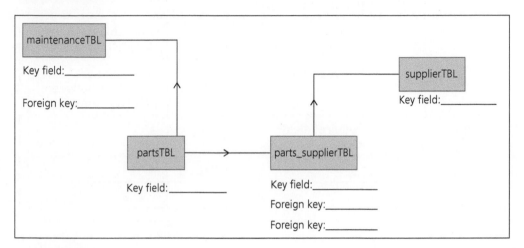

Tasks

1 Complete the ERD by identifying the key fields and foreign key fields in each table.

2 Describe the role played by parts_supplierTBL in the Airtime database solution.

NB The table names and the field headings for the Airtime database solution have already been provided for you in the scenario pages.

Tasks

Use the information provided in the Airtime scenario to produce a complete data dictionary for each of the tables identified in the Airtime scenario. Part of the data dictionary for maintenanceTBL and parts_supplierTBL has been completed for you. Review Chapter 15 Database development to help you complete details relating to possible validation checks, input masks and other such control elements.

parts_supplierTBL

Field name	Data type	Field length	Validation/Input masks	Default values	Description/Comment
ID	autonumber	n/a	n/a	n/a	Automatically assigned by database application.
PartID	number		n/a		Used to establish a link with partsTBL.
SupplierID					

maintenanceTBL

Field name	Data type	Field length	Validation/Input masks	Default values	Description/ Comment
ID	autonumber				
RepairDescription	text	40	>L<CCCCCCCCCCCC (for 40 characters)		
PartRequired					Look-up list using partsTBL as source.
Quantity			Between 1 and 30	1	Please ensure quantity is between 1 and 30 items.
DateNoted			Required field <=date()		
MaintenanceCompleted?				FALSE	
DateCompleted					

Tasks

Use your user requirements to complete the navigation structure diagram, right, to show what forms, queries and reports would be accessible to users from each menu option. You should list the options available to the user under each sub-menu.

Designing a menu system for navigation

Alexander would like to have a menu system to allow users to access forms for data input separately from queries and reports. When considering the navigation structure in a database, it is helpful to produce a navigation structure diagram similar to that used in designing multimedia solutions.

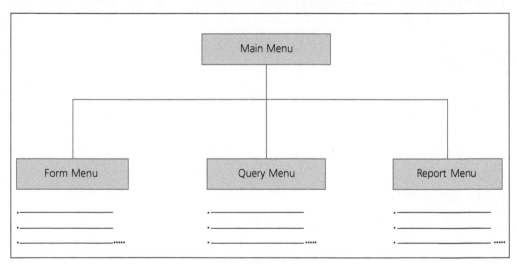

Designing simple and complex queries

A range of query types can be used to extract data from tables to be displayed.

The following examples show a range of simple and complex queries designs based on the Airtime database solution.

▼ maintenanceincompleteQRY

Field name	RepairDescription	PartRequired	Quantity	DateNoted	Maintenance Completed?
Table	maintenanceTBL	maintenanceTBL	maintenanceTBL	maintenanceTBL	maintenanceTBL
Sort					Ascending
Show	✓	✓	✓	✓	✓
Criteria					FALSE

▼ orderQRY

Field name	Repair Description	Part Required	Quantity	Price	PartsTotal: [Quantity] *[Price]	Supplier Name	StreetNum	Street Name
Table	mainte-nanceTBL	mainte-nanceTBL	mainte-nanceTBL	partsTBL	Calculated field	supplier TBL	supplier TBL	supplier TBL
Sort		Ascending						
Show		✓	✓	✓	✓	✓	✓	✓
Criteria								

▼ orderQRY continued

Field name	County	Postcode	TelNum	Email
Table	supplierTBL	supplierTBL	supplierTBL	supplierTBL
Sort				
Show	✓	✓	✓	✓
Criteria				

Tasks ✎

Review the user requirements for the Airtime scenario and design any queries you would expect to develop to meet the needs of the owner.

Try to include a range of queries including parameter-based queries, multi-query and multi-table queries and queries with calculated fields.

Designing forms and reports for data input and output

Wireframe diagrams illustrating the layout of the main menu screen and a form to allow data input into maintenanceTBL are shown below.

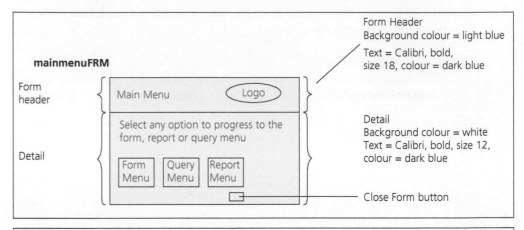

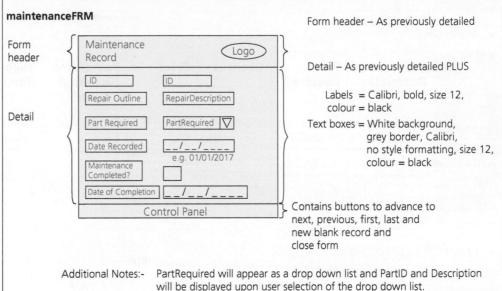

Practical tips ⚠

Input masks and hints are also provided to help the user complete the form.

Other control elements such as dropdown lists and check boxes are also shown at the design stage.

When completing wireframe diagrams for reports, remember to include any groupings, sorting or calculations to be included in the form. For an example of the use of calculations in reports, see Chapter 15 Database development, where the customer receipt contained calculations in the MemberID Footer.

Tasks

Review the section on Database design elements, in Chapter 11 Designing solutions. Use the design elements shown in that section to complete wireframe diagrams for each for the forms and reports required in the user requirements section above. Review Chapter 15 Database development for ideas to support your solution.

When developing your designs, consider how you would display the results of queries using reports. Think in particular about how orderQRY might be used as part of your solution.

Designing macros

Macros are an important part of ensuring the automation of tasks in any database solution. Consider carefully how you might use macros to help automate processes and aid navigation around the system for the end user.

The following macro design incorporates a number of steps which would allow the end user to print the list of orders needed at the end of a working day.

```
printorderMCR
  Action: OpenReport (orderRPT)
    View (Print)
  Action: PrintObject
End printorderMCR
```

Tasks

Produce a design plan for any macros you think would help improve automation and navigation for the system user. Macros could be used in the following ways:
▶ in forms and reports to support navigation between other forms and reports
▶ to automate print processes
▶ to close the application
▶ to open various objects forming part of the database solution.

Chapter 19 Building and testing a solution

This chapter should be reviewed in conjunction with Chapters 14 Multimedia authoring, 15 Database development and 16 Significance of testing and developing of appropriate text plans (Unit 2).

What this chapter covers

▶ Presenting a solution and developing a test strategy

▶ Test plan for a database solution

▶ Test plan for a multimedia solution

▶ Supporting the creation of your own solutions

▶ End user testing

▶ Testing for robustness

Presenting a solution and developing a test strategy

Practical tips

Evidence of completed solutions for this unit will be submitted in the form of working multimedia and database applications. The skills required to support the successful production of both applications have been presented in Unit 2 Chapters 14 Multimedia authoring and 15 Database development.

In this chapter, we shall focus on the more complex elements of the completed solutions to the Airtime scenario. Alongside examples of how to approach testing the key elements of both the database and multimedia parts of the completed solution. We will look at implementing scripted elements for the solution to the multimedia element of the Airtime problem.

The solution used to solve the Airtime database problem was based around the database structure shown below.

Note how the two foreign keys (PartID and SupplierID) in parts_supplierTBL are used to form a composite key in this format of the solution.

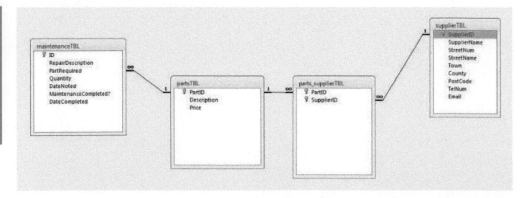

Presenting a test strategy for a database solution

The test strategy should include a description of the approaches taken to test each application, for example how black and white box testing, A/B testing, system testing or alpha and beta tests (if applicable) are being used as part of the process.

The test strategy for the database solution should detail how:

▶ white box testing will be carried out, which should specify that:
  – any database object (forms, reports, queries, macros) forming part of the solution will be tested
  – valid, invalid and extreme data will be used to test data validations
  – navigational elements will be tested
▶ system testing will be carried out
▶ the end user will be involved to help determine if user requirements have been met.

The test strategy for the multimedia solution should detail how, for example, A/B tests will be applied and how:

▶ navigational and accessibility elements will be tested
▶ performance issues within the application will be identified, including how load times for assets will be measured
▶ the robustness of the solution will be tested
▶ all interactive elements will be tested.

Practical tips (!)

Chapter 16 Significance of testing and developing appropriate test plans (Unit 2) includes an example of a test plan for part of a database solution. Note how expected outputs from the testing have been predicted. When carrying out testing, these outcomes should be compared to the actual output produced.

When devising a test plan for any solution it is important to evaluate if all user requirements are being met by the solution.

As the test plan is being applied to your completed solution, you should use screenshots to document the outcomes from each test. These should then be cross-referenced to your test plan using the test numbers identified in your test plan. This provides additional evidence of the production of a successful solution to the proposed problem.

Test plan for a database solution

The following table shows samples from a test plan for a potential Airtime database solution.

Practical tips (!)

Where the outcome from testing is not as predicted, it is important that the errors in the system are identified and that evidence of any corrective measures taken to rectify the situation is shown as part of the testing process.

Test number	Requirement number	Area to be tested	Test data	Expected outcome	Test results	Corrective measures
1	1	Main menu form menu option button	Click on form menu button in main menu.	Form menu will display when option clicked on.	Correct sub-menus were displayed following each button click.	n/a
...	...	...	...	...	...	...
9	3	Input mask for RepairDescription in MaintenanceTBL	spare net trampoline 2	Lower case s should be changed automatically to upper case.	Case is amended as expected.	n/a
10	3	Range check for quantity in MaintenanceTBL	0, 4, 45	0 and 45 should be rejected and message 'Order quantity must be between 1 and 30' displayed. 4 should be accepted.	Error message displayed when 0 and 45 entered. 4 accepted as correct data item.	n/a
11	3	Presence check for DateNoted field in MaintenanceTBL	Null data	A message should be displayed informing the user that a value must be entered into this field.	Error message displayed and user cannot continue entering data until value is entered.	n/a
...	...	...	...	...	...	...
15	23	maintenance completeQRY	Run query from object menu in application.	Spare net trampoline 29 should display with RepairDescription, PartRequired, Quantity, DateNoted and Maintenance Completed? DateCompleted fields displayed	All records fields displayed.	Criteria was not set to FALSE. Query criteria updated.
...	...	...	...	...	...	...

Test number	Requirement number	Area to be tested	Test data	Expected outcome	Test results	Corrective measures
27	14	printOrderMCR	Run macro from object menu in application.	Confirmation of printing message displayed on screen and order report printed without being opened on screen.	Appropriate message displayed on screen. Order report was sent to the printer without being opened on screen.	n/a
...	...	...	...	...	...	...
35	3	maintenanceFRM	Spare net trampoline 2, 8 ft trampoline net, 1, 27/02/2017, FALSE	When user closes form data should be evident in maintenanceTBL.	Data added correctly to maintenance TBL.	n/a
36	4	Dropdown list on maintenanceFRM	Click on arrow beside PartRequired field	All parts and prices are listed in a dropdown list for user to select.	All parts are listed and user can select any item from list.	n/a
...	...	...	...	...	...	...
45	Reports	*See task on page 172.*				
...	...	...	...	...	...	...

Test number 1

Form option clicked on Main Menu form.

User is navigated to the forms Menu.

Test number 9

Case is automatically updated for the user following input of lower case s.

0 and 45 both rejected and appropriate message displayed.

Test number 10

4 is accepted and the user can continue to enter data into the table.

Test number 11

No date entered. Error message displayed and will prevent user continuing with data entry process until required data item is entered.

Test number 15

All data displayed in first instance.

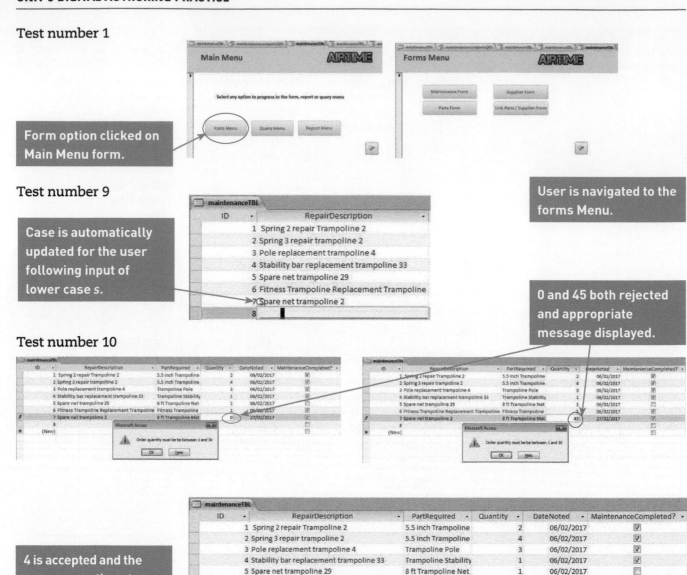

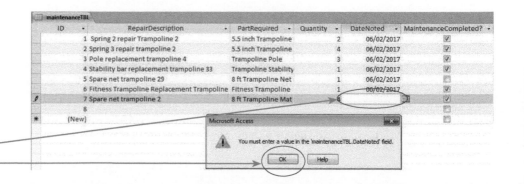

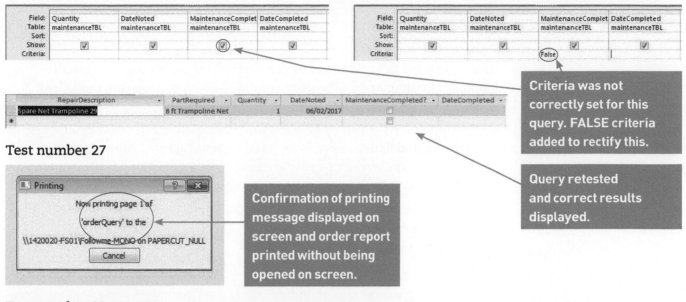

Criteria was not correctly set for this query. FALSE criteria added to rectify this.

Query retested and correct results displayed.

Test number 27

Confirmation of printing message displayed on screen and order report printed without being opened on screen.

Test number 35

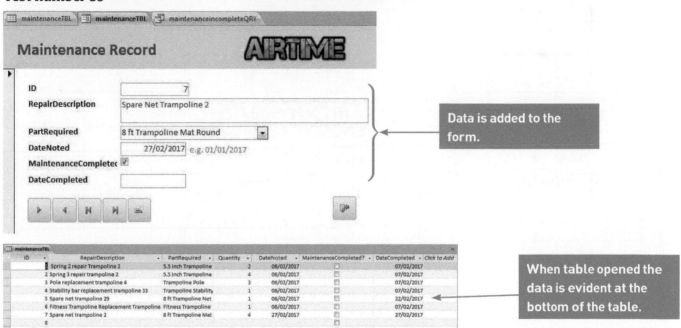

Data is added to the form.

When table opened the data is evident at the bottom of the table.

Test number 36

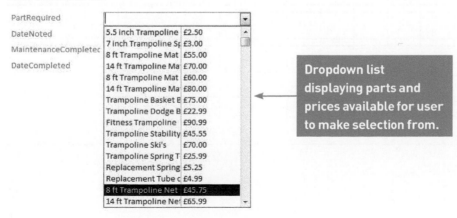

Dropdown list displaying parts and prices available for user to make selection from.

Tasks

Review the report below which is presented in Design View. Data used in this report has been combined from a variety of tables using orderQRY designed in Chapter 18 Designing solutions using appropriate tools (Unit 3).

1 If you have not already done so, recreate the query orderQRY and use it to generate the report layout shown below. Consider how groupings, headers and footers have been used to generate this report and think how you might make use of macros and control buttons to support the user in printing and closing the report.

2 a) Return to database test plan and complete the remaining columns for test number 45.

   b) Test the report.

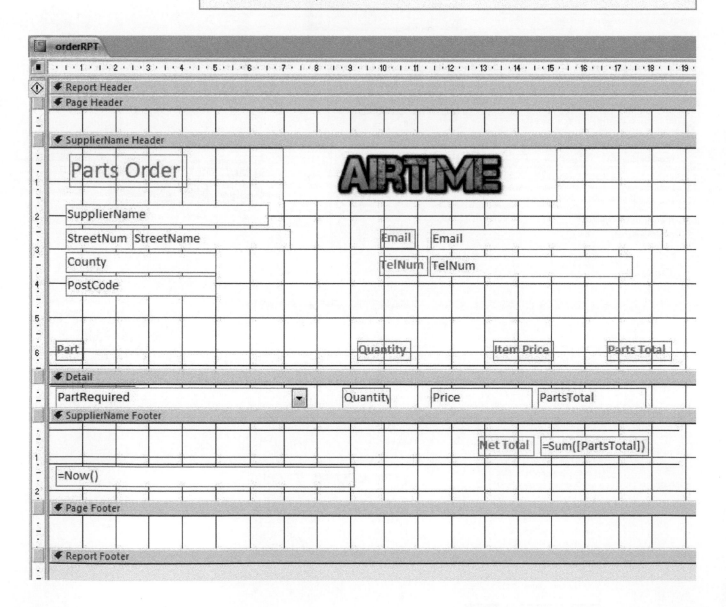

Test plan for a multimedia solution

The following tables show samples from a test plan for a potential Airtime multimedia solution.

Where evidence of testing of the multimedia application is required, this can be provided in the form of annotated screenshots (similar to those used for the database solution).

Where scripted elements or additional authoring package tools have been used to form part of the solution these are identified in the test plan using *. Details of how these elements were implemented follow the test plan and should be used to support the creation of your own solutions.

NB The objective numbers provided below are for example only. When you develop a test plan, the test descriptions and objective numbers should be specific to your own design document.

Test number	Requirement number	Area to be tested	Test data	Expected outcome	Test results	Corrective measures
1	10	Accessibility element – sound file on home page.	Click on microphone icon at end of each paragraph.	Paragraph content will be played for user with less than a 5 second delay while asset loads.	Sound files for all paragraphs were played successfully, except for paragraph 3 which failed to load.	The sound file was hyperlinked to the icon at the end of paragraph 3 and re-tested.
2	10	Accessibility element – alt text displayed with user mouse over on all images on home page.	Mouse over each image on home page.	Short description of image displayed is presented as a pop up and disappears when mouse rolled off image.	All alt text displayed for all images on the home page.	n/a
3	7	Navigation buttons on all pages.	Each navigation button to be clicked on to ensure correct destination page displayed.	Home page button destination is index.HTML. Facilities page button destination is facilities.HTML.	All navigation buttons took users to correct destination.	n/a
...	...	...	...	...	...	...
24	12	Image gallery on facilities page – next button.	Click next button to progress through four images in image gallery displaying.	Click on next should allow user to view four images of trampoline part size 200x200.	Clicking on next button allows user to view all images in continuous rotation.	n/a

Test number	Requirement number	Area to be tested	Test data	Expected outcome	Test results	Corrective measures
25	12	Image gallery on facilities page – thumbnail images*.	Click on each thumbnail image at top of image gallery.	Larger version of each image should be displayed.	Full size images shown for all but Wi-Fi café (image2).	Image was auto thumbnailed within authoring application and retested.
26	12	Form validation (title field) – cannot be blank	Complete form and leave title field blank.	Message – 'Please enter 'Mr', 'Miss, 'Ms', or other' should be displayed when submit button clicked.	Message – 'Please enter 'Mr', 'Miss, 'Ms', or other' correctly displayed.	n/a
...	...	...	...	...	...	...
40	29	Video displayed on facilities page loaded within 5 seconds of page loading.	Click on facilities page link from.	Video start image to display within 5 seconds of page loading.	Video start image loaded without delay.	n/a
...	...	...	...	...	...	...
50	10	Accessibility element – website displayed correctly in a range of web browsers.	Test website display on IE, Google Chrome and Opera.	All content should display on all web browsers.	Video file displayed on all but Opera.	Link to plugin for Windows Media Player added to page.

Adding multimedia elements to your multimedia solution

Throughout this section, we will be using MS Expression Web 4.

Adding an image gallery using the Next button (scripted elements that aid the interactivity of the package)

Tasks

Source four images to use as part of this task and save them in a folder called images.

Enter the code shown on the next page into a text editor like notepad or notepad++ in the first instance. When you are confident you understand the code you could try to integrate it into an existing webpage forming part of your Airtime solution.

```
1  <!DOCTYPE html>
2  <html>
3  <body>
4
5  <h1>Airtime Gallery</h1>
6
7  <img id="imgDisplay" src="./images/parkimage1.jpg"
8  alt="Park image"
9  width="200"
10 height="200"
11 >
12
13 <button onclick="nextImage()" id="nextButton">next</button>
14
15
16 <script>
17
18 var images = new Array("./images/parkimage1.jpg","./images/parkimage2.jpg",
19 "./images/parkimage3.jpg","./images/parkimage4.jpg");
20
21 var imgElement = document.getElementById("imgDisplay");
22 var imageCounter = 0;
23
24 function nextImage()
25 {
26      if(imageCounter < 3)
27          { imageCounter++;
28          }
29      else
30          { imageCounter=0;
31          }
32
33          imgElement.src = images[1mageCounter];
34 }
35
36 </script>
37
38 </body>
39 </html>
```

Display image called parkimage1.jpg (stored in images folder) on page load.

Assign an ID imgDisplay to the image and set properties for alt text, width and height as shown.

Add a button called nextButton to the page. It will display the next Next button.

When the button is clicked by the user it will call a scripted function called nextImage.

Reference your four images (and the correct pathway) here.

imgElement: calls the image named imgDisplay from within the html document and uses its properties when displaying the image at the end of the function.
imageCounter: used to determine which image is being displayed.

Function nextImage: checks if the last image is being displayed. If not, increases the imageCounter by 1 so it will point to the next image (referenced by var images).

If the last image is being displayed it will set imageCounter to 0 so the first image is the next to be displayed.

Adding thumbnail images

1. Set the default size for all thumbnail images.
2. Click on **Tools** > **Page Editor Options** > **AutoThumbnail**.
3. In the **Pixels** box enter your default size in pixels, for example 200.
4. Select any other appropriate options and then click **OK**.
5. Insert full size image into page in normal manner.
6. Right click on the image and select **Show Pictures toolbar**.
7. Select **Auto Thumbnail** button.
8. Click **File** > **Save** and select appropriate folder for thumbnail image to be saved to, then click **OK**.

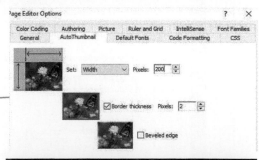

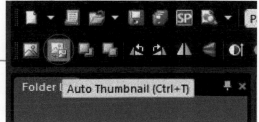

175

Tasks

Create a page which displays a series of thumbnail images in your Airtime multimedia solution.

Add the full-size image first and examine the code for the page. Complete the steps above to change the first image into a thumbnail image, then examine the code for the webpage to view the additional HTML added to the page following the creation of the thumbnail.

Adding a basic contact form and using scripted elements to validate contents

Tasks

1   Open a blank MS Expression Web 4 page and select the Form element from the Toolbox.

2   Add the Form element to your MS Expression page.

3   Right click on the Form element to display its Form Properties. Give the form a name, for example apply_form.

4   Use the Label and Input (Text) tools to add appropriate fields to your form. (We will only add a label for Title at this stage.)

5   Right click on the Input (Text) box and give it an appropriate name, for example Title. Label all Input (Text) boxes this way.

6   Use the Input (Button) tool to add a submit button to the form.

7   Add the script listed below to the head section of your HTML page.

```
2  <html xmlns="http://www.w3.org/1999/xhtml">
3
4  <head>
5  <meta content="en-gb" http-equiv="Content-Language" />
6  <meta content="text/html; charset=utf-8" http-equiv="Content-Type" />
7  <title>Contact Us</title>
8
9  <script type="text/javascript">
10
11
12      function validate_form()
13      {
14
15        if( document.apply_form.Title.value == "" )
16        {
17          alert( "Please enter Mr, Miss, Ms or alternative title" );
18          document.apply_form.Title.focus() ;
19          return false;
20        }
21
22            return( true );
23      }
24
25  </script>
```

Practical tips

In addition to the examples presented here, you can also use the html examples provided in Chapter 14 to enhance your multimedia solution.

Expand this example to include a complete form with all fields validated in the same way and incorporate a form element into your Airtime solution.

8   Add the following line of code to the body of your HTML page.

```
<form action="mailto:myemail@hotmail.com" name="apply _ form" onsubmit="return(validate _ form());">
```

(This will ensure the form contents will be sent to the email address given when the user clicks on the button. It will also call the validate_form function listed above to ensure in this case the Title field is not left blank.)

End user testing

Regardless of the type of solution developed, it is important that the end user is involved in the testing process so they can sign off on the solution and agree that their requirements have been met.

Evidence of end user involvement in the testing process must be presented during the testing stage. This may take the form of:

▶ completed questionnaires or a checklist where the user has ticked all of the user requirements they view as having been completed

▶ comments or witness statements from the end user confirming all requirements have been met and/or detailing areas where they feel the requirements have not been met

▶ details of observations from the user interacting with the application.

Testing for robustness

When we consider the **robustness** of a digital application we are assessing either the ability of the package to deal with errors or its ability to deal with exceptional circumstances. It is about ensuring that the application does not crash on the end user if either of these situations are encountered. Robustness of an application can be tested through black box testing where the functionality of the application is being assessed without considering internal processing.

When considering input of invalid data in a database solution, for example, a well-validated data entry system will ensure that appropriate feedback is presented to the user to support them in the correction of any errors which might prevent them from continuing processing. Appropriate feedback will ensure the user knows how to remedy the situation without having to close down the application. Exceptional circumstances in the use of a database application may include, for example, an increase in the amount of data to be processed at any given time or continued mouse clicks from an impatient user. Such events should be built into end user testing so the application is being used as it would be in a normal working environment.

In considering a multimedia application, the testing of the application on a range of platforms can help assess its robustness and could incorporate commentary on load times or situations where scripted elements fail to operate as expected.

Evidence detailing the robustness of the application can generally be gleaned from observing the system being used in a real-life working environment and should incorporate details on how quickly the system recovered, if indeed it did crash.

In Chapters 17 Evaluation of digitally authored systems (Unit 2) and 20 Evaluating a solution (Unit 3), how feedback collected from the end user at this stage can be used to support the evaluation of the success of the project is examined.

Tasks

Test a completed database and multimedia Airtime solution for a member of your class. Comment on the robustness of the solution by including commentary on areas such as:

▶ any situation where a digital asset or page in their multimedia solution failed to, or was slow to, load, or any interactive elements which did not work as anticipated

▶ whether the database solution was able to process all tasks and data you attempted to input (was there any time when you had to exit the application because appropriate feedback or a resolution to a problem was not provided by the system?).

Chapter 20 Evaluating a solution

Evaluating a solution

In an evaluation, end user involvement is key to ensuring the solution meets original user requirements. Evidence gathered during testing can be used to support comments made in the evaluation process, especially when explaining any improvements made to the solution or any deviations made from the original design. Sources of evidence include testing the design, structured testing of the final solution, dialogue with the user and observation of the system in use with real volumes of data.

The questions asked during the evaluation process may vary depending on the type of solution being evaluated.

Evaluation in general

An evaluation is a document which gives the development team an opportunity to justify design decisions. When completing your evaluation, you should include comments on:

▶ why certain design decisions were made (not how you achieved the final product)

▶ system robustness: for example how effective system-generated feedback was in supporting the user in continuing with processing following invalid data entry or whether any system crashes occurred during testing

▶ system performance: if the testing process identifies areas where a system generates inaccurate results or does not operate efficiently the solution will be improved upon or refined. The evaluation process should include a comment identifying any such refinements with an explanation as to why they are necessary

▶ possible improvements to the solution: following the implementation and testing of a completed solution it is often easy to identify areas where the solution could be improved upon. Such comments should be logged in the evaluation document to ensure ideas for improvement are recorded

> **The content of this chapter should be considered in conjunction with Chapter 17 Evaluation of digitally authored systems (Unit 2), which outlines the structure of an evaluation.**

> **Robustness is discussed further in Chapter 27 Evaluation of digitally authored systems (Unit 4).**

for future developers. You should also comment on any improvements already made to the solution. For example, during testing you may have identified code or scripted elements which did not generate the correct output, and which needed to be amended in some way. Reference should be made to those points during your evaluation

▶ deviations from original design: it may be necessary to deviate from the original design document. Comments in the evaluation should indicate how the final solution differs from the design and why this deviation was necessary

▶ strengths and weaknesses associated with the system: these should be identified and evidenced.

Evaluating a database solution

Alongside ensuring the user requirements have been met, the following should also be considered when evaluating database solutions.

Consistency of presentation

▶ Do all on-screen and printed reports have a similar layout? For example, do they all contain the company logo in the same location and at the same size?

▶ Is the font, text size and style consistent across all on-screen displays and printed elements of the application?

▶ Are all navigation buttons presented consistently?

Intuitiveness

▶ Can someone who is not familiar with the application easily navigate the application to complete the tasks required of the database?

Data integrity

▶ Are appropriate measures taken to help ensure data integrity? For example, is data validated whenever possible, are input masks, lookup lists and control elements used to support data entry whenever possible?

User-friendly error messages

▶ Do error message contain enough detail to help the user correct an error?

Many-to-many relationships

▶ To reduce data duplication and improve data consistency a database should not include any many-to-many relationships.

Field/table names

▶ Do all field and table names use a consistent naming convention and do they clearly describe the entities and attributes they represent? Field names in forms should be self-explanatory or contain examples where necessary.

▶ Do all reports, fields and data items display appropriately when opened by the user? For example, if a report is to be printed, is all content within the print margins of the selected page size for printing?

Task automation

▶ The end user should not need to access any elements of the underlying database to complete any task. For example, they should not have to create any queries or reports themselves. All tasks should be accessible from a menu option or an automated macro.

Appropriate presentation of processing results

▶ Does the database support presentation, for example on screen and or in printed format, as per the user's needs?

Evaluating a multimedia solution

Alongside ensuring the user requirements have been met, the following should also be considered when evaluating multimedia solutions.

Design choices

▶ During A/B testing, users are presented with alternative interfaces for the same application. The evaluation provides an opportunity to discuss the reasons behind the selection of the preferred interface, including:
  - use of colour and how variations in colour make the site more appealing to the target audience
  - choice of graphics and how they contribute to the application
  - choice of font, style and text size and how they appeal to the target audience (displayed on various platforms).

Balance of content

▶ Is there appropriate use of white space and balance of digital assets on pages and is all content of value to the end user?

Appropriateness of content

▶ Does the content help meet the needs of the target audience and is it fit for purpose?

Ease of use

▶ Is the application easy to navigate; are navigation buttons presented consistently?

Interface design and navigation

▶ Are all screens consistent in terms of presentation of text and other repeated elements? Are all hyperlinks within the application working correctly or were any broken hyperlinks found during the testing process?

Speed of download

▶ Do all pages in the application load quickly or is loading delayed while large multimedia assets are being downloaded? Comments should be made at this stage about the choice of file format selected for multimedia assets and why those formats were selected over any other format.

Quality of assets

▶ Are all multimedia assets relevant to the application? Did assets require compression? Are they stored in an optimised format?

Interactivity and feedback

▶ Is interactivity evident in all screens in the application? Is feedback instant, appropriate and informative? Does the correct element load and does it add to the content of the application? If there is an error in loading the interactive element, is the feedback informative?

Cross-platform compatibility

▶ To ensure the application runs on different platforms, amendments to the application may have been necessary, or additional plugins may be required. Comments should be included on these points at this stage.

Accessibility elements

▶ Is the application accessible to all users? For example, has the user included voice output of key points for users who are sight impaired? Is the user directed to download sites for additional plugins required to operate the application?

Tasks

1 The head coach in a local tennis club would like to introduce a database so he can easily manage lesson bookings at least four weeks in advance. He would like to use the system to:
   ▶ keep track of members of the club (including contact details), coaches, lessons and fees payable at the end of each month for any lessons given
   ▶ produce a printed invoice for all members at the end of each month
   ▶ produce a list of lessons for each coach at the start of each day
   ▶ search for members and staff details.

   As a class, discuss the possible user requirements for this system and produce a list of requirements which could be given to a design team, to help them produce a potential design for the system.

2 Evaluate your school's website or another digital application of your choice. Comment on the performance of the application and how the current solution can be improved upon. Identify the target audience for the application and produce a list of end user requirements you feel the application successfully fulfilled.

Chapter 21 Contemporary trends in software development

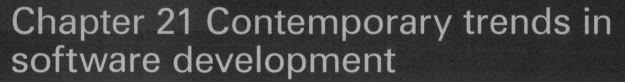

What this chapter covers

▶ Programming paradigms
▶ Software development environments

Programming paradigms

A program in its simplest form is a set of instructions that tells a computer what to do in order to solve a particular problem. There are a number of approaches to the programming process, and these are referred to as programming paradigms. Each paradigm adopts a different approach to building a solution using programming code. Two of the most important paradigms are the **procedural paradigm** and the **object-oriented paradigm**. These approaches are explained below.

Procedural programming

Procedural programming relies on implementing procedures (also known as functions or sub-routines). A procedure or function is a step-by-step set of instructions which performs a particular task or computation.

Top-down design involves breaking a complex problem down into smaller more manageable sub-problems. A procedural programming language provides features which allow the programmer to take a top-down approach to program development. These include variables, data structures and program structures. Functions are written to perform tasks on data and variables. A small sub-problem can be solved by writing a function. The order of the statements within a function is important. These functions can be called repeatedly. A program is made up of a number of functions or procedures.

Examples of procedural programming languages are C, COBOL and FORTRAN.

On the next page is an example of a C# program which takes a decimal number as input and outputs the cubed value of the number. In this program, there is a call to a function called 'cube' (in line 12).

```
1  using System;
2  using System.Collections.Generic;
3  using System.Linq;
4  using System.Text;
5  using System.Threading.Tasks;
6
7  namespace ConsoleApplication1
8  {
9      class Program
10     {
11         static void Main(string[] args)
12         {
13             //variables or data to be sed in the program are declared below
14             int value, cubedValue;
15
16             Console.WriteLine("Enter a number to calculate cubed value ");
17             value = Convert.ToInt32(Console.ReadLine());
18
19             //The function (or method) is called in the line below
20             cubedValue = cubed(value);
21
22             Console.WriteLine("The cubed value of " + value + " is " + cubedValue);
23             Console.ReadLine();
24
25         }
26
27
28         static int cubed(int x)//function (or method) definition
29         {
30             int p = x * x * x;
31             return p;
32
33         }
34     }
35 }
36
```

Object-oriented programming

Object-oriented programming uses the concept of **objects**. Here the object contains both the data (known as **properties**) being processed and the functions (known as **methods**) which will perform tasks on the data.

A **class** defines the properties and methods for a group of objects. It is like a template for an object. Relationships between one class and another can be implemented through **inheritance**. That is, one class can inherit the characteristics of another and therefore methods can be reused making code more efficient. If class 2 inherits class 1's properties and methods then only the differences in class 2 need to be reprogrammed.

Encapsulation or information hiding, hides the data belonging to an object. The object's data can only be directly accessed by the methods within the object itself. Users of the object do not need to understand *how* the object's methods are written, they can simply *use* the method. This is much like driving a car: you don't need to know how the engine and its components work, you just need to know how to drive the car. The object-oriented approach has these benefits.

▶ The code for an object can be programmed and maintained independently.

▶ The code for an object can be reused in different programs by different developers.

▶ The details of an object's internal implementation are hidden from the outside world, so direct access to the object's data is reduced.

Below is a simple example of the use of a class in C#.

```csharp
using System.Text;
using System.Threading.Tasks;
namespace ConsoleApplication1
{
  class Program
  {
    static void Main(string[] args)
    {
      Shape shape;
      shape = new Shape("Red", "Circle");
      Console.WriteLine(shape.Describe());
      shape = new Shape("Green","Square");
      Console.WriteLine(shape.Describe());
      Console.ReadLine();
    }
  }
  class Shape
  {
    private string shapename;
    private string colour;
    public Shape(string colour, string shapename)
    {
      this.colour = colour;
      this.shapename = shapename;
    }
    public string Describe()
    {
      return "This is a " + Colour + " " + ShapeName + "." ;
    }
    public string ShapeName
    {
      get { return shapename; }
      set { shapename = value; }
    }
    public string Colour
    {
      get { return colour; }
      set { colour = value; }
    }
  }
}
```

Tasks ✏

1 Describe how problems are solved using procedural programming languages.

2 How does object-oriented programming allow developers to create efficient solutions to problems?

In this C# code:

▶ the class name is Shape

▶ a shape has two attributes or pieces of data – shapename and colour

▶ the class Shape has one method called Describe

▶ the properties ShapeName and Colour allow the data within the class to be accessed.

Software development environments

The simplest program code can be written using a text or code editor. For example, Notepad can be used in most instances. **Software development environments** provide programmers with an integrated set of programming tools to build an application from coding through to testing. These are also known as integrated development environments (IDE), an example of which is Microsoft's Visual Studio. This software provides the programmer with tools for editing, debugging and compiling code as well as GUI features and tools for building forms.

Editing features of a software development environment

The editing window within an IDE allows the programmer to enter and edit code. It also provides access to objects, methods, properties and events at design time.

The image below shows a screenshot of the editing window in MS Visual Studio. You can see some features such as line numbers, colour coding of key words and collapsible code sections.

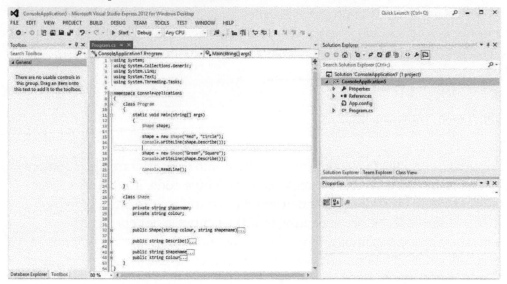

⌃ Using an integrated development to create a program

Most editors within software development environments provide the following features.

▶ Clipboard: used for copy and paste. The IDE remembers the last few chunks of code copied. Programmers can scroll through the copied items and select one to paste into the current window.

▶ Colour: used throughout the coding window to aid readability for the programmer. In Visual Studio, the editor uses different colours for keywords in the editing window. Errors are also colour-coded, for example, **syntax errors** are underlined in red in the C# coding editor. These are highlighted to programmers before compiling the program so that they can be corrected.

Tasks

1 Research the editing facilities provided by a software development environment of your choice. Create a short report detailing how these features can assist a programmer in the development process.

2 Write a program which will add two numbers together and output the result. Create a screenshot of the code and annotate it to illustrate the features provided by the source editor.

▶ Collapsible code sections: programmers can collapse/expand selected sections of code making viewing of large programs much easier.

▶ Line numbering: used to help programmers to distinguish between lines in long programs. Line numbers are also used by the compiler to reference the location of errors in the code.

▶ Code completion tools: when writing code there is instant, automatic, context-sensitive help. In Visual Studio this is known as IntelliSense. As a statement is entered, its full syntax is shown to the programmer. This helps ensure that the programmer knows how the statement should look and then enters it correctly. IntelliSense also provides lists of available functions, statements, constants, or values which the programmer can choose from.

High-level code translation and execution

Although program code can be read and understood by humans, it must be formally translated into **machine code** by a language compiler so that the computer can understand it and execute the instructions. The original program written by the programmer is called the **source code** and the translated version of the program is called the object code. The object code contains 1s and 0s and is the machine code version of the program.

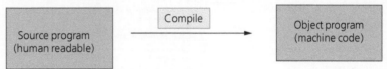

▲ The process of compilation

A language compiler is special software built into the software development environment that converts source code to machine code. It processes each statement in the source code and attempts to translate the whole program into machine code, before executing it. If the syntax is not correct, the translation process cannot be completed, therefore the program will not be executed. Once all syntax errors have been removed, the program can then be fully compiled.

During the compilation process, a number of tasks are performed such as the inclusion of library code, lexical analysis, syntax analysis and semantic analysis. If the program uses libraries (pre-compiled code which performs functions), the compiler will include any library code. This is called pre-processing. A pre-processor directive is used to include libraries in C#. In C# programs pre-processor directives are preceded by the '#' symbol for example #include.

Finally, the optimised machine code version of the source code is generated and can be executed. Executing, or 'running' a program means that the machine code instructions are loaded into memory and the computer performs the instructions.

Checkpoint

▷ The two most important programming paradigms are procedural and object-oriented programming.

▷ Procedural programming builds solutions based on procedures. A procedure is made up of a set of step-by-step computer instructions. Procedures operate on data and programs are made up of a number of procedures.

▷ Object-oriented programing builds solutions by grouping data and the functions that perform tasks on the data into classes. These functions are known as methods.

▷ Classes are a blueprint, or template, for creating objects.

▷ The object-oriented approach helps create reusable and more efficient code.

▷ A software development environment provides a programmer with a set of tools to create an application from coding through to testing.

▷ A source editor within a software environment provides many features to assist the programmer. These include the use of coloured text, collapsible code sections, code completion tools and line numbering.

▷ Source code must be compiled into machine code using a compiler.

▷ Compilers perform many tasks during compilation. These include pre-processing, lexical analysis, syntax analysis, semantic analysis.

Tasks

1 What does it mean to 'compile a program' and why is this necessary?

2 Describe the role of a compiler when developing programs.

3 Using a software development environment, compile and run a program. Record any errors generated and describe how the errors were corrected. Create a screenshot of the program as it is running showing how the program processes user input and produces output.

Practice questions

1 What is a computer program? [2 marks]

2 Describe the procedural programming paradigm. [2 marks]

3 Describe the main features and advantages of the object-oriented paradigm. [4 marks]

4 Name and describe four editing features that you would expect to find in a software development environment. [8 marks]

5 Describe the tasks performed by a compiler when translating a program from source code to machine code. [6 marks]

Chapter 22 Digital data

What this chapter covers

▶ Converting numbers into binary patterns

▶ Character representation

▶ Using binary, decimal and hexadecimal number systems

▶ Truth tables

▶ Using data types

Converting numbers into binary patterns

In Unit 1, the use of binary digits and **ASCII code** were discussed. Data must be converted to binary format so that it can be stored and understood by computers.

Numbers in the denary or base 10 system take one of ten values: 0, 1, 2, 3, 4, 5, 6, 7, 8, 9. Numbers in the base two or binary system can only take one of two values: 0 or 1. The base of a number can be shown by adding the base as a subscript. For example the number 147 can be shown as 147_{10}.

Numbers can be converted from one base to another. Consider converting the base 10 number 147_{10} to a base 2 number. There are two methods for doing this. The first is called divide by two and the second uses place values.

Understanding place values

The number 147_{10} is equal to one hundred, four tens, and seven units. Each digit in the number has a particular value, specified by its position. This is known as place value. In the denary system, place values are based on powers of 10 as shown here.

T	H	T	U
1000 (10^3)	100 (10^2)	10 (10^1)	1 (10^0)
	1	4	7

$(1 \times 10^2) + (4 \times 10^1) + (7 \times 10^0) = 147$ or $(1 \times 100) + (4 \times 10) + (7 \times 1) = 147$

Binary digits also have place values. Each bit (binary digit) in the pattern has a value. In the binary system, place values are based on powers of 2.

Using 147 as an example, the table below shows the place value of each binary digit along with the binary pattern for 147.

128	64	32	16	8	4	2	1
2^7	2^6	2^5	2^4	2^3	2^2	2^1	2^0
1	0	0	1	0	0	1	1

So, the denary number 147_{10} is equivalent to the binary pattern 10010011.

$(1 \times 2^7) + (1 \times 2^4) + (1 \times 2^1) + (1 \times 2^0) = 147$ or $(1 \times 128) + (1 \times 16) + (1 \times 2) + (1 \times 1) = 147$

Using divide by two to convert from denary to binary

	Remainder
2)147	1
2)73	1
2)36	0
2)18	0
2)9	1
2)4	0
2)2	0
2)1	1

Read the binary upwards

The resulting binary pattern is created by copying the bit values from the bottom up.

10010011

▲ Using divide by two

Using place value to create the binary number pattern

Another method of converting a denary number into a binary number is to make use of place values.

To create the binary number pattern for 147_{10}, write down the place values of each power of two.

Go to the highest value and check to see if that value can be taken away from 147. If so put a 1 beside the value. Then go to the next value; can it be taken away from the remainder? Continue in this way.

128 (2^7)	1	Can 128 be taken away from 147? Yes 147 - 128 = 19
64 (2^6)	0	Can 64 be taken away from 19? No
32 (2^5)	0	Can 32 be taken away from 19? No
16 (2^4)	1	Can 16 be taken away from 19? Yes 19 - 16 = 3
8 (2^3)	0	Can 8 be taken away from 3? No
4 (2^2)	0	Can 4 be taken away from 3? No
2 (2^1)	1	Can 2 be taken away from 3? Yes 3 - 2 = 1
1 (2^0)	1	Can 1 be taken away from 1? Yes 1 - 1 = 0

This time reading the binary digits from the top down gives the binary pattern 10010011, representing the denary value 147.

There are eight bits in this sequence. Eight bits is equivalent to 1 byte.

Binary coded decimal (BCD)

In this form of binary representation, each decimal digit is represented by a group of four binary digits. For example 147:

1	4	7
0001	0100	0111

So, 147_{10} = 000101000111 in BCD.

Character representation

ASCII code

In the early twentieth century, it became apparent that computers could be used to store and manipulate text as well as numbers. The original ASCII code table used seven bits to represent text. It was known as the **7-bit ASCII table**. There were 128 characters in the table (note that $2^7 = 128$). These characters include the letters A–Z and other common characters.

The **8-bit ASCII table** contains 256 characters ($2^8 = 256$); it makes use of the eighth bit in a byte. The 8-bit ASCII table includes all characters in the 7-bit table, plus regional characters and symbols, for example the Microsoft Windows Latin-1 extended characters.

The 8-bit ASCII table wasn't problem-free however. First, languages such as Japanese have thousands of characters and the limit of 256 meant that only some of the characters could be included. Second, the characters numbered 128 to 255 were used differently for different regions, leading to incompatibility between character sets.

Unicode

Unicode, a character-encoding standard, was created to get around the problems with 8-bit ASCII. Unicode provides a unique number for every character regardless of the language. The current Unicode set contains over 100 000 characters. The ASCII character codes are a subset of Unicode. Characters are called 'code points'. There are a number of encoding methods.

UTF-32 is fixed length encoding using 32 bits regardless of the character. This is inefficient when compared to ASCII which represents a character in 8 bits or one byte. Therefore variable length encoding was created.

UTF-8 is a variable-length encoding system. It uses one byte for the common characters, for example ASCII characters. Some other characters are encoded with two or more bytes. This typing of encoding is backward compatible with ASCII coding.

UTF-16 is another common encoding system making use of variable length encodings. It uses a minimum of 2-byte number units per character (16 bits per character).

Using binary, decimal and hexadecimal number systems

Hexadecimal number representation

Hexadecimal or **hex**, is a numbering system which uses the base 16. Hexadecimal values are expressed as the digits 0–9 and the letters A–F, giving 16 possibilities.

Hexadecimal number	0	1	2	3	4	5	6	7	8	9	A	B	C	D	E	F
Equivalent decimal number	0	1	2	3	4	5	6	7	8	9	10	11	12	13	14	15

Hexadecimal is generally used by programmers to simplify long binary patterns. One hexadecimal digit can represent a group of four bits. Computers do not work in hexadecimal but for every four bits in a binary pattern, only one hexadecimal value is required. This can be useful when looking at memory addresses. For example, if you want to look at a 64-bit memory address you can look at the 64-bit number pattern or the 16-digit hexadecimal pattern.

Converting a 16-bit binary pattern to hexadecimal

Place values in hexadecimal are arranged similarly to those in the denary and binary numbering systems. For example 17_{10} can be represent as 11_h using the hexadecimal numbering system. The table below shows some of the place values for hexadecimal numbers.

65536	4096	256	16	1
16^4	16^3	16^2	16^1	16^0
			1	1

That is $(1 \times 16^1) + (1 \times 16^0) = 16 + 1 = 17_{10}$

Hexadecimal is also used to represent colour codes on computers. The three primary colours (red, green and blue) have two-digit hexadecimal codes, ranging from 00 to FF (0 to 255 in decimal). These are placed together forming a six-digit hexadecimal code.

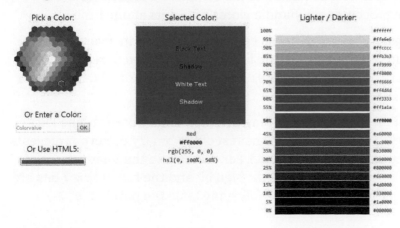

▲ Hexadecimal colour picker details

The values represent the colour mix between red, green and blue (RGB) in that order. For example, Black is #000000 and white is #FFFFFF. Red is given by #FF0000 (the sequence tells us that is no green or blue are added to the mix).

Converting between denary, binary and hexadecimal

Consider the binary pattern 10011011.

To convert from binary to hexadecimal, first split the binary pattern into 4-bit groups.

1001 1011

Establish the denary value for each group, using binary place values (see page 189).

$(8 + 1 = 9_{10})$ $(8 + 2 + 1 = 11_{10})$

Convert from denary to hexadecimal using the hexadecimal numbering system.

9 is 9 in hex and 11 is B in hex, therefore 10011011 is $9B_{16}$.

Converting from hexadecimal to denary can be done using two methods.

1   Convert each hexadecimal value into its binary equivalent and then convert the binary number into decimal.

$9B = 10011011 = (1 \times 128) + (0 \times 64) + (0 \times 32) + (1 \times 16) + (1 \times 8) + (0 \times 4) + (1 \times 2) + (1 \times 1) = 155_{10}$

2   Use place values for the base 16.

65536	4096	256	16	1
16^4	16^3	16^2	16^1	16^0
			9	B
			9 x 16 = 144	11

So, 9B = 144 + 11 = 155

Sign and magnitude and complementation

The maximum unit of data that a computer can process at one time is called 'a word'. The size of a word is related to the computer's architecture. For example a 16-bit processor can handle words of 16-bits at one time.

Positive and negative binary patterns can be represented in a variety of different ways. In general, one bit, the left-most bit, is used to represent the sign of the pattern. Usually, 1 indicates a negative number and 0 indicates a positive number.

Sign and magnitude is one way of doing this. In a binary pattern, the left-most bit is reserved for the sign and the rest of the binary pattern represents the size of the number (the magnitude). For example in the 8-bit pattern, 10000111, the left-most 1 represents the sign bit and the remaining 7 bits are the magnitude of the number. In the following table the number is –7.

Most significant bit MSB (+/–)	64	32	16	8	4	2	1
1	0	0	0	0	1	1	1

Complementation is another way of representing positive and negative numbers. Again, the left most bit (MSB) usually indicates the sign of the binary pattern.

When using **one's complement**, each bit is inverted, so a 1 bit changes to a 0 bit, and each 0 bit changes to a 1 bit.

For example:

+37 in binary is 00100101

Using one's complement: –37 =11011010

For one's complement using 8 bits it is possible to represent the denary numbers –127 to +127.

Two's complement is used more often.

The two's complement is obtained by:

▶ first changing the bit pattern to one's complement (inverting the bits)

▶ then adding 1 to the resulting binary pattern.

So, the two's complement of +37 is:

       11011010
             1 +
       11011011 (= –37)

Note that the most significant bit (left-most) is a 1 indicating a negative number.

Using 8 bits in two's complement, it is possible to represent the denary numbers –128 to +127.

Tasks

1 Find the binary pattern for each of these denary numbers and convert them to one's and two's complement.

 a) 64

 b) 43

 c) 70

 d) 127

 e) 110

2 Using 4 bits in two's complement, create a table showing the range of denary values that can be represented.

Adding two bytes together

Binary addition is carried out in a similar way to denary addition. However, a binary digit can only take on values of 0 or 1 therefore, a 'carry' is generated when two bits of value 1 are added. Consider the simple example below.

Add the binary patterns 101 and 001.

What about adding 111 to 111?

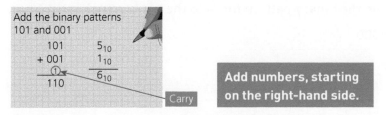

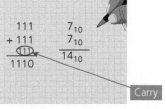

Adding the bits 1 + 1 gives 0 and a carry of 1.

Adding the bits 1 + 1 + 1 gives 1 and a carry of 1.

Note that in this example, we have had to add an additional bit to the pattern. The result is a 4-bit pattern.

Bytes (8-bit patterns) are added together in the same way.

Consider a computer which uses 8-bit word format. The maximum number that can be represented in a byte (8-bit word) is 255_{10}. That is 11111111 $(128 + 64 + 32 + 16 + 8 + 4 + 2 + 1 = 255)$.

Using 8-bit unsigned binary numbers, add 64 to 14.

$$01000000 + (64)$$
$$00001110 \quad (14)$$
$$01001110 \quad (78 = 64 + 8 + 4 + 2)$$

However, consider adding 129 to 129 (giving 258).

1							1		Carry
	1	0	0	0	0	0	0	1	129
	1	0	0	0	0	0	0	1	129
	0	0	0	0	0	0	1	0	Result (2)

$$10000001$$
$$10000001 +$$
$$(1) \quad 00000010$$

A problem has occurred. The sum is incorrect and there is an additional 1 generated. This extra bit is known as **overflow**. Overflow occurs when the magnitude of the number is greater than the maximum number that can be represented by the computer, in this case 255. The left-most 1 cannot be stored and is lost, therefore the result generated by this addition is 2_{10} which is incorrect.

Consider using 8-bit two's complement numbers to calculate 48 – 24.

This is achieved by calculating 48 + (–24).

Convert 48 to binary: 00110000

Convert 24 to binary: 00011000

Find –24 by converting the binary pattern for 24 to the two's complement form:

11100111 + 1 = 11101000

1	1	1							Carry
	0	0	1	1	0	0	0	0	48
	1	1	1	0	1	0	0	0	–24
	0	0	0	1	1	0	0	0	24 (Result)

The ninth bit is ignored. In order to determine if overflow occurred, it is necessary to examine the last two carry bits. If these are the same, overflow has not occurred and the result is correct. If the last two bits of the carry are different then overflow has occurred. In this case overflow has not occurred and the result is correct.

Consider the calculation –125 – 4 using 8-bit two's complement numbers.

▶ Find 125 in binary = 01111101

▶ Invert the bits = 10000010

▶ Add 1 = 10000011

▶ –125 = 10000011

▶ Find 4 in binary = 00000100

▶ Flip the bits = 11111011

▶ Add 1 = 11111100

1	0	0	0	0	0	0	0		Carry
	1	0	0	0	0	0	1	1	–125
	1	1	1	1	1	1	0	0	–4
	0	1	1	1	1	1	1	1	Result 127 incorrect

In the above case, overflow has occurred since the last two bits of the carry are different. The result therefore is incorrect. This is because –125 – 4 = –129 which is beyond the range of numbers that can be represented using 8-bit two's complement numbers.

Truth tables

Computers must carry out logical operations as well as arithmetical calculations. The computer will apply logical operators such as AND, NOT and OR to Boolean variables. A Boolean variable can take only one of two values, 1 or 0. These can be also expressed as true or false respectively.

NOT operator

The NOT operator has one input. The truth table for the NOT operator is shown, right.

X	NOT X
0	1
1	0

AND operator

The AND operator can have any number of inputs. All inputs must be equal to 1 (true) in order for an overall output of 1 or true to be obtained. The truth table for the AND operator is shown, right, using a 2-bit input sequence.

X	Y	X AND Y
0	0	0
0	1	0
1	0	0
1	1	1

Tasks

Perform binary addition on these 8-bit two's complement numbers:

1011 1101

1110 0101

Is the answer correct or not?

OR operator

The OR operator can have any number of inputs. At least one input must be equal to 1 (true) in order for an overall output of 1 (true) to be obtained. The truth table for the OR operator is shown below using a 2-bit input sequence.

X	Y	X OR Y
0	0	0
0	1	1
1	0	1
1	1	1

XOR operator

The XOR (exclusive OR) operator can have any number of inputs. However, an output of 1 will be obtained if only 1, not all of the input values, is equal to 1. The truth table for the XOR operator is shown below using a 2-bit input sequence.

X	Y	X OR Y
0	0	0
0	1	1
1	0	1
1	1	0

Complex logic gates are used to determine the results of evaluating Boolean expressions. Consider a logic gate which has three inputs: X, Y and Z. There are eight possible combinations of input. What values should appear in column P?

X	Y	Z	M = NOT Z	N = Y AND M	P = N OR M
0	0	0	1	0	
0	0	1	0	0	
0	1	0	1	1	
0	1	1	0	0	
1	0	0	1	0	
1	0	1	0	0	
1	1	0	1	1	
1	1	1	0	0	

This type of logic is used in programming during selection, when parts of the program will be executed based on evaluating a Boolean expression.

For example, if A = 4 and B = 6 and C = 10 which of the following statements will be output?

```
IF (A>B and A>C)
OUTPUT 'A is the largest value'
ELSE IF (B>A and B>C)
OUTPUT 'B is the largest value'
ELSE
OUTPUT 'C is the largest value'
END-IF
Tasks
```

Copy and complete the following for 3-bit input (the first row has been done for you).

X	Y	Z	M = X OR Y	N = Y AND Z	P = M AND N
0	0	0	0	0	0

Using data types

When writing a program or developing a software application, any data used must be given a data type so that it can be stored and processed correctly as a binary pattern. Data used in a program can also be called variables.

All variables are given names and data types and this determines how the bits representing the data are stored in memory. Most programming languages have built-in data types. These primitive data types include integers, strings and characters. Date/time values can be retrieved using special functions within the programming language. The program shown makes use of all of these data types.

> The following data types are described in Chapter 1 Digital data (Unit 1): numeric (integer and real), date/time, character and string.

```csharp
class Program
{
    static void Main(string[] args)
    {
        //declare variables
        DateTime today = new DateTime();
        string studentName = "";
        double courseWorkMark = 0.0;
        double examMark = 0.0;
        double totalMark;
        char overallGrade = ' ';

        Console.Write("Enter Student Name ");
        studentName = Console.ReadLine();
        Console.Write("Enter coursework mark ");
        courseWorkMark = Convert.ToDouble(Console.ReadLine());
        Console.Write("Enter exam mark ");
        examMark = Convert.ToDouble(Console.ReadLine());

        totalMark = examMark + courseWorkMark;

        if (totalMark > 75)
            overallGrade = 'A';
        else if (totalMark > 65)
            overallGrade = 'B';
        else if (totalMark > 55)
            overallGrade = 'C';
        else overallGrade = 'D';

        Console.WriteLine("Student " + studentName + " has achieved an overall mark of " + totalMark);
        Console.WriteLine(" This is a Grade " + overallGrade + ".  This has been achieved on " + today.DayOfWeek.ToString() +".");
        Console.ReadKey();
    }
}
```

▲ C# program which uses different data types

```
Enter Student Name Anthony
Enter coursework mark 44
Enter exam mark 45
Student Anthony has achieved an overall mark of 89
 This is a Grade A.  This has been achieved on Monday.
```

▲ Output from the program shown above

Checkpoint

▷ Data is stored in binary format on a computer.

▷ Numbers can be converted from denary to binary using the divide by two method or by making use of place values.

▷ When using binary coded decimal, each decimal digit is represented by a group of four binary digits.

▷ Character representation made use of ASCII code, but a larger character set was required for special characters and languages. Unicode provides a unique number for every character regardless of the language. Forms of Unicode, UTF-8 and UTF-16, are used for character representation.

▷ Hexadecimal is a number system which uses the base 16. Hexadecimal values can be generated using groups of four bits. The hexadecimal numbering system provides a concise way of representing long bit patterns. Colour codes make use of the hexadecimal numbering system.

▷ Numbers can be represented in a computer system in signed or unsigned format.

▷ Sign and magnitude uses the most significant bit (MSB) for the sign and the rest of the bit pattern to represent the magnitude or size of the number.

▷ One's complement can be used to represent binary numbers. To change a binary pattern to one's complement, each bit is inverted.

▷ Two's complement is used to represent positive and negative binary number patterns. Two's complement is achieved by changing the bit pattern to one's complement and adding 1.

▷ Binary addition can result in overflow. Overflow occurs because the value generated by the arithmetic operation is outside of the range that can be stored by the bit pattern.

▷ Truth tables apply the rules of logic to input values. They include AND, OR, NOT and XOR.

▷ All data used in a program or application must be given a data type. Programming languages have built-in data types such as integer, real, string, character. Date and time values can be retrieved from the system using special functions.

Practice questions ?

1 Describe two methods for converting denary numbers to binary format. [4 marks]

2 Computer systems use encoding for character representation.
   a) Why was ASCII code not sufficient for character representation? [3 marks]
   b) Describe a form of encoding that did not have the shortcomings of ASCII code. [4 marks]

3 Describe how hexadecimal numbering is utilised in computer systems. [4 marks]

4 What methods are available for representing negative numbers in a computer system? [6 marks]

5 What is overflow and how can it be detected when performing binary addition of two bytes? [5 marks]

5 Create AND, OR, and XOR truth tables for a 3-bit system. [6 marks]

6 Modify the program provided in this chapter to find the average mark achieved by the student and output the full date of the achievement. [6 marks]

Chapter 23 Digital design principles

What this chapter covers

▶ The underlying concepts of computational thinking

▶ Using algorithms, flowcharts and pseudo-code

▶ Algorithms for sorting and searching

▶ Refining a solution to a problem during design

▶ Identifying data requirements for a solution

▶ Developing an appropriate user interface

▶ Using a dry run to test a solution

> This chapter can be reviewed in conjunction with Chapter 28 Designing solutions using appropriate tools (Unit 5), which gives examples of the tools being used.

The underlying concepts of computational thinking

Computational thinking is an approach to problem solving that people use to define a problem and create a solution which can be carried out by a computer or individual. Computational thinking is not computer programming! Students in all subject areas can use computational thinking to help them solve problems.

There are four key elements to computational thinking. They are **decomposition**, **pattern recognition**, **abstraction** and **algorithm design**.

▶ Decomposition involves breaking the large complex problem into smaller sub-problems and then examining each sub-problem to provide a solution. The small solutions can be brought together to provide an overall solution to the complex problem.

▶ Pattern recognition involves observing key characteristics, patterns and trends in the data that is being considered.

▶ Abstraction involves removing specific details from a problem which are not needed to solve it.

▶ An **algorithm** is a step-by-step set of instructions which specifies how the problem is going to be solved. The order of the instructions in an algorithm is important. Both **flowcharts** and **pseudo-code** can be used in algorithm design.

Computational thinking provides a way for a computer programmer to look at a problem and begin to design a solution.

Tasks

1 Apply computational thinking to making a pizza. Document each stage in the development process.

2 A local pizza delivery service, Great Pizzas, applies these charges to pizza deliveries.

Distance from Great Pizzas	Cost for basic range delivery
Less than 2 miles	£3.00
2–4 miles	£5.00
More than 4 miles	£6.50

Luxury range pizzas require a special thermal box to ensure they are kept warm. If a customer orders from the luxury range, they must pay an additional £1.00 per luxury pizza for the use of the thermal box.

An additional 10 per cent is applied to the total delivery cost if the customer orders more than 10 pizzas. Apply computational thinking to produce a solution which will calculate the delivery cost for a customer regardless of what they order.

Using algorithms, flowcharts and pseudo-code

Flow diagrams and pseudo-code are methods of representing solutions to a problem. Pseudo-code is a way of describing a solution to a problem. A program can be written directly using pseudo-code. It uses keywords and control structures in a similar way to a programming language. However, pseudo-code is language-independent and can be used to write a program in any programming language.

A flow diagram or **flowchart** is a graphical representation of the solution to a problem. The flowchart uses special symbols to represent different operations, flow lines represent the sequence of operations and arrows on the flow lines represent the direction of flow from top to bottom or left to right.

Graphic	Symbol	Purpose
→	Flow line	Indicates the flow of logic and connects the different symbols together.
⬭	Terminal (Stop/Start)	Represents the start and end of the flowchart.
▱	Input/Output	Indicates input or output of data.
▭	Process	Indicates that an operation is to be done. There is usually text in the rectangle.
◇	Decision	Asks a question. There are a number of alternative answers and a pathway is selected based on the response to the question.
▯	Sub-routine symbol	Represents a call to a sub-routine.
▢	Document/ Report	Indicates that a report or document is used or produced.

▲ Symbols used for flowcharts

Consider the following problem. A weather station containing a rain gauge measures rainfall in millimetres. Readings are taken every three hours. A program is required that will take as input the eight readings and calculate the average rainfall in a period of 24 hours. The average reading must be output at the end of the day.

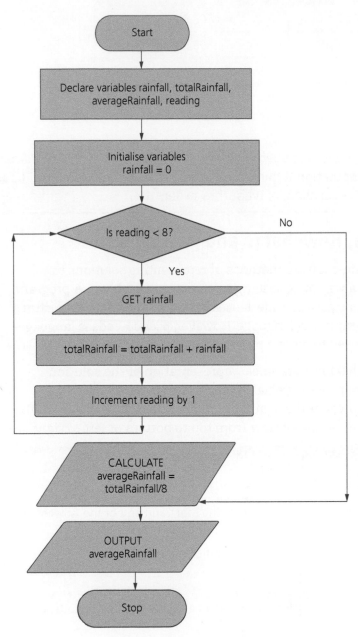

▲ Flowchart showing how the average rainfall for the weather station is calculated

The flowchart shows the use of a decision box which is used to decide whether or not to take another reading. This means that the solution includes a 'loop'. A loop is a programming construct which allows sections of code to be repeated. Different data items are used in the solution (totalRainfall, rainfall, reading, averageRainfall); these can be referred to as variables. All variables used in the solution are set to zero.

Solutions can also be represented using pseudo-code. Pseudo-code describes the solution using a set of instructions that is not related to any programming language.

```
Initialise rainfall, totalRainfall, averageRainfall, reading
WHILE reading is less than 8
  INPUT rainfall
  totalRainfall = totalRainfall + rainfall
  increment reading by 1
END WHILE
CALCULATE AVERAGE
OUTPUT averageRainfall

CALCULATE AVERAGE
averageRainfall=totalRainfall/8
```

▲ Pseudo-code showing how the average rainfall for the weather station is calculated

Compare both the flowchart and the pseudo-code. Note that each provides a pathway to the solution for the problem. Both the flowchart and the pseudo-code could be used to produce a program, in any programming language, to solve the problem.

Tasks

Create both flowchart and pseudo-code solutions for each of the following problems.

1 A student wishes to calculate and output the area and perimeter of a rectangle.

2 An organisation wants to calculate and output the pay due to workers. The basic rate of pay is £12.00 per hour. If a worker works more than 10 hours, additional hours are paid at £14.00 per hour. If a worker earns more than £90.00, tax is applied at a rate of 22 per cent.

3 An insurance company wishes to apply these weightings to people applying for insurance. The weightings are based on the engine size of the car and whether or not they have any convictions. An appropriate message will be displayed, using the rules in the table below. In your solutions use a reference to a sub-routine called DISPLAY MESSAGE which will show the appropriate message.

Age	Engine size	Convictions?	Percentage policy weighting
>=18	>=1200	Y	40
>=18	>=1200	N	20
>=18	<1200	Y	30
>=18	<1200	N	0
<18	>=1200	Y	Refuse application

Age	Engine size	Convictions?	Percentage policy weighting
<18	>=1200	N	55
<18	<1200	Y	50
<18	<1200	N	10

4 Explain how the data in the above table could be described as a truth table.

Algorithms for sorting

Sorting algorithms are used by computers to sort data in a particular order, for example numerical or alphabetical. There are many different sorting algorithms and each has its own advantages and limitations. Sorting algorithms can be evaluated in terms of the:

▶ speed at which they sort large amounts of data

▶ amount of memory used during the sorting process

▶ number of comparisons carried out within a sort

▶ number of exchanges carried out during a sort

▶ stability of the sort. A sorting algorithm is said to be stable if two equivalent objects appear in the same order in the input list to be sorted as they appear in the sorted output.

Simple sorting algorithms include the **bubble sort** and the **insertion sort**. More complex sorts include the quick sort and the merge sort.

The bubble sort and the insertion sort

The table below shows how the bubble and insertion sorts differ with regard to the number of comparisons and the number of exchanges.

Sort type	Number of comparisons		Number of exchanges	
	Average case	Worst case	Average case	Worst case
Bubble sort	$N^2/2$	$N^2/2$	$N^2/2$	$N^2/2$
Insertion sort	$N^2/4$	$N^2/2$	$N^2/8$	$N^2/4$

N = number of data items.

A comparison is when two items of data are compared to each other.

An exchange is when items of data swap their position in the list.

The insertion sort can be more efficient than the bubble sort in terms of comparisons and exchanges.

Bubble sort

▶ Inefficient for sorting large amounts of data. The time taken to sort data is related to the square of the number of items to be sorted.

▶ The algorithm works by swapping adjacent data items until they are in the correct order.

▶ Data items 'bubble' up through the list until they are in the correct order.

Insertion sort

▶ Adaptive: the performance of the algorithm adapts to the initial order of the elements. This algorithm may be used when the data items are nearly sorted.

▶ Stable: retains the relative order of the same elements.

▶ Requires a constant amount of memory as the entire sort occurs in internal memory.

Storing data for sorting

An array is used to store the data items to be sorted. An array is a data structure which holds a set of data items all of the same type. It is given a name and the data items or elements are accessed using the array name followed by their position in the array. Usually, an array is zero indexed, meaning that the first element can be accessed by giving the following details Arrayname[0].

How does the bubble sort work?

Imagine an array called myNumbers which has the following six integers stored: 47, 69, 12, 34, 25, 39.

The data needs to be sorted using the bubble sort method.

The table below shows the results after one full pass through the array of data. One full pass involves five comparisons. Each comparison examines two adjacent elements in the array of data. The two elements being compared are shaded in the table below. Exchanges are highlighted.

Comparison	myNum-bers[0]	myNum-bers[1]	myNum-bers[2]	myNum-bers[3]	myNum-bers[4]	myNum-bers[5]	Exchange
1	**47**	**69**	12	34	25	39	47 > 69? No No swap
2	47	**69**	**12**	34	25	39	69 > 12? Yes Swap
3	47	12	**69**	**34**	25	39	69 > 34? Yes Swap
4	47	12	34	**69**	**25**	39	69 > 25? Yes Swap
5	47	12	34	25	**69**	**39**	69 > 39? Yes Swap
	47	12	34	25	39	**69**	

This process is repeated. On the second pass, the second largest value will be moved to the second last array position and so on.

> **Tasks** 🖉
>
> **Consider the data above.**
>
> 1 Using the data in the last row of the table above, create a new table to represent a second pass through the array of data. The column and row headings will be the same.
>
> 2 Continue creating tables each representing another pass until the data is sorted.
>
> 3 How many passes through the array are required to ensure the array is sorted?
>
> 4 How many comparisons are required to sort the data?

How does the insertion sort work?

Consider the same data in an insertion sort.

The tables below show the results after one full pass using the insertion sort algorithm. Each comparison examines two adjacent elements in the array of data. When a data item is swapped it is added to the sorted sub-list in the correct order. At the end of one full pass the array of data is fully sorted.

Com-parison	myNum-bers[0]	myNum-bers[1]	myNum-bers[2]	myNum-bers[3]	myNum-bers[4]	myNum-bers[5]	Exchange
1	47	69	12	34	25	39	47 > 69? No No change

Com-parison	myNum-bers[0]	myNum-bers[1]	myNum-bers[2]	myNum-bers[3]	myNum-bers[4]	myNum-bers[5]	Exchange
2	47	69	12	34	25	39	69>12? Yes Swap and add to sorted sublist
3	47	12	69	34	25	39	check new sorted sublist. 47>12? Yes Swap
4	12	47	69	34	25	39	Note that the sorted sublist now contains two values

Comparison	myNumbers[0]	myNumbers[1]	myNumbers[2]	myNumbers[3]	myNumbers[4]	myNumbers[5]	Exchange
5	12	47	**69**	**34**	25	39	69>34? Yes Swap and add to sorted sublist
6	12	**47**	**34**	69	25	39	check new sorted sublist. 47>34? Yes Swap
7	**12**	**34**	47	69	25	39	Check new sorted sublist 12>34 ? No No change in sorted sublist order. Note that the sorted sublist now contains three values

Comparison	myNumbers[0]	myNumbers[1]	myNumbers[2]	myNumbers[3]	myNumbers[4]	myNumbers[5]	Exchange
8	12	34	47	**69**	**25**	39	69>25? Yes Swap and add 25 to sorted sublist
9	12	34	**47**	**25**	69	39	check new sorted sublist. 47>25? Yes Swap
10	12	**34**	**25**	47	69	39	Check new sorted sublist 34>25 ? Yes Swap
11	**12**	**25**	**34**	47	69	39	Check new sorted sublist 12>25 ? No No change in sorted sublist Note that the sorted sublist now contains four values

Comparison	myNumbers[0]	myNumbers[1]	myNumbers[2]	myNumbers[3]	myNumbers[4]	myNumbers[5]	
12	12	25	34	47	**69**	**39**	69>39? Yes Swap and add 39 to sorted sublist
13	12	25	34	**47**	**39**	69	check new sorted sublist. 47>39? Yes Swap
14	12	25	**34**	**39**	47	69	Check new sorted sublist 34>39 ? No No Swap No further comparisons required in this pass.
	12	25	34	39	47	69	Data is now sorted

> **Tasks** ✎
>
> 1 How does this compare to the bubble sort in terms of the number of comparisons and number of exchanges?
> 2 Describe how a sort algorithm can be evaluated.

Possible algorithms for both the bubble sort and the insertion sort are shown below using pseudo-code.

Bubble sort pseudo-code

```
For i= 0 to 4
  For j=0 to 4
    if myNumbers[j] > myNumbers [j+1]
      SWAP NUMBERS
  end for
end for
SWAP NUMBERS
temp = myNumbers [j]
myNumbers [j] = myNumbers [j+1]
myNumbers [j+1] = temp
```

The bubble sort uses a loop (inside j loop) to move through an array comparing adjacent data items as it moves along. If an array element a[j] is greater than the element immediately to its right a[j+1], it swaps them. The first time around, this process will bubble the largest value to the end of the array. After N-1 passes the data will be sorted.

Insertion sort pseudo-code

```
For i= 0 to 5
  positionOfMin=i
  For j= i to 5
    If myNumbers[positionOfMin]>myNumbers[j]
      positionOfMin = j
  end for
  SWAP NUMBERS
end for
SWAP NUMBERS
Temp= myNumbers[i]
myNumbers[i]=myNumbers[positionOfMin]
myNumbers[positionOfMin] = temp
```

The insertion sort uses two loops. The first loop goes from 0 to 5, and the second loop goes from i to 5, so it goes from 0 to 5, then from 1 to 5, then from 2 to 5 and so on.

This sort inserts each element of the array into its proper position, leaving larger stretches of the array sorted (the sorted sub-list); then, the current element of the array is inserted into the proper position at the head of the array.

> **Tasks** ✎
>
> 1 Research the 'modified bubble sort' and describe how the bubble sort algorithm can be improved to make it more efficient.
> 2 Create flowchart solutions for the bubble and insertion sort algorithms shown above.

Algorithms for searching

Search algorithms are used to locate and return data given certain criteria. Each search algorithm has benefits and limitations. When searching through large amounts of data it is important to apply an efficient search method, as the time taken to find the data may mean a slower return of results. Sorting the data in advance of searching can make the search more efficient. Search algorithms work with data structures such as arrays.

The linear search algorithm

This is a simple search technique. Every data item is examined in order to see if it matches the target value being searched for. In a **linear search**, the average number of attempts required to find a target value is half the number of data items. So, to find a target value in a set of 20 data items could take on average 10 attempts.

For example, in the data structure 47, 69, 12, 34, 25, 39 a linear search for 25 would look like this:

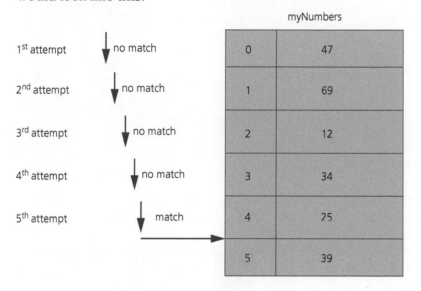

5 attempts in total to find 25.

Pseudo-code for a linear search through an array called myNumbers holding six data items might look like this:

```
Declare array myNumbers
i=0
found = false
  For i= 0 to 5
    if myNumbers[i] = targetValue
      found=true
    endif
  end for
  If found = true
    OUTPUT MESSAGE "Target value found"
  Else
    OUTPUT MESSAGE "Target value not found"
```

The binary search algorithm

The **binary search** algorithm is much more efficient than the linear search algorithm. It only works on data that is already sorted. The binary search starts by finding the middle location in the list. The middle location value is compared to the target value. If the target value is not found, the search determines if the target value is below or above the middle location value. This process is repeated and the number of items being searched through,

Tasks

Write down a list of surnames from your class in any order and discuss how many attempts are needed to find a given name. Sort the list into alphabetical order. How does this help the searching process?

Tasks

In pairs, play 'Think of a number' in the range 1–100. One person sets the target value and the other person attempts to guess the number. After every guess the setter of the number should tell the person guessing whether they should go higher or lower. Record the guesses made. Discuss the strategy that the person used to guess the number.

the 'search space', is decreased until eventually there is only one item to be searched through.

In a binary search, the maximum number of attempts required to find a target value is $\log_2$number of items. So, to find a target value in a set of 20 data items, the maximum number of attempts would be four. Compare this to the linear search.

Consider the array myNumbers, which now contains 11 numbers sorted in numerical order.

The target value = 85

myNumbers

Location	0	1	2	3	4	5	6	7	8	9	10
Value	12	25	34	39	47	69	72	78	85	90	99

To find 85:

Find the mid-point location

```
start _ location = 0
end _ location = 10
mid = start _ location + (end _ location - start _ location)/2
mid = 0 + ((10-0)/2) = 5
```

Location	0	1	2	3	4	5	6	7	8	9	10
Value	12	25	34	39	47	69	72	78	85	90	99

```
Is the value in location 5 = to the target value? No
Is the value in location 5 < target value? Yes
  Calculate a new start _ location
    Start _ location = mid + 1 = 5 + 1 = 6
    end _ location remains the same = 10
```

The search space has been decreased. It is now from location 6 to location 10 and includes only five data items.

Location	6	7	8	9	10
Value	72	78	85	90	99

Find the mid-point location

```
start _ location = 6
end _ location = 10
mid = start _ location + (end _ location - start _ location)/2
mid = 6 + ((10-6)/2) = 8
```

location	6	7	8	9	10
value	72	78	85	90	99

Is the value in location 8 = to the target value? Yes

The target value has been found after two attempts. This is much more efficient than applying a linear search, which would have taken nine attempts.

Pseudo-code for a binary search which uses an array of N numbers sorted in descending order and handles the situation when a number is not found might look like this.

```
Declare array myNumbers
start_location =0
end_location= N-1
found = false
While (start_location <= end_location)
mid = start_location + ((start_location + end_location) / 2)
  if myNumbers[mid]==target
      found=true
  else
    if (target < myNumbers[mid])
      start_location = mid + 1;
      else
      if (target > myNumbers[mid])
        end_location = mid - 1;
      end if
    endif
  end if
END While
If found = true
  OUTPUT MESSAGE "Target value found"
Else
  OUTPUT MESSAGE "Target value not found"
```

Tasks

1 Using the array myNumbers in the above example, try searching for the number 34. Produce the same diagrams and calculations as outlined above.

2 Try searching for 100 using the same array. The search must stop when the start_location exceeds the end_location.

Tasks

Implement the binary sort in a programming language of your choice.

Refining a solution to a problem during design

Refining a solution to a problem starts with defining an initial solution. This is unlikely to be perfect and will need some modification to ensure that it meets a set of requirements. For example, it may omit aspects of functionality required by a user or may be inefficient. During the design process, a solution can be refined using the principles of computational thinking and by testing the solution before writing any code.

Defining and refining a solution

Consider the following problem: A butcher has recently received a consignment of 24 steaks from a supplier. He wishes to categorise the steaks into each of the following weight classes.

Class	Grams
A	>1000
B	> 750
C	> 500
D	> 400
E	> 250
F	<= 250

At the end of weighing, he requires a report containing the supplier's name, the total number of steaks in each category, what percentage of the total weight each category is, and the total weight of the steaks in kilograms. The butcher does not accept steaks below 100 g and above 1.25 kg.

Create an algorithm which will solve the problem. It should allow the input of the supplier's name (at least five characters in length), the weights of the 24 steaks (in grams) and output the required statistics. All input should be validated.

Using decomposition, a list of sub-problems can be created as follows:

```
OUTPUT prompt to input name
INPUT name
Validate name
For i = 1 to 24
  OUTPUT prompt to input weightOfSteak
  INPUT weightOfSteak
  Validate weightOfSteak
Assign steak to category
Calculate percentage weight of each category
End for
OUTPUT Report
```

These are the main tasks required to solve the problem. Those underlined can be further divided up. That means that the design can be further refined.

Refining and designing a solution

The sub-problems can be further defined as follows, to show each single step required to ensure the task is completed.

<u>Validate name</u>
```
do
  valid=true
  OUTPUT prompt
  INPUT name
  if length(name) =0
    valid=false
    OUTPUT error message
  end if
  clear error message
WHILE valid=false
```

<u>Validate weightOfSteak</u>
```
do
  valid=true
  OUTPUT prompt
  INPUT weightOfSteak
  if (weightOfSteak < 100) OR (weightOfSteak>1250)
    valid=false
    OUTPUT error message
  end if
  clear error message
WHILE valid=false
```

<u>Assign steak to category</u>
```
If (weightOfSteak>1000)
  category='A'
else
  If (weightOfSteak>750)
    category='B'
  else
    If (weightOfSteak>500)
      category='C'
    else
      If (weightOfSteak>400)
        category='D'
      else
        If (weightOfSteak>250)
          category='E'
        else
          category='F'
        end if
      end if
    end if
  end if
end if
```

<u>Calculate Percentage Weight of each category</u>
```
If (weightOfSteak>1000)
  Add weightOfSteak to categoryAWeight
else
  If (weightOfSteak>750)
    Add weightOfSteak to categoryBWeight
  else
    If (weightOfSteak>500)
      Add weightOfSteak to categoryCWeight
    else
      If (weightOfSteak>400)
        Add weightOfSteak to categoryDWeight
      else
        If (weightOfSteak>250)
          Add weightOfSteak to categoryEWeight
        else
          Add weightOfSteak to categoryFWeight
        end if
      end if
    end if
  end if
end if
```

totalWeightOfSteak = categoryAWeight + categoryBWeight + categoryCWeight + categoryDWeight + categoryEWeight + categoryFWeight

percentageA = (categoryAWeight/totalWeightOfSteak) * 100

percentageB = (categoryBWeight/totalWeightOfSteak) * 100

percentageC = (categoryCWeight/totalWeightOfSteak) * 100

percentageD = (categoryDWeight/totalWeightOfSteak) * 100

percentageE = (categoryEWeight/totalWeightOfSteak) * 100

percentageF = (categoryFWeight/totalWeightOfSteak) * 100

Look at <u>Assign steak to category</u> and <u>Calculate Percentage Weight of each category</u>.

If the code is written in two separate sections, there is some duplication of code. This could be avoided by creating a procedure or subroutine called <u>Classify and Count Steak</u>. This will make the code more efficient and avoid the repetition of code.

The new algorithm would be:

```
OUTPUT prompt to input name
INPUT name
Validate name
For I = 1 to 24
  OUTPUT prompt to input weightOfSteak
  INPUT weightOfSteak
  Validate weightOfSteak
  Classify and Count Steak
End for
Calculate Percentage Weight of each category
OUTPUT REPORT
```

The refined sub-problem, Classify and Count Steaks, now becomes:

```
Classify and Count Steaks
  If (weightOfSteak>1000)
    category='A'
    Add weightOfSteak to categoryAWeight
    Add 1 to categoryATotal
  else
    If (weightOfSteak>750)
      category='B'
      Add weightOfSteak to categoryBWeight
      Add 1 to categoryBTotal
    else
    If (weightOfSteak>500)
      category='C'
      Add weightOfSteak to categoryCWeight
      Add 1 to categoryCTotal
    else
      If (weightOfSteak>400)
        category='D'
        Add weightOfSteak to categoryDWeight
        Add 1 to categoryDTotal
      else
        If (weightOfSteak>250)
          category='E'
          Add weightOfSteak to categoryEWeight
          Add 1 to categoryETotal
        else
          Add weightOfSteak to categoryFWeight
          category='F'
          Add 1 to categoryFTotal
```

```
        Add weightOfSteak to categoryEWeight
      end if
    end if
   end if
  end if
 end if
```

Calculate Percentage Weight of each category now becomes

Calculate Percentage Weight of each category

totalWeightOfSteak = categoryAWeight + categoryBWeight + categoryCWeight + categoryDWeight + categoryEWeight + categoryFWeight

percentageA = (categoryAWeight/totalWeightOfSteak) * 100

percentageB = (categoryBWeight/totalWeightOfSteak) * 100

percentageC = (categoryCWeight/totalWeightOfSteak) * 100

percentageD = (categoryDWeight/totalWeightOfSteak) * 100

percentageE = (categoryEWeight/totalWeightOfSteak) * 100

percentageF = (categoryFWeight/totalWeightOfSteak) * 100

OUTPUT Report

OUTPUT "Supplier name: " + name

OUTPUT "The total number of steaks in Category A is" + categoryATotal + "This category makes up " + percentageA + "of the total weight"

OUTPUT "The total number of steaks in Category B is" + categoryBTotal + "This category makes up " + percentageB + "of the total weight"

OUTPUT "The total number of steaks in Category C is" + categoryCTotal + "This category makes up " + percentageC + "of the total weight"

OUTPUT "The total number of steaks in Category D is" + categoryDTotal + "This category makes up " + percentageD + "of the total weight"

OUTPUT "The total number of steaks in Category E is" + categoryETotal + "This category makes up " + percentageE + "of the total weight"

OUTPUT "The total number of steaks in Category F is" + categoryFTotal + "This category makes up " + percentageF + "of the total weight"

OUTPUT "There are " + totalNoOfSteaks + "steaks."

OUTPUT "The overall steak weight is " + totalWeightOfSteak

When reviewing the design using test data, it was noted that the value for totalNoOfSteaks had not been calculated. A further refinement to the design was required.

CalculateTotal number of steaks

totalnoOfSteaks = categoryATotal + categoryBTotal + categoryCTotal + categoryDTotal + categoryETotal + categoryFTotal

Tasks

Examine the OUTPUT Report section. What is wrong with the totalWeightOfSteak output? What modification is required to the calculation to ensure the output meets the user requirements? Hint: Is it in grams or kilograms?

The top level algorithm is now:

```
OUTPUT prompt to input name
INPUT name
Validate name
For I = 1 to 24
  OUTPUT prompt to input weightOfSteak
  INPUT weightOfSteak
  Validate weightOfSteak
  Classify and Count Steak
End for
Calculate Percentage Weight of each category
Calculate Total Number of Steaks
OUTPUT REPORT
```

> The role played by the end user when developing prototypes of a digital system is discussed further in Chapter 11 Designing solutions (Unit 2).

In the above case, several refinements were made to the design. Refinement during the design stage is to be expected. Additional refinements can also come from the user if they are part of the design team or if the designer produces wireframe diagrams of screens to be included and allows the user to review them. Refinement at this stage is easily carried out and ensures that the user will receive a product that meets their needs.

Models for designing solutions

There are different models for designing solutions. **Traditional development** involves following a development life-cycle from beginning to end. The developer will perform analysis to determine the user requirements and then work through designing a solution. Programmers will then code (implement) the solution and perform different types of testing on it before releasing the system to the user. One drawback of this approach is that the user is not involved after the analysis stage.

Agile development methods allow the user to be closely involved with the developers and development of the system is done in sections. Each section is designed, built and tested before the user sees it. The user is allowed to review each section and give feedback to the developer who can then make the necessary changes.

Identifying data requirements for a solution

Part of the design process involves identifying **data requirements**. This is the data that will be input to the system, output by the system and any data that is used to store values temporarily when the system is running. Using the previous steak example, we can list the data items.

It is important to plan the data requirements for the solution in advance. This is needed to produce a test plan for the system. The test plan will be used to check that the program works as expected and is a very important part of developing the system, as it identifies errors in the logic of the design. These can be corrected and the design improved as a result.

	Data item	Data type	Sample valid data	Function of data item
1	Name	String	Mr Mattwell	Stores the supplier's name for use in the report.
2	weightOfSteak	Integer	750	Stores the weight of an individual steak as input.
3	Category	Character	A	Stores the derived category of a steak based on its weight.
4	categoryAWeight	Integer	2000	Stores the total weight of steaks in category A. Calculated by adding the weight of the category A steak to a running total.
5	categoryATotal	Integer	45	Stores the total number of steaks in category A. Calculated by adding 1 to a running total each time a steak in category A is entered.
6	percentageA	Real/ double/ float	93.2	Stores the percentage weight of category A compared with the overall weight of all steaks. Calculated as follows: (categoryAWeight/ totalWeightOfSteak)*100
7	totalWeightOfSteak	Integer	12500	Stores the total weight of all steaks. Calculated by adding the weight of every steak to a running total.
8	totalNoOfSteaks	Integer	22	Stores the total number of steaks. Calculated by adding 1 to a running total each time a steak weight is entered.

▲ Table showing some of the data requirements for the solution

Developing an appropriate user interface

The user interface is the part of the system the user will interact with and use to operate the different functions. It is important that the user interface is user-friendly. This can be achieved by:

▶ presenting information clearly and concisely

▶ using colours, icons and messages in a consistent manner to help the user learn how to use the system

▶ placing menus, messages, buttons in the same place throughout the system

▶ designing an efficient system which is responsive and does not have lengthy loading times

▶ supporting the user if they make a mistake through providing helpful messages and feedback

▶ designing an interface which focuses on user experience, has visual appeal and is attractive to the user.

During design, the interface should be drawn using wireframes or sketches. This can be shown to the user who can make suggestions about changes and the addition of features.

Tasks

Complete the table above by including the rest of the data requirements for the butcher's solution.

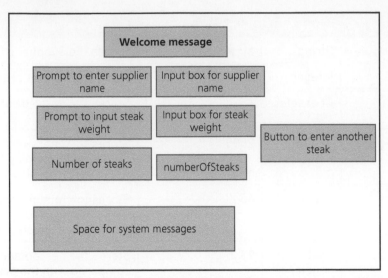

▲ Simple wireframe of the data collection form for the butcher's problem

Solutions can provide the user with a graphical user interface (GUI) or a simple text-based screen that prompts the user for input.

GUIs are discussed further in Chapter 12 Digital development considerations (Unit 2).

A GUI provides the user with an interactive environment. It is navigated using a mouse and the user makes selections by pointing and clicking on windows, menus and icons. The Windows operating system provides a good example of a GUI. A system which operates using a GUI is likely to be larger in size than a similar one which uses simple text-based screens.

Consider the butcher's problem. Two different interfaces could be provided: one is a simple text-based user interface and the other is a graphical user interface.

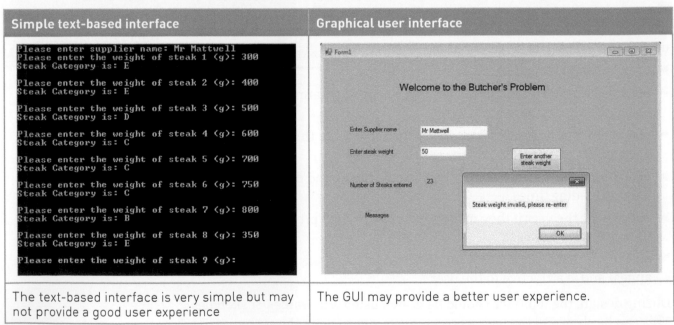

Simple text-based interface	Graphical user interface
The text-based interface is very simple but may not provide a good user experience	The GUI may provide a better user experience.

Tasks

Examine the text-based screen and the GUI. Which provides the best user experience? Give reasons for your choice.

Using a dry run to test a solution

A dry run is a paper-based exercise which allows the programmer to work through a solution using test data. The programmer can make use of a dry run at the design or coding stages. It involves creating a trace table with a list of variables and checking the value of the variables after each line of code has been executed. This can identify errors in the logic of the design and any omissions and incorrect results. A dry run is particularly useful when designing a solution.

Many programming environments provide debugging facilities to enable programmers to watch the value of variables whilst the program is running. This is a more common way of tracing the values of variables.

To create a trace table:

▶ number each line of code or pseudo-code

▶ create a table structure

▶ create a column for each variable in the section of code

▶ add an output column to show any output generated from the code.

Consider the section of pseudo-code used to validate the weight of a steak.

Validate weightOfSteak

```
1  do
2    valid=true
3    OUTPUT prompt
4    INPUT weightOfSteak
5     if (weightOfSteak < 100) OR (weightOfSteak>1250)
6       valid=false
7        OUTPUT error message
8      end if
9    clear error message
10 WHILE valid=false
```

Line no.	Valid	Weightofsteak	Output
1			
2	True		
3	True		Prompt
4	True	1400	
5	True	1400	
6	False	1400	
7	False	1400	Error message
8	False	1400	
9	False	1400	Cleared screen
10	False	1400	

→

Line no.	Valid	Weightofsteak	Output
1	False		
2	True		
3	True		Prompt
4	True	750	
5	True	750	
9	True	750	Cleared screen
10	True		Loop ended

▲ Trace table

Tasks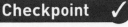

Use a dry run to test the solution to Classify and Count Steak using these seven values:

250, 750, 300, 560, 250, 1200, 1100.

Checkpoint ✓

▷ The four key elements of computational thinking are decomposition, pattern recognition, abstraction and algorithm design. Used together these tools can help design solutions to complex problems.

▷ Algorithms represent solutions to problems. An algorithm can be created using flowcharts or pseudo-code.

▷ A flowchart is a graphical representation of a solution whereas pseudo-code uses keywords and control structure, like programming languages, to represent a solution.

▷ The bubble sort and the insertion sort are simple sorting algorithms. The insertion sort can be more efficient than the bubble sort in terms of comparisons and exchanges.

▷ Searching data can be done using a linear search in which every data item is checked. This is an inefficient search. A binary search operates on data that has been sorted. It searches by using the mid location and checking the data value found here against the target value sought. The number of attempts needed to find the target value, if it exists, is greatly reduced. The binary search is more efficient than the linear search.

▷ A solution can be refined at the design stage by reviewing and testing the solution using test data. Input from the user is also valuable at this stage. Refinements can include breaking the problem into smaller sub-problems, changing the nature of the solution to make the code more efficient, correcting logic errors or redesigning aspects of the user interface.

▷ The data requirements for a system must be identified at design time. Data items or variables should be given a name and assigned a data type. All data used for input, output or processing should be specified in the data requirements.

▷ The user interface is the point at which the user 'meets' the system. Any part of the system with which the user can interact, is part of the interface. Interfaces can take the form of a graphical user interface or a simple text-based data capture screen.

▷ A dry run is a paper-based exercise carried out by a programmer to test the logic of a section of code. A trace table is used and each line of code is numbered. The trace table contains a reference to each line of code and all variables or data items used within the section of code are included as columns. A column for output data is also included.

Practice questions ?

1 A small organisation hires out coaches. A solution is required which will calculate the hire charge for a coach. The charge depends on the size of the coach, the length of time the coach is being hired for and the distance travelled. There are three different sizes of coach: 60 seater, 40 seater and a 20 seater. The basic charges for these are £120.50, £100.50 and £81.00 respectively. All coaches are charged at £30 per hour. The mileage charges for the coaches are 60p per mile for a 60 seater, 45p per mile for a 40 seater and 20p per mile for a 20 seater.

The solution should take as input the size of the coach, the departure time and return time (departure and return can only take place on the hour and should be entered as hours on the 24 hour clock, i.e. 3 p.m. should be entered as 1500) and the estimated mileage. All input is to be validated. The solution is to output the calculated hire charge.

   a) Using decomposition, create an algorithm to solve the problem. You may use a flowchart or pseudo-code. [10 marks]

   b) Identify the data requirements for the system using a suitable table to present them. [8 marks]

   c) Create an interface design for the system. [4 marks]

   d) Use a dry run to test the logic of your solution for a client who wishes to hire a 20 seater bus from 3 p.m. to 10 p.m. to travel 150 miles. [4 marks]

   e) Implement the solution using a programming language of your choice. [20 marks]

2 Describe the main elements of computational thinking and how they can be used in the creation of a solution. [6 marks]

3 Evaluate the bubble sort algorithm and the insertion sort algorithm in terms of efficiency of sorting. [4 marks]

4 Describe two methods of searching through data for a target value. Comment on the efficiency of each. [6 marks]

Chapter 24 Programming constructs

What this chapter covers

▶ Features of programming languages

▶ Program control structures

▶ One-dimensional arrays

▶ Programming sort and search algorithms

▶ String manipulation

▶ Building reusable code

▶ Basic file handling

> This chapter can be reviewed in conjunction with Chapter 29 Building and testing a solution (Unit 5), which provides additional examples of building and testing.

Features of programming languages

Programs make use of a combination of features available in a programming language. Some of these key features are defined below.

Term	Definition	Example
Variable	A variable is a named location in computer memory used to hold data when a program is running. The value of a variable can change whilst the program is running. When declaring a variable it must be given a name and a data type.	Declare a variable called *number* to hold an integer value. C#: int number Python: number=0 NB Variables do not need to be declared explicitly in Python in order to reserve memory space. The memory space is reserved as soon as the variable is assigned a value.
Constant	A constant is a named location in computer memory used to hold data when a program is running. The value of the constant remains the same whilst the program is running. When declaring a constant it must be given a name and a data type.	Declare a constant to hold a decimal value. C#: Const float rateOfPay =11.55 Python: there is no constant keyword.
Boolean operator	An operator which allows conditions to be combined and then evaluated. The outcome is a Boolean variable.	C#: the AND operator is denoted by &&. The or operator is denoted by ||. Python: AND OR
Arithmetic operator	Enables arithmetic operations to be carried out on variables. Arithmetic operators include +, -, *(multiply), /.	b*c
Input statement	A statement used to capture data which is to be used in the program.	C#: Student Name = Console. Readline(); Python: Student Name = Input ("Enter your name")

Term	Definition	Example
Output statement	A statement used to output data and information from the program.	C#: Console.Write Python: print
Assignment statement	A statement which assigns a value to a variable, constant or other data structure. The value on the right-hand side of an assignment statement can contain a calculation.	a=b*c assigns the value of b*c to the variable named a.

Examples of each of these features can be seen in the code samples within this chapter.

Program control structures

Sequence

Sequence denotes the order in which instructions are carried out by the computer. The simplest programs run from beginning to end and each statement is carried out one after the other in sequence.

The following simple programs take as input a number representing the radius of a circle and output the circumference and area of the circle.

C#	Output

```
sequence.Program                                    Main(string[] args)
 9  {
10      class Program
11      {
12          static void Main(string[] args)
13          {
14              //using double precision floating point numbers
15              double radius, area, circumference;
16
17              //declare a constant pi.
18              const double pi =3.14;
19
20              //prompt the use for input
21              Console.Write("Enter the radius of the circle in cms: ");
22              //read the value for the radius from the screen and
23              //convert it to a value of type double for use in the calculations
24              radius=Convert.ToDouble(Console.ReadLine());
25
26
27              //perform the calculations
28              area = 2 * pi * radius;
29              circumference = pi * radius * radius;
30
31              //output the results
32              //note that {0:F2} is a formatting placeholder used to out the value to 2 decimal places
33              Console.WriteLine ("Given a radius of : {0:F2}", radius, "cms");
34              Console.WriteLine ("The circumference is: {0:F2} " , circumference);
35              Console.WriteLine("The area is: {0:F2}", area);
36
37              //this statement keeps the console window open until the user presses a key
38              //it prevents the output from disappearing.
39              Console.ReadKey();
40
41          }
42      }
43  }
44
```

```
Enter the radius of the circle in cms: 5
Given a radius of : 5.00
The circumference is: 78.50
The area is: 31.40
```

Python	

```python
# a simple program to calculate the area and circumference of
# a circle given the radius

pi=3.14

radius = float(input ("Enter the radius of the circle in cms: "))

circumference = 2 * pi* radius

area=pi * radius * radius
print ("Given a radius of " , "{:6.2f}".format(radius) , "cms")
print ("The circumference is: " ,"{:6.2f}".format(circumference), "cms")
print ("The area is: ", "{:6.2f}".format(area), "cms")
```

```
Enter the radius of the circle in cms: 5
Given a radius of     5.00 cms
The circumference is:    31.40 cms
The area is:    78.50 cms
>>>
```

Tasks 🖉

1 Identify these in the samples of code above:
   a) variable
   b) constants
   c) Boolean operators
   d) arithmetic operators
   e) assignment statements
   f) input statements
   g) output statements

2 Examine the Python program above. Using the comments in the C# version of the code, explain each of the statements in the Python version.

3 Most programming languages have mathematical functions and constants available for programmers to use.
   a) Implement the program in a programming language of your choice.
   b) Research how the mathematical functions provided by your chosen programming language could be used to improve the code.
   c) Change your code to include the mathematical functions you have found in b).

Selection

The sequence of instructions within a program can be changed based on the value of variables within that program. This means that certain statements are selected based on a value. This is achieved through the use of IF-statements and Boolean operators.

IF-statement

When a condition in an IF-statement evaluates to true, the statements following IF are executed. Otherwise, the statements following Else are executed. IF-statements can be nested and conditions can be combined using Boolean operators to form complex selection statements.

Consider a simple program to find the largest of three numbers. The IF-statement is required to select the appropriate assignment statement.

C#	Output

```csharp
0 references
class Program
{
    0 references
    static void Main(string[] args)
    {
        int a, b, c;
        int largest;

        Console.Write("\n\n\n\n Enter the first number and press return : ");
        a = Int32.Parse(Console.ReadLine());
        Console.Write("Enter the second number and press return : ");
        b = Int32.Parse(Console.ReadLine());
        Console.Write("Enter the third number and press return : ");
        c = Int32.Parse(Console.ReadLine());

        if (a > b && a > c)
        {
            largest = a;
        }
        else if (b > a && b > c)
        {
            largest = b;
        }
        else
        {
            largest = c;
        }

        Console.WriteLine("\n\n The largest is {0}", largest);
        //{0} is a place holder in the output string for the value of largest
        Console.ReadKey();
    }
}
```

Output:
```
Enter the first number and press return : 7
Enter the second number and press return : 9
Enter the third number and press return : 5

 The largest is 9
```

Python	

```python
a = int(input("Enter the first number and press return: "))
b = int(input("Enter the second number and press return: "))
c = int(input("Enter the third number and press return:"))

if (a > b) and (a > c):
    largest = a
elif (b > a) and (b > c):
    largest = b
else:
    largest = c

print("The largest number is ",largest)
```

Output:
```
>>>
Enter the first number and press return: 7
Enter the second number and press return: 9
Enter the third number and press return:5
The largest number is  9
>>>
```

Iteration

Iteration is another word for repetition. Repetition is used when a section of code is to be carried out more than once. Programming languages facilitate repetition through loops. Repetition comes in two forms: **unconditional** and **conditional repetition**.

Unconditional or bounded repetition

This loop is used when we know in advance how many times the loop is to be carried out. There is a start value and a stop value for the loop. For example, write a program to output all the multiples of three between 3 and 99. This is unconditional repetition as the loop will repeat 97 times. Most programming languages use a FOR loop for this purpose. The basic structure of a FOR loop is as follows:

```
FOR loopcontrolvariable = startvalue TO stopvalue
    section of code to be repeated
END For
```

The loopcontrolvariable will be incremented by 1 each time the loop is executed. An increment of 1 is the default. It is possible to change the increment value within the FOR loop by adding additional code to the FOR statement.

C#	Output

```csharp
 1  using System;
 2  using System.Collections.Generic;
 3  using System.Linq;
 4  using System.Text;
 5  using System.Threading.Tasks;
 6
 7  namespace ConsoleApplication1
 8  {
 9      class Program
10      {
11          static void Main(string[] args)
12          {
13              for (int i = 3; i <= 99; i++)
14              {
15                  if (i % 3 == 0)
16                      Console.WriteLine(i + " is a multiple of 3");
17              }
18              Console.ReadKey();
19          }
20
21      }
22  }
```

```
3 is a multiple of 3
6 is a multiple of 3
9 is a multiple of 3
12 is a multiple of 3
15 is a multiple of 3
18 is a multiple of 3
21 is a multiple of 3
24 is a multiple of 3
27 is a multiple of 3
30 is a multiple of 3
33 is a multiple of 3
36 is a multiple of 3
```

In C# the FOR loop is structured: for(initialise;condition;increment)
Initialise: the loop control variable is initialised to the starting value once during the execution of the loop.
Condition: the condition is evaluated during each execution of the loop.
Increment: this part of the statement is used to update or change the loop control variable.

Python	

```python
for number in range(3,99):   #to iterate between 3 to 99
# use the modulus function which returns the remainder after division
    if number%3 == 0:
        print (str(number) + " is a multiple of 3")
```

```
3 is a multiple of 3
6 is a multiple of 3
9 is a multiple of 3
12 is a multiple of 3
15 is a multiple of 3
18 is a multiple of 3
21 is a multiple of 3
24 is a multiple of 3
27 is a multiple of 3
30 is a multiple of 3
33 is a multiple of 3
36 is a multiple of 3
```

Conditional or unbounded repetition

This is when the loop will run until a particular condition is true or false.

Consider writing a program which allows a user to enter an integer value between 1 and 50. The user is prompted to enter the value until a value in the correct range is entered.

How many times will the user have to enter a value? Until they get the value correct! We cannot determine in advance how many times the loop will run. In this case we must evaluate a condition in order to determine whether or not the code inside the loop should be executed another time. This is conditional repetition.

So for the example outlined above, the algorithm may be as follows:

```
OUTPUT Enter an integer value in the range 1 to 50
INPUT number
```

We need to repeat these two lines until the value entered is in the correct range. That is, while the value is less than 1 or greater than 50.

Formulate a condition for this: number<1 or number>50.

Enclose the lines within a loop which contains this condition:

```
while(number < 1 or number > 50)
    OUTPUT Enter an integer value in the range 1 to 50
    INPUT number
End While
```

If this section of code is to be used for validation purposes, then it can be constructed as a range check. A Boolean variable can be used to control the loop. Using a Boolean variable called 'valid', the algorithm could be:

```
number=0
valid=False
While (valid=False)
    OUTPUT "Enter a number in the range 1-50"
    If (number >=1 AND number <=50)
        valid=True
    Else
        OUTPUT Error Message
    END-IF
END WHILE
```

C#	Output
``,WhileValid.Program   ▾ ◎ₐ Main(string[] args)
1 ⊟using System;
2   using System.Collections.Generic;
3   using System.Linq;
4   using System.Text;
5   using System.Threading.Tasks;
6
7 ⊟namespace WhileValid
8   {
9 ⊟   class Program
10   {
11 ⊟   static void Main(string[] args)
12   {
13   //declare an integer variable called number
14   int number=0;
15   //declare a boolean variable called valid
16   Boolean valid=false;
17
18   //repeat the loop while valid is false
19   while (valid == false)
20   {
21   //output a prompt to the user to enter the number
22   Console.Write("Enter a number in the range 1 - 50 ");
23   //read the number from the screen and convert it to an integer
24   number= Convert.ToInt32(Console.ReadLine());
25
26   //use a range chaeck on the number entered
27   if ((number >= 1) && (number <= 50))
28   valid = true; //set valid to true if the number is within the correct range
29   else
30   //if the number is not in the correct range then output an error message
31   Console.WriteLine("Error - number entered out of range");
32
33   }
34   Console.ReadKey();
35   }
36   }
``` | ```
Enter a number in the range 1 - 50 88
Error - number entered out of range
Enter a number in the range 1 - 50 9
``` |

Loop using Boolean variable

Python	
| ```
number=0
while (number < 1) or (number > 50):
    number=int(input("Enter a number in the range 1-50"))
```<br><br>Simple loop structure | ```
Enter a number in the range 1-5067
Enter a number in the range 1-5099
Enter a number in the range 1-506
```<br>. |
| ```
number=0;
valid=False;
while (valid==False):
    number=int(input("Enter a number in the range 1-50 "))
    if (number >=1) and (number<=50):
        valid=True
    else:
        print("Error - number entered out of range")
```<br><br>Loop using Boolean variable | ```
Enter a number in the range 1-50 -6
Error - number entered out of range
Enter a number in the range 1-50 99
Error - number entered out of range
Enter a number in the range 1-50 12
``` |

The loop shown in the examples above tests the condition at the beginning of the loop. Most programming languages provide a loop which tests the condition at the end of the loop.

```
number=0
valid=False
do
  OUTPUT "Enter a number in the range 1-50"
  If (number >=1 AND number <=50)
    valid=True
  Else
    OUTPUT Error Message
  END-IF
While (valid is False)
```

The code within a loop with the test at the beginning may not be executed at all if the condition evaluates to false.

The code within a loop with the test at the end will be executed at least once because the condition is not tested until after the code is executed.

Tasks

Create an algorithm which represents a solution to this problem. Implement your solution in a programming language of your choice.

A student studying computer science at a college is examined by coursework and written examination. Both components of the assessment carry a maximum of 50 marks.
The following rules are used by the examiners in order to grade students.
▶ A student must score a total of 40 or more to pass.
▶ A total mark of 39 is moderated to 40.
▶ Grades are awarded on marks that fall into the following categories:

100–70	69–60	59–50	49–40	39–0
A	B+	B	C	F

Extension task

This rule for passing has been added. Modify your program to take account of the new rule.

Each component must be passed with a minimum mark of 20. If a student scores 40 or more but does not achieve the minimum mark in either component he/she is given a technical fail of 39 (this mark is not moderated to 40).

One-dimensional arrays

An array is a data structure which holds a set of data items of the same data type. The array is assigned a name, a size (representing the number of data items to be stored) and a data type by the programmer.

More information about arrays can be found in Chapter 23 Digital design principles (Unit 4).

For example, an array of integers called myNumbers has been used in the sorting algorithms in the previous chapter.

Here is a representation of the array myNumbers. The array has six integer values stored: 47, 69, 12, 34, 25, 39. An individual data item or element is accessed by referring to the array name and the index of the element.

Element	myNumbers[0]	myNumbers[1]	myNumbers[2]	myNumbers[3]	myNumbers[4]	myNumbers[5]
Position in array [index]	0	1	2	3	4	5
Value	47	69	12	34	25	39

When an array is used in a program, the computer reserves a set of memory locations, one for each element in the array. The memory locations are next to each other or **contiguous**.

In many programming languages, arrays are zero-indexed. That means that the index of the first element in the array is 0. So, myNumbers[0] holds a value of 47.

Elements can be assigned values, for example myNumbers[2]=99.

An array is described using a declaration statement. For example, declare an array called myNumbers which will hold six integers: C# int[ ] myNumbers = new int[6].

Python does not support arrays in the way other languages do. Data structures called **lists and tuples** are used. The difference is that arrays can only hold data items of the same data type. Lists and tuples can hold mixed data types. For example, declare a list called myNumbers and populate the list with six integer values: myNumbers = [47, 69, 12, 34, 25].

To access every element in the array, a loop can be used. Most commonly a FOR loop is used to go through the entire array, one element at a time. Examples of this are shown in the bubble and insertion sort examples on page 208.

Tasks ✏️

1 Write a program which makes use of an array structure. The array should hold 20 integers, representing the marks of 20 students in an exam. The program should allow the user to input the 20 values and store them in the array. It should then calculate and output the average.

2 Write a program that accepts a set of digits (0 to 9) as input and prints a horizontal histogram representing the number of occurrences of each digit. Test your program with this set of digits: 1, 7, 2, 9, 6, 7, 1, 3, 7, 5, 7, 9, 0.

Programming sort algorithms

Sort algorithms make extensive use of arrays to store data while it is being sorted. In this section we will examine the algorithms outlined in the previous chapter.

Programming the bubble sort

The bubble sort is a simple sort which compares adjacent elements. Below is one implementation of the bubble sort.

C#	Output
ConsoleApplication1.Program	After pass 1

```csharp
1  using System;
2  using System.Collections.Generic;
3  using System.Linq;
4  using System.Text;
5  using System.Threading.Tasks;
6
7  namespace ConsoleApplication1
8  {
9      class Program
10     {
11         static void Main(string[] args)
12         {
13             int[]  mynumbers = {47, 69, 12, 34, 25, 39};
14             int temp;
15             for (int i=0;i<mynumbers.Length-1;i++)
16             {
17                 for (int j=0;j<mynumbers.Length-1-i;j++)
18                     if (mynumbers[j] > mynumbers[j + 1])
19                     {
20                         temp = mynumbers[j];
21                         mynumbers[j] = mynumbers[j + 1];
22                         mynumbers[j + 1] = temp;
23                     }
24                 Console.WriteLine("After pass {0}", i + 1);
25                 for (int k = 0; k < mynumbers.Length; k++)
26                     Console.Write(mynumbers[k] +" ");
27                 Console.WriteLine();
28
29             }
30             Console.WriteLine("Sorted List");
31             for (int i = 0; i < mynumbers.Length; i++)
32                 Console.Write(mynumbers[i]+ " ");
33             Console.WriteLine();
34             Console.ReadKey();
35
36         }
37     }
38  }
```

Output:
```
After pass 1
47 12 34 25 39 69
After pass 2
12 34 25 39 47 69
After pass 3
12 25 34 39 47 69
After pass 4
12 25 34 39 47 69
After pass 5
12 25 34 39 47 69
Sorted List
12 25 34 39 47 69
```

➡️

Python

```
# Programming the Bubble Sort
mynumbers = [47, 69, 12, 34, 25, 39]
for i in range(0,len(mynumbers)-1):
    for j in range(0, len(mynumbers) - i - 1):
        if mynumbers[j] > mynumbers[j + 1]:
            temp = mynumbers[j]
            mynumbers[j] = mynumbers[j + 1]
            mynumbers[j + 1] = temp
    # Print mynumbers array after every pass
    print ("After pass " + str(i+1) +":")
    print(mynumbers)

print ("The sorted list : ")
print(mynumbers)
```

```
After pass 1:
[47, 12, 34, 25, 39, 69]
After pass 2:
[12, 34, 25, 39, 47, 69]
After pass 3:
[12, 25, 34, 39, 47, 69]
After pass 4:
[12, 25, 34, 39, 47, 69]
After pass 5:
[12, 25, 34, 39, 47, 69]
The sorted list :
[12, 25, 34, 39, 47, 69]
>>>
```

Programming the insertion sort

The algorithm for the insertion sort has been discussed in the previous chapter. Below is one implementation of this sort.

C#

```
 9   class Program
10   {
11       static void Main(string[] args)
12       {
13
14           //declare an array which will hold a set of integer values
15           int[] mynumbers = {47, 69, 12, 34, 25, 39};
16           //declare the variables to be used in the sorting code
17           int currentvalue, position, index;
18
19           //for loop to go from first number to last number
20           for (index=0;index<mynumbers.Length; index++)
21           {
22               currentvalue = mynumbers[index];
23               position = index;
24               //while loop to find where to insert the value in the sublist
25               while ((position>0) && (mynumbers[position-1]>currentvalue))
26               {
27               mynumbers[position]=mynumbers[position-1];
28               position = position-1;
29               }
30
31               mynumbers[position]=currentvalue;
32               Console.WriteLine ("After pass {0} ", index+1);
33               for (int i=0;i<mynumbers.Length;i++)
34                   Console.Write(mynumbers[i] + " ");
35               Console.WriteLine();
36           }
37
38           Console.WriteLine("The sorted list is: ");
39           //note that the code below is repeated from above
40           //this is not good coding practice.  In this case the code should be
41           //written as a function and called when required.  This will be addressed
42           // later in the chapter.
43           for (int i=0;i<mynumbers.Length;i++)
44               Console.Write(mynumbers[i] + " ");
45           Console.WriteLine();
46           Console.ReadKey();
47
48       }
```

Output

```
After pass 1
47 69 12 34 25 39
After pass 2
47 69 12 34 25 39
After pass 3
12 47 69 34 25 39
After pass 4
12 34 47 69 25 39
After pass 5
12 25 34 47 69 39
After pass 6
12 25 34 39 47 69
The sorted list is:
12 25 34 39 47 69
```

Python

```python
mynumbers = [47, 69, 12, 34, 25, 39]
for index in range(1,len(mynumbers)):

    currentvalue = mynumbers[index]
    position = index

    while position>0 and mynumbers[position-1]>currentvalue:
        mynumbers[position]=mynumbers[position-1]
        position = position-1

    mynumbers[position]=currentvalue
    print ("After pass " + str(index)+ " "),
    print(mynumbers)

print("The sorted list is : "),
print(mynumbers)
```

```
After pass 1
[47, 69, 12, 34, 25, 39]
After pass 2
[12, 47, 69, 34, 25, 39]
After pass 3
[12, 34, 47, 69, 25, 39]
After pass 4
[12, 25, 34, 47, 69, 39]
After pass 5
[12, 25, 34, 39, 47, 69]
The sorted list is :
[12, 25, 34, 39, 47, 69]
>>>
```

Programming the linear search

A linear search is not efficient as it compares all elements in the array during a search. Below is the code for the algorithms discussed in the previous chapter.

C#

```csharp
ConsoleApplication1.Program                                    Main(string[] args)
 1  using System;
 2  using System.Collections.Generic;
 3  using System.Linq;
 4  using System.Text;
 5  using System.Threading.Tasks;
 6
 7  namespace ConsoleApplication1
 8  {
 9      class Program
10      {
11          static void Main(string[] args)
12          {
13              int[] mynumbers = new int[20];
14              Boolean found = false;
15
16              Console.WriteLine("Enter the twenty numbers to be stored in the array");
17              for (int i = 0; i < 20; i++)
18              {
19                  mynumbers[i] = Convert.ToInt32(Console.ReadLine());
20              }
21
22              Console.WriteLine("Enter a number that you wish to search for\n");
23              int searchNumber = Convert.ToInt32(Console.ReadLine());
24              for (int i = 0; i<20; i++)
25              {
26                  if (mynumbers[i] == searchNumber)
27                  {
28                      Console.Write("Number {0} found ", searchNumber );
29                      Console.WriteLine("at location {0}\n",i + 1);
30                      found = true;
31                  }
32              }
33
34              if (found==false)
35                  Console.WriteLine("Number not found");
36              Console.ReadKey();
37
38          }
39      }
40  }
```

Output

```
Enter the twenty numbers to be stored in the array
1
2
3
4
5
6
7
8
9
10
11
12
13
14
15
16
17
17
18
19
20
21
Enter a number that you wish to search for

6
Number not found
```

Python	

``python
mynumbers=[47,69,12,34,25,39]
foundmatch=False
searchnum=int(input("Enter number to search for "))
for i in range(1,len(mynumbers)):
    if (mynumbers[i]==searchnum):
            foundmatch=True
            print("Number found at position ", i)
if(foundmatch==False):
    print ("number not found")
``
	``
	Enter number to search for 6
	6
	number not found
	>>> |
	``

Programming the binary search

The algorithm for the binary search has been discussed in the previous chapter. Below is an implementation of the binary search using a sorted one-dimensional array of integers.

C#	Output

``csharp
10   {
11   static void Main(string[] args)
12   {
13
14   int[] mynumbers = { 6, 5, 4, 3, 2, 1 };
15   Boolean found = false;
16   int mid=0, first = 0, last = mynumbers.Length - 1;
17   Console.WriteLine("What number are you looking for");
18   string item = Console.ReadLine();
19   int target = Convert.ToInt16(item);
20
21   //for a sorted array with descending values
22   while((first <= last) && (found==false))
23   {
24   mid = first + (last-first) / 2;
25   if (mynumbers[mid]==target)
26   found=true;
27   else
28   if (target < mynumbers[mid])
29   first = mid + 1;
30   else
31   if (target > mynumbers[mid])
32   last = mid - 1;
33   }
34
35   if (found == true)
36   Console.WriteLine("Value found at position " + mid);
37   else
38   Console.WriteLine("Value not found");
39   Console.ReadKey();
40   }
41   }
42 }
``
	``
	What number are you looking for
	6
	Value found at position 0
	``

Python	
| ```
mynumbers = ( 6, 5, 4, 3, 2, 1 )
found = False
mid=0
first = 0
last = len(mynumbers) - 1
target=int (input("What number are you looking for"))
#for a sorted array with descending values
while(first <= last) and (found==False):
            mid = int(first + (last-first) / 2);
            if ( mynumbers[mid]==target) :
                found=True
            elif (target < mynumbers[mid]):
                first = mid + 1
            elif (target > mynumbers[mid]):
                last = mid - 1
if (found == True):
    print("Value found at position ", mid)
else:
    print("Value not found")
``` | ```
What number are you looking for 2
Value found at position  4
>>> |
``` |

String manipulation

Data containing text, letters or a mixture of letters and numbers are known as strings. Strings can be processed and manipulated using string functions. Most programming languages make use of string data and provide in-built functions so that the user can manipulate them. Examples of these functions are listed in the table below.

String data is **immutable**. This means that a string cannot be changed once it is created, instead a new string must be created to reflect a change.

Consider two strings:

string1="WELL DONE"

string2="award-winning performance"

Strings can be considered as an array of characters. Each character in the string has a position and a value. Strings are zero-indexed.

Position	0	1	2	3	4	5	6	7	8
	string1[0]	string1[1]	string1[2]	string1[3]	string1[4]	string1[5]	string1[6]	string1[7]	string1[8]
Value	W	E	L	L		D	O	N	E

There are many string handling functions available. Some of the more common functions are listed below.

String handling function	C#	Python
Splitting a string	string1.split(" ") Split string one at the first space. Result : "WELL"	String1.split(' ') Split string one at the first space Result : ['WELL', 'DONE']
Concatenating string: appending strings together using the relevant function or symbol.	string1 + " " + string2 Concatenate string1, a space and string2. Result: "WELL DONE award-winning performance"	string1 + " " + string2 Concatenate string1, a space and string 2. Result: "WELL DONE award-winning performance"

String handling function	C#	Python
Character and substring searching in a string for the occurrence of a character or substring. This search returns an integer representing the starting position of the substring or position of the character in the string being searched.	string1.IndexOf("D") Find the position of the first letter "D" in string1. Result: 5	string1.index('D') Find the position of the first letter "D" in string1. Result: 5
Substring searching: using a start position and a length, return a substring.	string2.Substring(6, 7) start at position 6 in string2 and return the next 7 characters result: "winning"	string2[6:13] Start at position 6 in string2 and return the next 7 characters. result: "winning"
Lower case: change all the characters in a string to lower case.	string1.ToLower(); Change all letters in string1 to lower case. Result: "well done"	string1.lower() change all letters in string1 to lower case Result: "well done"
Upper case: change all the characters in a string to upper case.	string2.ToUpper(); Change all letters in string2 to upper case. Result: "AWARD-WINNING PERFORMANCE"	string2.upper() Change all letters in string2 to upper case. Result: "AWARD-WINNING PERFORMANCE"
Length: return an integer value representing the length of a string.	string2.Length(); Return the length of string2. Result: 25	len(string2) Return the length of string2. Result: 25

C#

```
12      {
13          string string1 = "WELL DONE";
14          string string2 = "award winning performance";
15
16          //finding the length of a string
17          Console.WriteLine("String 1 has {0} characters\n", string1.Length);
18          Console.WriteLine("String 2 has {0} characters\n", string2.Length);
19
20
21          //split a string up into smaller strings
22          //this statement splits string1 each time a space is found and puts the resulting
23          //string into an array of type string
24          string[] thewords = string1.Split(' ');
25
26          Console.WriteLine("Splitting string 1 into words gives:");
27
28          foreach (string s in thewords) //using the foreach loop to print the contents of thewords
29              Console.WriteLine(s);
30
31          //concatenating two strings places the strings together as one string
32          string fullstring = string1 + " " + string2;
33
34          //search for the occurence of a word or character
35          int wordposition = fullstring.IndexOf("winning");
36          Console.WriteLine("The word winning has been found at position {0} in this string", wordposition);
37
38          //copy string1 to a new string called copystring1
39          string copystring1 = string.Copy(string1);
40          Console.WriteLine("copystring1= "+ copystring1);
41
42          //replace the word "done" in string 1 with "completed"
43          string newstring1 = copystring1.Replace("DONE", "completed");
44          Console.WriteLine("newstring1= " + newstring1);
45
46          //copy 7 letters from string2 starting at position 6 in the string and place them into mysubstring
47          string mysubstring = string2.Substring(6, 7);
48          Console.WriteLine("mysubstring = "+ mysubstring);
49
50          string1 = string1.ToLower();
51          Console.WriteLine("Lower case string1= "+ string1);
52          string2 = string2.ToUpper();
53          Console.WriteLine("Upper case string2= " + string2);
54          Console.ReadKey();
55      }
56  }
```

Output

```
String 1 has 9 characters

String 2 has 25 characters

Splitting string 1 into words gives:
WELL
DONE
The word winning has been found at position 16 in this string
copystring1= WELL DONE
newstring1= WELL completed
mysubstring = winning
Lower case string1= well done
Upper case string2= AWARD WINNING PERFORMANCE
```

Python

```
string1 = 'WELL DONE'
string2 = 'award winning performance'

#finding the length of a string
print("String 1 has ", len(string1), "characters")
print("String 2 has ", len(string2), "characters")


#split a string up into smaller strings
#this statement splits string1 each time a space is found and puts the resulting
#string into an array of type string
thewords = string1.split(' ')

print("Splitting string 1 into words gives:");
print (thewords)

#concatenating two strings places the strings together as one string
fullstring = string1+" "+ string2
#search for the occurence of a word or character
wordposition = fullstring.index("winning")
print("The word winning has been found at position ", wordposition, " in this string")

#copy string1 to a new string called copystring1
copystring1 = string1
print("copystring1= "+ copystring1)

#replace the word "done" in string 1 with "completed"
newstring1 = copystring1.replace("DONE", "completed");
print("newstring1= " + newstring1);

#copy 7 letters from string2 starting at position 6 in the string and place them into mysubstring
#string mysubstring = string2.Substring(6, 7);
#Console.WriteLine("mysubstring = "+ mysubstring);

string1 = string1.lower()
string2 = string2.upper()
print ("Lower case string1 = ", string1)
print ("Upper case string2 = ", string2)
```

```
String 1 has  9 characters
String 2 has  25 characters
Splitting string 1 into words gives:
['WELL', 'DONE']
The word winning has been found at position  16  in this string
copystring1= WELL DONE
newstring1= WELL completed
Lower case string1 =  well done
Upper case string2 =  AWARD WINNING PERFORMANCE
>>>
```

Tasks

1 What string functions could be used to ensure the valid entry of a:
   a) blood type (which can be O+, AB+, AB-, O-, B-, B+, A+, A-)?
   b) surname?
   c) customer code made up of one letter and two numbers, for example A29?

2 A program is required which will take as input a string of characters and output the length of the string and the number of vowels in the string. Create an algorithm to solve the problem. You may use pseudo-code or a flowchart to represent the solution.

Building reusable code

When developing a solution it is important to make the code as efficient as possible. If a section of code is to be used in more than one place, a function can be written. Functions are blocks of code that can be reused within the program. They are written to perform a particular task and can be 'called' when required within the program.

Below is an example of a C# program which implements the bubble sort. The code now contains two functions, printnumbers and sortnumbers. Note that printnumbers is reused within the code.

```csharp
5  using System.Threading.Tasks;
6
7  namespace Binary_Search_Function
8  {
9      class Program
10     {
11         static void Main(string[] args)
12         {
13             int[]  mynumbers = {47, 69, 12, 34, 25, 39};
14             Console.WriteLine("Before sorting");
15             printnumbers(mynumbers);
16             sortnumbers(mynumbers);
17
18             Console.WriteLine("Sorted List");
19             printnumbers(mynumbers);
20             Console.WriteLine();
21             Console.ReadKey();
22
23         }
24
25         static void printnumbers(int[] mynumbers)
26         {
27             for (int i = 0; i < mynumbers.Length; i++)
28                 Console.Write(mynumbers[i] + " ");
29         }
30
31         static void sortnumbers(int [] mynumbers)
32         {
33         for (int i=0;i<mynumbers.Length-1;i++)
34             {
35                 int temp;
36                 for (int j=0;j<mynumbers.Length-1-i;j++)
37                     if (mynumbers[j] > mynumbers[j + 1])
38                     {
39                         temp = mynumbers[j];
40                         mynumbers[j] = mynumbers[j + 1];
41                         mynumbers[j + 1] = temp;
42                     }
43                 Console.WriteLine("After pass {0}", i + 1);
44                 for (int k = 0; k < mynumbers.Length; k++)
45                     Console.Write(mynumbers[k] +" ");
46                 Console.WriteLine();
47
48             }
49
50         }
51
52     }
```

Below is an example of a python program which implements the bubble sort. The code now contains a function called bubblesort.

```python
# Programming the Bubble Sort

# use a function called bubblesort and pass mynumbers as a parameter
def bubblesort(mynumbers):

    for i in range(0,len(mynumbers)-1):
        for j in range(0, len(mynumbers) - i - 1):
            if mynumbers[j] > mynumbers[j + 1]:
                temp = mynumbers[j]
                mynumbers[j] = mynumbers[j + 1]
                mynumbers[j + 1] = temp
        # Print mynumbers array after every pass
        print ("After pass " + str(i+1) +":")
        print (mynumbers)
mynumbers = [47, 69, 12, 34, 25, 39]
print ("Initial numbers : ")
print (mynumbers)
#call the bubblesort function
bubblesort(mynumbers)
```

Basic file handling

Files provide a means of permanently storing data. When a program uses data, it is lost after the program stops running. Files allow data to be stored permanently after the program closes. The data in the file can be used as input to the program also.

In C# a file stream is opened. A filestream is used to read from, write to, open and close files. The filestream makes use of Filemodes and FileAccess as follows:

▶ FileMode.Append: open and append to a file. If the file does not already exists this mode will cause the creation of a new file

▶ FileMode.Create: create a new file. If the file already exists it will be overwritten

▶ FileMode.CreateNew: create a new file

▶ FileMode.Open: open an existing file

▶ FileAccess.Read: data can be read from the file

▶ FileAccess.ReadWrite: data can be read from and written to the file

▶ FileAccess.Write: data can be written to the file.

```
11      class Program
12      {
13          static void ReadData()
14          {
15              FileStream myFile = new FileStream("test.txt", FileMode.Open, FileAccess.Read);
16              StreamReader myStream = new StreamReader(myFile);
17              Console.WriteLine("Program to show content of test file");
18              myStream.BaseStream.Seek(0, SeekOrigin.Begin);
19              string str = myStream.ReadLine();
20
21              while (str != null)
22              {
23                  Console.WriteLine(str);
24                  str = myStream.ReadLine();
25              }
26
27              Console.ReadKey();
28              myStream.Close();
29              myFile.Close();
30
31          }
32
33          static void WriteData()
34          {
35              //create a filestream
36              FileStream myFile = new FileStream("test.txt", FileMode.Append, FileAccess.Write);
37              StreamWriter myStream = new StreamWriter(myFile);
38              Console.WriteLine("Enter the text which you want to write to the file");
39              string str = Console.ReadLine();
40              myStream.WriteLine(str);
41              myStream.Flush();
42              myStream.Close();
43              myFile.Close();
44          }
45
46          static void Main(string[] args)
47
48          {
49              WriteData();
50              ReadData();
51          }
52
53      }
54
55  }
```

▲ Sample C# program showing simple file-handling operations

In Python, files can be opened for reading ('r') and writing ('w').

```python
#Open a text file
myFile = open("myFile.txt", "r")

#reading from a text file:
myFile = open("myFile.txt","r")
print (myFile.read())

#reading lines from the file
myFile = open("myFile.txt", "r")
print (myFile.readline())

#reading a set of lines from the file
myFile = open("myFile.txt.", "r")
print (myFile.readlines())

f = open("myFile.txt")
next = f.read(1)
while next != "":
    print(next)
    next = f.read(1)

#writing to a file
myFile = open("myFile.txt","w")
myFile.write("This is a test\n")
myFile.close()

#writing multiple lines of text to a file
myFile = open("myFile.txt", "w")
lines_of_text = ["This is the second test", "This is the third test", "This is the fourth test"]
myFile.writelines(lines_of_text)
myFile.close()

#appending data to the file
myFile = open("myFile.txt", "a")
myFile.write("A fourth test")
myFile.close


#closing a file
myFile = open("myFile.txt", "r")
print(myFile.read())
myFile.close()
```

▲ Sample Python program showing simple file-handling operations

Checkpoint

▷ Most programing languages provide for three main structures. Sequence, where instructions are carried out one after the other in sequence; selection where if-statements and conditions are used to select the statements which are to be executed; and repetition, where sections of the code are repeated based on the outcome of a condition.

▷ A one-dimensional array is a data structure which holds data of one type. The array is given a name, a size and a data type. Individual elements of the array are accessed using the array name and the index of that element in the array. Arrays are zero-indexed meaning that the index of the first element in the array is zero.

▷ Sorting can be carried out on arrays of data. There are a number of ways of implementing a sort. The bubble sort and the insertion sort are two possible methods.

▷ Searching can be done using the binary search or the linear search. The binary search is a much more efficient method of searching through data.

▷ String variables hold text. The string data type is zero-indexed meaning that each element in the string can be accessed using the string name and the index of the element. The index is numbered from 0. There are many in-built functions for manipulating strings including the length function.

▷ Program code can be improved by writing functions to do particular tasks. These functions can be reused, ensuring that code is not repeated unnecessarily. A function has a name, a list of parameters and a return type.

▷ Most programming languages facilitate file handling. This allows the permanent storage of data between runs of the program.

Practice questions

Write a program which uses a function to take as input a set of characters from a text file. The function should count the number of occurrences of vowels, consonants, numbers and other symbols. Another function should set up a suitable output screen and a third function should output the details of each of the counts together with a count of the total numbers of characters in the file.

You need to submit a:
▶ top-down algorithm representing a solution to the problem   [10 marks]
▶ print out of the completed program code   [30 marks]
▶ set of test data which will thoroughly test the program.   [10 marks]

Chapter 25 Simple error-handling techniques

What this chapter covers

▶ Data validation

▶ Detection and correction techniques

▶ Simple error-trapping techniques

Data validation

During data entry it is necessary to ensure that all data entered is valid. Data validation is the process of checking that the data entered is complete, falls within a set of boundaries specified and is sensible. Validation aims to reduce the amount of erroneous data captured by the program or system. Validation is not solely about detecting invalid data; it cannot eliminate erroneous data completely. For example, when entering a name, a misspelling is unlikely to be detected by a validation routine.

This chapter can be reviewed in conjunction with Chapter 29 Building and testing a solution (Unit 5), which provides additional examples of building and testing.

Data validation checks

Different validation checks can be used to detect errors in data when it is entered.

More information on data validation can be found in Chapter 3 Database applications (Unit 1).

Presence check

This is used to ensure that the user has not left a value or field blank. This is commonly used in forms to ensure that all fields are completed.

Range check

This is used to ensure that the data entered is in the correct range. Range checks make use of upper and lower boundaries. For example, when entering percentages, the value must be in the range 0 to 100.

Length check

This is used to ensure that the data entered does not exceed or is not shorter than a particular number of characters. This type of check is commonly used when entering a password to ensure that it contains a minimum amount of characters.

Type check

This is used to ensure that the data entered is of the correct data type. For example, numeric, string, date.

Format check

This is used to ensure that data entered is in the correct format. This means that the data must conform to a pattern. For example, a postcode must have the following pattern XX99 9XX, such as BT67 8LH.

Detection and correction techniques

Syntax errors

A syntax error is an error in the code entered into a coding editor. It may be a misspelling or the omission of a symbol. A program containing syntax errors cannot be compiled into machine code until the errors have been removed. Some programming languages like C# will provide assistance when a programmer is entering the code. Others do not alert the programmer until the program is being compiled.

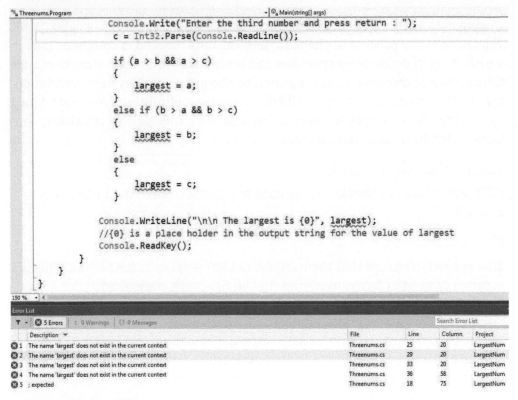

▲ A section of code showing syntax errors

Execution errors

An execution or run-time error occurs when a problem in a program causes it to crash as it is being executed. The program has no syntax errors and appears correct. Such problems include trying to append data to a file which does not exist, trying to write to an array element which is out of range, or when a calculation includes a division by zero.

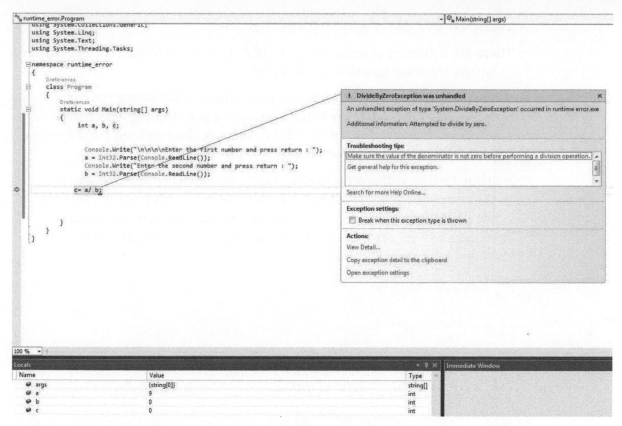

```
runtime_error.Program                                                          Main(string[] args)
    using System.Collections.Generic;
    using System.Linq;
    using System.Text;
    using System.Threading.Tasks;

  namespace runtime_error
  {
      0 references
      class Program
      {
          0 references
          static void Main(string[] args)
          {
              int a, b, c;

              Console.Write("\n\n\n\nEnter the first number and press return : ");
              a = Int32.Parse(Console.ReadLine());
              Console.Write("Enter the second number and press return : ");
              b = Int32.Parse(Console.ReadLine());

              c= a/ b;

          }
      }
  }
```

```
DivideByZeroException was unhandled                                    ✕

An unhandled exception of type 'System.DivideByZeroException' occurred in runtime error.exe

Additional information: Attempted to divide by zero.

Troubleshooting tips:
Make sure the value of the denominator is not zero before performing a division operation.
Get general help for this exception.

Search for more Help Online...

Exception settings:
  ☐ Break when this exception type is thrown

Actions:
View Detail...

Copy exception detail to the clipboard

Open exception settings
```

```
Locals                                                    ▾ ╳    Immediate Window
  Name              Value                    Type
    args            {string[0]}              string[]
    a               9                        int
    b               0                        int
    c               0                        int
```

▲ A section of code showing a run-time error

Logic errors

Logic errors occur when the application or program is being used. A logic error generally results in the output of unexpected or incorrect results. A program with logic errors will compile and run, but the output from the program may be incorrect.

```
namespace Logic_Error
{
    0 references
    class Program
    {
        0 references
        static void Main(string[] args)
        {
            int[] mynumbers = new int[] { 1, 2, 3, 4, 5, 6, 7, 8, 9, 10 };
            int total = 0;

            for (int i = 0; i < 10; i++)
            {
                total += mynumbers[1];          ⟵  Logic error
            }
            Console.WriteLine("Result is " + total);
            Console.ReadKey();

        }
```

▲ A section of code showing a logic error

> **Tasks** ✎
>
> Look at each of the screenshots above and describe what the errors are in each case.

Simple error-trapping techniques

There are a number of techniques available to help detect and correct errors to ensure software functions as expected.

When errors occur in a program, the programmer must debug the code. This may mean going through each line of code and determining where the error has occurred, or creating a trace table to see how the expected output varies from the actual output at each line.

A debug facility (debugger) identifies errors and allows the programmer to step through each line of the program code and to inspect the values of variables. The programmer can set breakpoints in the code. The program execution will stop at these breakpoints and the programmer will be able to view and edit variable values.

```
namespace Logic_Error
{
    0 references
    class Program
    {
        0 references
        static void Main(string[] args)
        {
            int[] mynumbers = new int[] { 1, 2, 3, 4, 5, 6, 7, 8, 9, 10 };
            int total = 0;

            for (int i = 0; i < 10; i++)
            {
                total += mynumbers[1];
            }
            Console.WriteLine("Result is " + total);
            Console.ReadKey();

        }
    }
}
```

150 %

Locals		
Name	Value	Type
args	{string[0]}	string[]
i	0	int
▷ mynumbers	{int[10]}	int[]
total	2	int

Autos Locals Watch 1

▲ A section of code showing a breakpoint and the Locals window which allows the programmer to inspect the values of each variable

Exceptions

Error handling can be included within a program. This means that the program will attempt to deal with an error generated at run time so that the program does not crash. When the error occurs, an exception is raised which 'calls' code to handle the error. An unhandled exception will still cause the program to crash. Programmers can make use of in-built exception-handling features and write customised code to handle specific errors.

```
0 references
class Program
{
    0 references
    static void Main(string[] args)
    {
        int a, b, c;

        Console.Write("\n\n\n\nEnter the first number and press return : ");
        a = Int32.Parse(Console.ReadLine());
        Console.Write("Enter the second number and press return : ");
        b = Int32.Parse(Console.ReadLine());
        try
        {
            c = a / b;
        }
        catch (Exception e)
        {
            Console.WriteLine("Cannot divide by zero");
        }

        Console.ReadKey();
    }
}
```

```
Enter the first number and press return : 9
Enter the second number and press return : 0
Cannot divide by zero
```

▲ A section of code showing the use of exception handling in a C# program

In the section of code above, the try catch statement is used to 'handle' the exception, which outputs a message to the user and prevents the program from crashing.

Tasks

Investigate the debug feature of a programming language of your choice. Set breakpoints and examine the value of variables. Produce a presentation containing screenshots of your activities and provide a brief explanation below each screenshot.

Checkpoint ✓

▷ Data validation is necessary to ensure that data entered is complete, falls within a set of boundaries specified and is sensible.

▷ Data validation can be performed using presence, range, type, length and format checks.

▷ Syntax errors occur when the program is being entered into the editor and are detected when the program is being compiled. A program with syntax errors will not compile.

▷ Execution errors or run-time errors occur during program execution and will cause the program to crash. Division by zero will cause a run-time error.

▷ Logic errors arise in programs that compile and run without error. However, the actual output produced by the program does not match the expected output.

▷ Debugging is the process of removing errors from the code. It may involve using the debug feature of the programming language, creating breakpoints and stepping through code one line at a time.

Practice questions ?

1 Describe the main types of data validation and suggest suitable validation checks for these fields.

a) Customer number which must lie between 1 and 100. [3 marks]

b) A surname which must be entered onto a form. [3 marks]

c) A date of birth which must indicate that the individual is over 18 years of age. [4 marks]

d) A national insurance number which must be in the form XX 99 99 99 X (where X is a letter in the range 'A' to 'Z'). [6 marks]

2 Complete this table about errors. [9 marks]

Error type	Explanation	Example
Syntax		
Execution		
Logic		

a) What is error handling and how does it improve the quality of the code written? [4 marks]

b) Research how error handling and exceptions are used in any programming language. [4 marks]

Chapter 26 Developing test plans and testing a solution

What this chapter covers

▶ White box testing

▶ Black box testing

▶ Unit, integration and system testing

▶ Creating and using a test plan

▶ Devising and using valid, invalid and extreme test data

This chapter can be reviewed in conjunction with Chapter 29 Building and testing a solution (Unit 5), which provides additional examples of testing.

The overall aim of testing is to improve the quality of the software by ensuring that it is bug-free, meets the user requirements and operates efficiently. This is done by executing the code and entering test data. The outcome of the testing is observed and potential gaps, errors or bugs are identified and subsequently fixed.

Testing is not a single activity but is carried out throughout the development of a software system. Testing needs to be planned, designed, executed and recorded.

It is impossible to test every scenario, so developers build a number of **test cases** which represent a wide variety of possible inputs to the program. Modern software development encourages an early start to testing. The earlier errors are discovered, the less it will cost to fix the problems.

There are a number of testing techniques which can be used.

White box testing

White box testing involves detailed testing of the internal logic of a section of code. It is used to identify errors in syntax, logic and data flow within the code. The tester needs to know how the code works and the internal structure of the code. Therefore, it is generally a programmer who will complete this testing. White box tests are carried out on units of code. Every possible pathway through the code is tested. Test cases should be built so that every statement is executed at least once. For example, all branches of an IF-statement should be completed, loops should be executed zero, one and more than one time.

```
if (a > b && a > c)
{
  largest = a;
}
else if (b > a && b > c)
{
  largest = b;
}
else
{
  largest = c;
}
```

▲ IF-statement with three branches

The IF-statement above has three branches. All branches of the code should be tested. The test case for this example should include data where:

▶ a is the largest
▶ b is the largest
▶ c is the largest
▶ a = b = c.

Advantages of white box testing

▶ This type of testing is thorough because it allows each line of code to be tested.
▶ Hidden errors are identified and the code is modified and optimised.
▶ Programmers who know the code can easily identify suitable test data.

Disadvantages of white box testing

▶ Experienced programmers are required to undertake the testing.
▶ Large scale applications require complex test cases, which is time-consuming.
▶ Some conditions may not be tested as it is not possible to test every possibility.

Black box testing

Black box testing focuses on inputs and outputs. It is used to identify errors in data structures, problems with user interfaces, errors in reports, missing functionality and behaviour errors. The tester has no knowledge of the internal code and interacts with the system's user interface. The unit, sub-system or system being tested is viewed as a black box (the tester cannot see inside the box). A variety of users will carry out this type of testing.

Advantages of black box testing

▶ This type of testing can help identify where the user requirements are not being met.

▶ Testers do not need to know about the code and so the tester can be independent of the developer.

▶ Test cases can be designed as soon as the specification for the unit is completed.

Disadvantages of black box testing

▶ Not all program pathways will be tested as only a small number of input cases will be used.

▶ The reason for a test failure cannot always be determined.

▶ Repetition of tests already carried out by the programmer may occur.

Unit, integration and system testing

Unit testing

In **unit testing**, one module of code in the program is tested to ensure that it works as expected. The unit test will have no relationship to code outside of the unit being tested. Unit testing starts with the module specification and includes detailed testing of the code. Therefore, it is a form of white box testing with a narrow scope limited to one unit.

Integration testing

Integration testing occurs after unit testing. A number of tested units are combined together to form a sub-system. Integration testing is then used to ensure that the units are working together as expected, for example there will be a focus on the data passed between units. Integration tests therefore identify problems with interfaces or with the interactions between units. This testing focuses on the input, output and code associated with the units in the sub-system.

System testing

System testing is carried out after integration testing. All sub-systems are brought together to form a complete software system. The system is tested as a whole to ensure that it meets the user requirements. The system is treated like a black box and the internal code is not tested. This testing can help identify missing functionality or issues related to performance. The tests should be carried out in a real-life setting with real volumes of data.

Creating and using a test plan

A test plan is a document which describes in detail the activities to be undertaken when testing is carried out. It identifies the features to be tested, provides a description or reason for each test, and specifies the data to be

Tasks

In groups, consider the butcher's problem outlined in the previous chapter.

1 Create a black box test plan for the system and state how you would check to ensure that all functions are present within the program.

2 Create a white box test plan to test the logic of the function which will calculate Percentage Weight of each category.

Waterfall and iterative methods of software development are discussed in Chapter 16 Significance of testing and developing of appropriate test plans (Unit 2).

Test plans are discussed in more detail in Chapter 16 Significance of testing and developing of appropriate test plans (Unit 2).

entered and the expected output following data entry. It is a record of the test planning process.

Testing can be carried out at any stage in the software development process. However, it must be well planned, designed, executed and recorded. The manner in which this is done will be determined by the approach taken, the waterfall method or an iterative approach.

The list below details the expected contents of a test plan.

Introduction: a summary of the application or particular area of the application to be tested.

Features to be tested/not tested: any area not being tested should be identified with an explanation as to why it is not being tested, for example an existing application unaffected by new developments may not need to be tested at this point.

Testing approach (white box, black box. integration, system, unit).

Test environment (the hardware and software platform being used to support testing).

Staff involvement (details of any staff involved in the testing process).

Test schedule (details of any key dates in the testing schedule, for example a timeline detailing start and completion dates for different types of tests to be carried out).

Test strategy: this should include:

▶ a number for each individual test so that each test can be identified separately in the testing evidence

▶ a description of the area to be tested, for example whether it is a particular query or a navigational element of the application

▶ examples of the test data to be applied to the particular area of the application

▶ expected outcomes from the completed test

▶ actual test outcomes

▶ comments about the outcome of the test or details of any corrections made to the application.

Testing during development is largely carried out by the development team and involves white box and black box testing.

Testing carried out after development should confirm that the software meets the user requirements and operates efficiently and effectively. The user may have specified other **non-functional requirements** such as performance or response times for the processing of data and particular requirements in terms of usability.

Devising and using valid, invalid and extreme test data

Test cases, in the form of test data, must be created in order to test the system as fully as possible. The behaviour of the system is observed, recorded and compared to the expected outcome in the test plan. These test cases should include extreme data, valid data, **invalid data** and null data.

Extreme data

This is used to test that the system can cope with very large or very small data values. This can also include data on the boundary. For example if a student number has to be in the range 1–100, the test data would normally include the numbers 1 and 100 as extreme values.

Valid data

This is used to test that the system operates as expected with normal data. Invalid data is used to test that the system can process invalid data and does not crash when invalid data is entered.

Null data is used to test that the system can cope when no data is entered.

A simple test plan for the code which validates the student number in the range 1–100 is shown below.

Test number	Reason for test	Test data	Expected output	Observed output	Does observed match expected? (Y/N)
1	Extreme value	1	Value accepted		
2	Extreme value	100	Value accepted		
3	Invalid data	-23	Error message		
4	Valid data	25	Value accepted		
5	NULL test	No data – press Enter	Error message		

Checkpoint ✓

▷ Testing is a continuous process which is carried out throughout the development process. Developers build test cases to represent a wide range of input values.

▷ White box testing is testing the internal logic of a module of code.

▷ Black box testing is only concerned with inputs and outputs. The tester has no knowledge about the code, hence the term 'black box'.

▷ Unit testing tests one unit of code in the system.

▷ Integration testing tests a series of units which have been grouped together to ensure that the units work together and pass data to each other as expected.   ➡

▷ System testing is carried out on the entire system when all functionality has been added.

▷ A good test plan is structured, states what is being tested, who is responsible, the approach being used, the test environment, the test schedule and the testing strategy.

▷ Testing should always be cross-referenced to the user requirements and seek to determine to what extent the user requirements were met.

▷ Test data should include extreme, valid, invalid and null data to help determine how the program behaves in a range of situations.

Practice questions

A spa has a number of different types of equipment for use by clients. Clients must enter a four-digit PIN to use the equipment. A computer system logs the length of time spent on each item of equipment by each client. This information is used to create an itemised bill for clients.

1 Complete the test plan below to enable full testing of the PIN entry. [6 marks]

Test number	Reason for test	Test data	Expected output	Observed output	Match

2 Describe how null, valid, invalid and extreme data could be used when testing the PIN entry system. [6 marks]

3 Describe how unit and integration testing could be used when developing the system. [4 marks]

Chapter 27 Evaluation of digitally authored systems

What this chapter covers

▶ Functional and non-functional user requirements

▶ Robustness

In Chapter 17, where general points on evaluation are considered, the importance of evaluation throughout the design process was mentioned. A thorough test plan must be created which will enable the developer to test the algorithm proposed as a solution. This may highlight problems with an algorithm's logic or areas where the user requirements are not being met. The evaluation will assess the degree to which the final product meets the functional and non-functional requirements.

Evaluation helps ensure a solution meets the original design, is a full and complete solution, is efficient, robust and operates on an appropriate platform.

> **User requirements are discussed in Chapter 11 Designing solutions (Unit 2).**

Functional and non-functional user requirements

The design criteria for any software system is driven by the user requirements. User requirements can be divided into functional and non-functional.

Functional requirements describe the things that the system should be able to do, such as produce a total value or output a particular report.

Non-functional requirements describe the way in which the system should work. For example, the performance of the system in terms of user response time, the usability of the system and the reliability of the system.

Robustness

Evaluating the robustness of a system ensures a true evaluation of its performance. Any system may operate well when valid data is being entered. The ability of a system to handle invalid and exceptional data is a measure of its robustness. If the system does not crash when processing high volumes of valid, invalid or exceptional data, then we can say it is robust.

Practice questions

1 What is the difference between functional and non-functional requirements when developing software systems? [4 marks]

2 How will the development team participate in evaluation at the close of the project? [5 marks]

> **Tasks**
>
> 1 Using a program solution which you have already created, prepare a test plan which will determine whether it is a full, complete, efficient and robust solution.
>
> 2 Prepare a structured evaluation report. Swap your evaluation report with another student and evaluate each other's program. Is the evaluation report accurate and objective?

Airtime scenario 2

Remind yourself of the Airtime scenario, found at the beginning of Unit 3 on page 153.

Alexander must ensure that the employees of Airtime are trained in health and safety awareness. All staff must attend a two-day health and safety training course and pass an examination at the end of the two days. Employees who pass are awarded a certificate. In order to ensure that employees remain familiar with their health and safety responsibilities, each employee must also take a computer-based test in health and safety practices every three months.

Alexander wants a computer program which will test the employees' knowledge of health and safety policies within the organisation every four months, over the period of a year.

He has designed three tests containing ten multiple choice questions. Employees will be required to take and pass each test over the course of a year. Details about the three tests are shown below.

Test number	Test code	Pass mark
1	HS1	85%
2	HS2	80%
3	HS3	90%

Employees will log on to complete the test and will need:

▶ Employee number: a number between 1000 and 1200

▶ Test code (from table above)

▶ Passcode: to be set by Alexander and provided to employees as they enter the test centre. The passcode will be four digits long and should be randomly generated by the computer. (Alexander will keep a record of which employees have been given passcodes, to prevent employees taking the test more than once.) Alexander should be able to use the computer program to generate the passcodes for each test.

The test should work as follows.

▶ The employee should be presented with the correct test starting with an introductory information screen. Each question should be shown on screen with possible answers A, B, C or D.

▶ The employee's score should be displayed on screen while the test is being taken.

▶ At the end of the test the employee number, test code, date, score and 'pass' or 'fail' should be stored.

▶ A final screen showing these details should be presented to the employee.

▶ All input should be validated and error messages should be helpful and user-friendly.

The following reports are required.

▶ For each test (Test 1, Test 2, Test 3):
 – a list of all employees tested, their score and whether they have passed or failed. The average score for that test and the name of the highest scoring employee should be included.

▶ For every employee:
 – an end-of-year certificate showing the score obtained in each test and the average mark achieved by that employee.

Chapter 28 Designing solutions using appropriate tools

What this chapter covers

▶ Use algorithms to design a fully decomposed solution

▶ Specify the data requirements

▶ Include suitable input, output and navigation design

▶ Use dry runs to evaluate a solution

▶ Refine the design solution

Use algorithms to design a fully decomposed solution

> The content of this chapter should be considered in conjunction with Chapter 23 Digital design principles and Chapter 25 Simple error-handling techniques (Unit 4).

In this chapter we are going to use decomposition to create a list of sub-problems to be solved for the Airtime scenario 2.

The main sub-problems could be listed as follows:

▶ Set Pass Codes for Tests

▶ Employ ee Logon

▶ Employee Take Test

▶ Generate Reports

These problems can be solved individually by developing algorithms for each one. At this point it is important to note that there are many different paths to solving a problem. Each individual will adopt their own approach. This is an important consideration when working on controlled assessment.

When considering a solution, you must choose a method of representing the solution. This can be a flowchart or pseudo-code.

Possible algorithms for Airtime scenario 2

Data needed to solve the problem has been highlighted in red.

> **Create logonPassCode**
>
> Start random number generator.
>
> Generate a number between 0 and 9999.
>
> Return PassCode.

```
Set Pass Codes for Tests
Declare an array passCodes to hold pass codes
Declare Boolean variable unique
For loop1 =0 to 2
  Create logonPassCode
  Set Boolean variable unique=false
  Repeat
    for loop2 = 0 to 2
      If passCodes[loop2]=logonPassCode
        unique=false
      End If
      Create logonPassCode
  Until unique=true
End For
```

```
Input and Validate Employee Number
do
  valid=true
  OUTPUT prompt
  INPUT Employee Number
  if Employee Number<1000 OR Employee Number> 1200
   valid=false
   OUTPUT error message
  end if
  clear error message
WHILE valid=false
```

Employee logon
Input and Validate Employee Number
Input and Validate Test Code
Input and Validate Logon Pass Code
Assign Correct Test to Employee

Note that validation must be included throughout the design to ensure that the program is robust and does not crash or fail if the user enters unpredicted values. Validation checks outlined in Chapter 25 should be considered. For example, in the algorithm above, a range check has been used to ensure the employee number is entered correctly. Other validation checks to be considered are: presence, length, type and format.

Tasks

Using algorithms, create a solution for:
▶ Input and Validate Test Code
▶ Input and Validate Logon Pass Code
▶ Assign Correct Test to Employee.

Highlight any new data so that you are able to use this for the data requirements later.

Ensure that you have considered all of the possible validation checks that are required when inputting data.

Record Employee Result Details
Open Employee textfile for writing
Go to the bottom of the file
Write Employee Number, Test Code Date, Score, Grade
Close the file

Here is an algorithm which represents a solution to the employe taking the test.

```
Employee Take Test
  Show Introductory screen
  FOR each question
   Show Question details
   Output prompt to get employeeAnswer
   Input employeeAnswer
   Validate employeeAnswer
   If employeeAnswer=correctAnswer
     add 1 to score
   Endif
   OUTPUT score
  End For
  Assign Pass or Fail Grade
  Record Employee Result Details
```

Tasks

Using algorithms create a solution for:
▶ Show Introductory Screen
▶ Show Question Details
▶ Validate employeeAnswer
▶ Assign Pass or Fail Grade

257

Generate reports

This sub-problem involves looking at the contents of the employee text file and processing the data stored there. There are two reports required. For the first report, one piece of reusable code (a function, method or procedure) can be used to generate the required report when given the required test code.

Generate Reports
Generate Test Report
Generate Employee End of Year Certificate

Generate Test Report
Generate Test Report for HS1
Generate Test Report for HS2
Generate Test Report for HS3

```
Generate Test Report (for the requiredTest)
Output Report Headings
declare integer highScore=0
declare integer totalScore=0
declare integer employeeCount=0
declare real averageScore
Open Employee text file
While Not End of File
  Read the first line of data from the file
  If TestCode= requiredTest
    OUTPUT EmployeeNumber, score, grade
    totalScore=totalScore+score
    employeeCount=employeeCount+1
    If score> highScore
      topEmployee = EmployeeNumber
      highScore = score
    end IF
End If
End While
Close Employee text file
averageScore=totalScore/employeeCount
OUTPUT averageScore
```

Tasks 🖊

Create an algorithm which represents a solution to Generate Employee End of Year Certificate. You will need pseudo-code to GenerateEmployee End of Year Certificate (for the requiredEmployeeNo). Use the algorithm Generate Test Report (for the requiredTest) to help you.

Specify the data requirements

The table below shows data requirements for Set Pass Codes.

	Data item	Data type	Sample valid data	Function of data item
1	passCodes	Array of integer Size 3	2345	To store the three passcodes generated for the health and safety tests.
2	logonPassCode	integer	2345	To store the passcode entered by the employee when taking the test.
3	loop1	integer	1	A loop counter for assigning unique passcodes to the correct position in the array.
4	loop2	integer	2	A loop counter for checking through the array to ensure the passcode is unique.

➡

	Data item	Data type	Sample valid data	Function of data item
5	unique	Boolean	TRUE	A variable which is set to TRUE or FALSE depending on whether the passcode generated is unique. It controls the Repeat Until loop.

Tasks

Using the headings in the table above, create a data requirements table for:
▶ Employee Logon
▶ Employee TakeTest including the sub-problems:
 – Show Introductory Screen
 – Show Question Details
 – Validate employeeAnswer
 – Assign Pass or Fail Grade
▶ Generate Reports

Include suitable input, output and navigation design

The user interface must be designed and discussed with the user. In the first instance, simple sketches can be used to illustrate ideas before the formal wireframes (or storyboards) are drawn up.

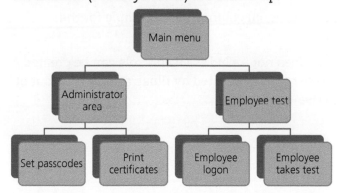

▲ The main processes for Airtime's user interface

Consider a design for the menu options associated with the Airtime computer program.

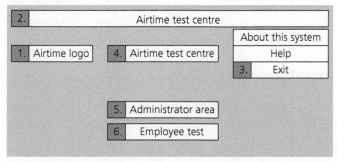

▲ Simple wireframe for initial menu screen at Airtime

If a GUI solution is proposed, a control table which details the names and purpose of any controls used on the form should be included.

Number	Control name	Control type	Purpose of control	Control value
1	pctLogo	Picture box (or a control capable of holding a graphic)	To show Airtime logo on screen.	airtimelogo.jpg
2	Mnubar1	Menu (or a control which can be shown along the top of the screen and which can provide dropdown options)	To allow user to navigate to help, exit and information.	
3		Sub-menu items	To navigate to About, Help, Exit.	About this system Help Exit
4	LblTitle	Label (or a control capable of holding text; the user should not be able to edit the text)	To store and show the title on screen.	Airtime test centre
5	btnAdmin	Button (or a control which can be clicked)	The user can click the button and go to the admin area.	Administrator area
6	btnEmployee	Button (or a control which can be clicked)	The user can click the button and go to the employee logon screen.	Employee test

▲ Control table for wireframe 1

Tasks ✎

1 Create wireframes or screen layout designs for the Administrator area and Employee test options of the Airtime site.

2 Create control tables for each wireframe you have designed.

The control table may include additional columns, for example for the position of each control on screen.

Alternatively, a solution which does not include GUI controls can be created. The design for such an interface could be created by illustrating the layout of the menu to be presented to the user.

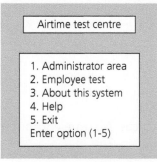

Airtime test centre

1. Administrator area
2. Employee test
3. About this system
4. Help
5. Exit
Enter option (1-5)

▲ A simple screen design for text-based menu options. The screen co-ordinates for the starting position of each option could also be shown.

Use dry runs to evaluate a solution

All algorithm design should be reviewed and tested prior to creating the computer program. This can be done using a trace table which creates a paper-based, dry run of the solution. It enables the programmer to see if the algorithm designed provides the correct solution to the problem.

Consider Validate Employee Number and the associated trace table.

Line number	Valid	Employee number	Output
1			
2	True		
3	True		Prompt
4	True	900	
5	True	900	
6	False	900	
7	False	900	Error message
8	False	900	
9			Cleared error message
10	False		
1	False		
2	True		
3			Prompt
4	True	1100	
5	True	1100	
8	True	1100	
9	True	1100	Cleared error message
10	True		Loop ended

```
Validate Employee Number
1  do
2  valid=true
3  OUTPUT prompt
4  INPUT Employee Number
5    if Employee Number<1000 OR Employee Number> 1200
6      valid=false
7      OUTPUT error message
8    end if
9  clear error message
10 WHILE valid=false
```

Error-trapping proposals should also be specified during the design stage. A trace table used at the design stage may help identify logical errors, but what will happen if, for example, a user enters a character instead of a number? The program may crash. During design, you should consider how to avoid these types of execution errors. Most programming languages provide error-handling routines which can be used to trap an error like this. You should include some simple error-handling proposals when designing your solution as discussed in Chapter 25 Simple error-handling techniques.

Refine the design solution

Testing a solution begins with design. During design, it is important to consider the solution in terms of accuracy, completeness and usability.

A design may be revised or refined because of these considerations. When the solution design is complete, it is important to use all available tools to evaluate the design. Trace tables and discussion can help identify potential problems in the design. These problems can then be corrected and the solution improved.

Tasks

1 In groups of four, review the wireframes created by each person for the Administrator area and Employee test options.

   a) Discuss how effective the computer program would be if the designs were used.

   b) Propose changes to improve the design.

2 As an individual, make changes to your design which will improve the user's experience.

3 Review and create a trace table for the algorithm ValidateEmployeeAnswer. Use the trace table to prove that there are no potential errors in this design.

4 Create a list of four error traps that you will use to ensure that execution errors are minimised. Explain why each is required.

Chapter 29 Building and testing a solution

What this chapter covers

▶ Integrated development environment (IDE)

▶ Building a solution

▶ Testing a solution

Integrated development environment (IDE)

An integrated development environment is a software application which consists of a range of tools to support the development and testing of a computer program.

Source code editor

This is the area where the programmer enters program code. Features such as copy and paste, find and replace and line numbers are available. A source editor is a text editor program designed specifically for editing source code. It may be a standalone application, built into an integrated development environment (IDE) or web browser. More sophisticated code editors provide:

▶ code outlining where sections of the program code can be collapsed and expanded

▶ 'intellisense' which prompts the programmer with the correct syntax

▶ syntax error assistance which highlights syntax errors in the code being entered.

The source code editor ensures that brackets are matched and automatically indents lines of code where necessary.

Debugger

This helps to diagnose errors within the program code. The programmer can advance through the program one line at a time and inspect the value of variables at any given point. Breakpoints, which stop the code at specific lines, can be set and the programmer can view the code to ensure it is functioning as expected.

Compiler

A compiler is needed to convert the original source code of a program into machine code (code a computer can understand) before executing it. The syntax of each statement is checked and if a statement is not constructed

> The content of this chapter should be considered in conjunction with Chapters 24 Programming constructs, 25 Simple error-handling techniques and 26 Developing test plans and testing a solution (Unit 4).

correctly the compiler will generate an error. Source code cannot be fully compiled until it is error-free. The compiler produces an executable file in machine code format (1s and 0s).

Additional tools

The IDE may have a GUI through which the programmer can utilise the tools available. The GUI can include a solution explorer, where the programmer can see a graphical representation of all files associated with the solution, and where files can be edited and added.

Some IDEs also enable the development of GUI applications. In this case, the user has access to a toolbox of controls such as textboxes, labels, list-boxes and radio buttons. These are dragged and positioned onto a form. Each control has a set of properties which can be set and events which can be programmed.

For an example of controls, see the Control table on page 260 of Chapter 28 Designing solutions using appropriate tools (Unit 5).

Building a solution

Practical tips

Evidence of your completed solutions for this unit will be submitted in the form of a working computer program based on a given scenario. The skills required to support the successful production of the program have been presented in Chapters 23 Digital design principles and 24 Programming constructs.

In this chapter, we shall focus on the development and testing of some of the more complex aspects of the Airtime solution. The main elements of developing the solution are:

▶ creating the interface

▶ adding functionality to the system

▶ testing the solution.

Creating the interface

Use the design wireframes created in the previous chapter to create the interface for Airtime.

A section of a possible solution is shown on the next page. The different sections in the IDE (the solution explorer, the design window for the form, the toolbox and the properties window) can be seen in the image. Three forms (screens) have been added to the project. Their names can be seen in the solution explorer. Each has been named appropriately and controls have been added. Controls, such as buttons, labels and textboxes enable the user to interact with the system. It is also possible to create a menu-driven solution which does not make use of forms and controls.

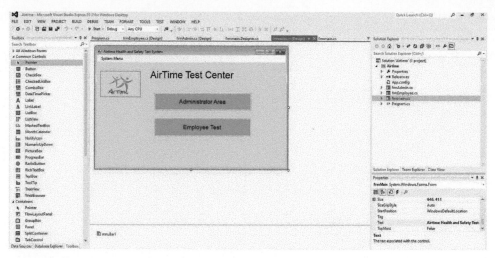

▲ An IDE

To insert a new form

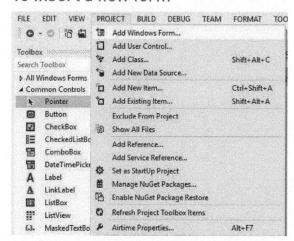

Select 'Add windows form' and name the form appropriately.

To add a control

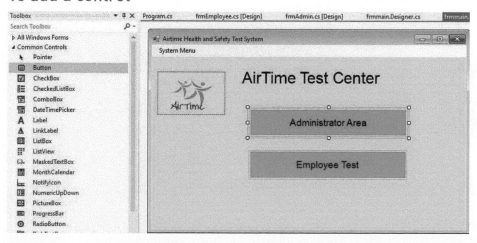

Select the control from the toolbox and draw it onto the form. Name the form appropriately.

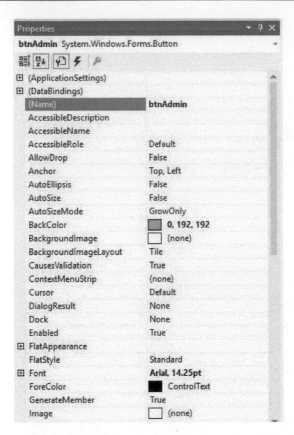

Set the properties of the control. Above you can see a section of the controls for btnAdmin.

Tasks

1. Research how you can display text on screen and capture input from users, using controls, in a programming language of your choice.

2. Create two screens or forms.

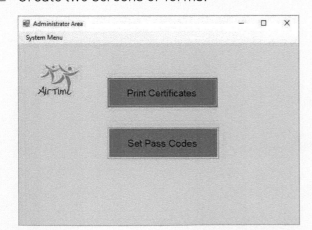

Administrator screen which contains buttons to carry out the tasks shown.

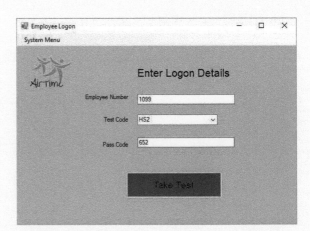

Employee logon screen which contains labels, textboxes and a combo box for displaying and entering data. The employee should be taken to the introductory screen.

If you use forms and controls, ensure that each control is appropriately named, for example:

▶ buttons should start with btn, for example btnAdmin

▶ textboxes should start with txt, for example txtemployeeNo

▶ labels should start with lbl, for example lblLogon

▶ comboboxes should start with cbo eg cbotestCode.

3 Create the quiz introduction screen. One possible design is shown.

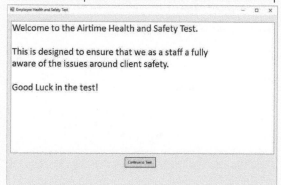

4 Finally, create the quiz page. A simple version of this is shown.

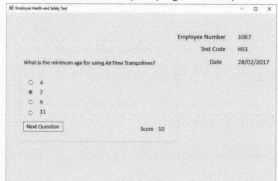

Adding functionality to the system

In order to add functionality, consider the content of the data requirements table and the algorithms created in the previous chapter. Use each of these to help you code the solution for each bit of the problem.

Set pass codes for tests

Part of the code for setting the passcodes is shown on the next page. The passcodes are stored in an array then the content of the array is written to a file.

Airtime.frmAdmin
button2

```
20
21   private void button2_Click(object sender, EventArgs e)
22   {
23       Random randompasscode = new Random();
24       Boolean unique;
25       int logonpassCode=0;
26
27       int[] passCodearray = new int[3];
28       for (int loop1 = 0; loop1 < 3; loop1++)
29       {
30           do
31           {
32               logonpassCode = randompasscode.Next(1, 9999);
33               unique = true;
34               for (int loop2 = 0; loop2 < 3; loop2++)
35                   if (passCodearray[loop2] == logonpassCode)
36                       unique = false;
37
38           } while (unique == false);
39           passCodearray[loop1] = logonpassCode;
40           MessageBox.Show(passCodearray[loop1].ToString());
41       }
42       WriteData(passCodearray);
43
44   }
45   static void WriteData(int [] passCodes)
46   {
47       //create a filestream
48       FileStream myFile = new FileStream("passcodes.txt", FileMode.Append, FileAccess.Write);
49       StreamWriter myStream = new StreamWriter(myFile);
50       string str;
51       for (int i = 0; i < 3; i++)
52       {
53           str = passCodes[i].ToString();
54           myStream.WriteLine(str);
55       }
56       myStream.Flush();
57       myStream.Close();
58       myFile.Close();
```

Tasks

1 List the data types used in this part of the solution.

2 List the data structures used in this part of the solution.

3 List the program structures used in this part of the solution.

Employee logon

Two sections of code are shown below. They are for validating the employee number and matching test codes with passcodes.

```
73
74   private void txtEmployeeNo_Validating(object sender, CancelEventArgs e)
75   {
76       int num;
77       Boolean valid = Int32.TryParse(txtEmployeeNo.Text, out num);
78       if ((valid == false) || (num < 1000 || num > 1200))
79       {
80           MessageBox.Show("Enter a valid employee number");
81           e.Cancel = true;
82       }
83   }
84
85   private void btnTakeTest_Click(object sender, EventArgs e)
86   {
87       Boolean match=true;
88       if (cboTestCode.Text == "HS1" && txtPassCode.Text != passCodes[0].ToString())
89           match = false;
90       else if (cboTestCode.Text == "HS2" && txtPassCode.Text != passCodes[1].ToString())
91           match = false;
92       else if (cboTestCode.Text == "HS3" && txtPassCode.Text != passCodes[2].ToString())
93           match = false;
94
95       /* Below is an alternative simplified version of the above if statement using
96          pass codes that are decided by the user and hard coded into the program
97          Here HS1=1234; HS2=2345 and HS3=3456
98
99       if (cboTestCode.Text == "HS1" && txtPassCode.Text != "1234")
100          match = false;
101      else if (cboTestCode.Text == "HS2" && txtPassCode.Text != "2345")
102          match = false;
103      else if (cboTestCode.Text == "HS3" && txtPassCode.Text != "3456")
104          match = false;     */
105
106      if (match == false)
107      {
108          MessageBox.Show("Test Code and Pass Code do not match");
109      }
110      else
111      {
112          GlobalVariables.employeenumber = Convert.ToInt32(txtEmployeeNo.Text);
113          GlobalVariables.testcode = cboTestCode.Text;
114          MessageBox.Show("Valid details entered you may proceed to the test");
115          frmTest1 myform = new frmTest1();
116          myform.Show();
117      }
118
119  }
```

Employee take test

To add this functionality you will need to consider the questions below.

How will you assign the correct test?

Using the test code.

How you will store the quiz questions?

▶ In a text file.

▶ In an array or string.

▶ Place each question on a different form.

```
private void btnContinue_Click(object sender, EventArgs e)
{
    listBox1.Visible = false;
    btnContinue.Visible = false;
    groupBox1.Visible = true;

    if (lblTestCode.Text == "HS1")
        setFirstQuestion(GlobalVariables.HS1, ref testarray);
```

```
public static string[,]  HS1 = new string[10,6] {{"How often are Trampolines serviced at Airtime?", "Weekly", "Monthly", "Yearly", "Never", "B"},
                        {"What is the minimum age for using AirTime Trampolines?", "4", "7", "9", "11", "B"},
                        {"What is the maximum number of users allowed on one trampoline?", "2", "3", "4", "5", "B"},
```

Part of the quiz for test HS1 stored in an array of string.

How will you count the score?

▶ Using a local integer variable called score.

▶ Compare the user's answer to a stored correct answer.

```
private void button1_Click(object sender, EventArgs e)
{
    questionno++;

    if (useranswer == correctanswer)
    {
        score = score + 10;
        lblScore.Text = score.ToString();
    }

    if (questionno < 10)
    {
        lblQuestion.Text = testarray[questionno, 0];
        lblAnswerA.Text = testarray[questionno, 1];
        lblAnswerB.Text = testarray[questionno, 2];
        lblAnswerC.Text = testarray[questionno, 3];
        lblAnswerD.Text = testarray[questionno, 4];
        correctanswer = Convert.ToChar(testarray[questionno, 5]);
    }
    else
    {
        MessageBox.Show("Test Completed");
        btnNext.Enabled = false;
        MessageBox.Show("You have scored " + score + ".  Your result has been submitted",lbldate.Text);
        string Grade = CalculateGrade(score, lblTestCode.Text);
        writeToFile(GlobalVariables.employeenumber, score, lbldate.Text, Grade);
    }
}
```

How will you assign a grade?

▶ Set the pass mark based on the test code.

▶ Compare the score with the pass mark.

```
static string CalculateGrade(int score, string testCode)
{
        int passmark=0;

        switch (testCode)
        {
            case "HS1": passmark = 85; break;
            case "HS2": passmark = 80; break;
            case "HS3": passmark = 75; break;
        }

        if (score > passmark)
            return "Pass";
        else
            return "Fail";

}
```

This is a function which will take the score and the test code and return the words 'pass' or 'fail'.

How will you write the data for an employee to the file?

```
static void writeToFile(int employeeNo, int score, string datedone, string grade)
{
    FileStream myFile = new FileStream("Results.txt", FileMode.Append, FileAccess.Write);
    StreamWriter myStream = new StreamWriter(myFile);
    string str;

        str = Convert.ToString(employeeNo)+","+Convert.ToString(score)+ "," + datedone + "," + grade;

        myStream.WriteLine(str);

    myStream.Flush();
    myStream.Close();
    myFile.Close();
}
```

This is a function which takes the relevant data and opens a file called 'Results.txt' and writes the data to the file.

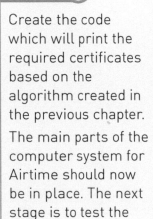

Tasks

Create the code which will print the required certificates based on the algorithm created in the previous chapter.

The main parts of the computer system for Airtime should now be in place. The next stage is to test the system.

Tasks

Describe the features of the programming language you have used for each of the main processes in the functionality section. Structure your answer under these headings:
▶ Data types
▶ Control structures
▶ Functions
▶ Data structures
▶ String handling
▶ Arithmetic
▶ Logical and relational operators

Testing a solution

A test plan for any solution should be presented in tabular format. It should incorporate black box and white box testing, and list appropriate test data and expected output.

The testing should identify errors in the logic of the code and establish the general robustness of the system. The testing phase will also measure the extent to which the user requirements have been met.

The test strategy for the solution should detail how:
▶ black box and white box testing will be carried out
  − all forms will be tested
  − valid, invalid, extreme and null data will be used to test the solution
  − the navigation through the system will be tested
▶ system testing will be carried out
▶ the end user will be involved to help determine if user requirements have been met
▶ performance issues with the application will be identified
▶ the robustness of the solution will be tested.

Practical tips (!)

Chapter 26 Developing test plans and testing a solution includes an example of a test strategy for part of a solution. Note how expected outputs from the testing have been predicted. When carrying out testing, these outcomes should be compared to the actual output produced. Each section of the program should be tested.

The test plan should be cross referenced to the original user requirements.

Airtime user requirements

1 Employees will log on to complete the test using: Employee number (a number between 1000 and 1200), Test code and Pass code. All to be provided by Alexander on entering the test centre.

2 Alexander should be able to use the computer program to generate, set and change the passcode for each test.

3 The employee should be presented with the correct test, starting with an introductory information screen. Following this, each question should be shown on screen with possible answers A, B, C or D.

4 The employee's score should be displayed on screen whilst the test is being taken.

5 At the end of the test, the Employee number, Test code, date, score and 'pass' or 'fail' should be recorded.

6 A final screen showing these details should be presented to the employee. The employee should be given the option to print a certificate of completion for their own records.

7 Employees should have access to simple help about the testing system throughout the test.

8 All input should be validated and error messages should be helpful and user-friendly.

9 The following reports are required
   a) For each test (HS1, HS2, HS3): a list of all employees tested, their score and whether they have passed or failed. The average score for that test and the name of the highest scoring employee should be included.
   b) For a given employee: an end-of-year certificate showing the score obtained in each test and the average mark achieved by that employee.

During testing, where the actual outcome does not match the expected outcome, it is important that any errors in the system are identified and that evidence of any corrective measures taken to rectify the errors is also shown.

Consider a test plan for the Employee logon screen. If a user requirement column is included, the test plan can show to what extent the user requirements have been met.

In order to fully test this screen, it is necessary to generate the Pass codes.

Test number	Reason for test	Test data	Expected output	Observed output	Match/ Corrective measures	User requirement
1	Generate passcodes	Click 'Set Pass Codes' [Set Pass Codes]	Pass codes written to file	passcodes - Notepad File Edit Format View Help 652 3312 8304 Three codes generated, one for each test. HS1 = 652	✓	2
2	Extreme value	employeeNo=1000	Value accepted	Enter a valid employee number [OK]	No condition incorrect (<=1000) Correct condition to >=1000	1
3	Extreme value	employeeNo=1000	Value accepted	Enter Logon Details Employee Number 1000	✓	1
4	Extreme value	employeeNo=1200	Value accepted	Enter Logon Details Employee Number 1200	✓	1
5	Invalid data	employeeNo=-10	Error message	Enter a valid employee number [OK]	✓	1
6	Valid data	employeeNo=1055	Value accepted	Enter Logon Details Employee Number 1055	✓	1
7	NULL test	employeeNo=No Data – press Enter	Error message	Enter a valid employee number [OK]	✓	1
8	Check that Pass codes match test codes.	testCode=HS1 PassCode=601	Error message	Enter Logon Details ... Test Code and Pass Code do not match [OK]	✓	1
9	Check that Pass codes match test.	testCode=HS1 PassCode=555	Error message	Enter Logon Details ... Test Code and Pass Code do not match [OK]	✓	1
10	Check that Pass codes match test.	testCode=HS1 PassCode=652	Value accepted	Enter Logon Details ... Valid details entered you may proceed to the test [OK]	✓	1

Thoughts on testing a solution

▶ It is best to test the software as early in the development process as possible.

▶ Using white box testing requires an understanding of the program code. Therefore developers or programmers are best placed to design the test data for white box testing.

▶ A well-thought-out test plan will help to confirm the robustness of the code. Test cases should cover a wide range of scenarios to test the behaviour of the code.

▶ Validation and error handling techniques should be built in to the program for maximum performance.

▶ The end user must always be involved in the testing process. The user will accept the product created based on the user requirements set down at the beginning of the project. The end user should be involved from the beginning of the development process. For example, if you develop the interface first, without any functionality, the user can feedback on the structure and usability of menus and screens. This will improve the computer system from their point of view.

▶ All functional aspects of the system should be tested to ensure they work as expected and produce accurate output.

▶ Non-functional requirements, such as performance or response times for the processing of data and requirements in terms of usability, should also be tested. Evidence to support success in this area can be obtained by using high volumes of data for testing and by observing the computer system in a real-life environment.

In Chapter 27, we identified the importance of user feedback at the testing stage and we will examine how the user requirements form the basis for evaluation in the next chapter.

Tasks

1 Using the headings below, create a test plan to test the <u>Employee Take Test</u> section of the Airtime computer program. Your test plan should include valid, invalid, extreme and null data. The test plan should also check the accuracy of the score produced.

Test number	Reason for test	Test data	Expected output	Observed output	Match/Corrective measures	User requirement
1						

2 Implement your test plan and evidence the outcome from each test using screenshots. Indicate which user requirements are being met through each test.

3 Comment on the robustness of the solution by referring to the test data used and the behaviour of the system, given particular test cases.

4 Suggest improvements to the system in terms of error handling and validation procedures.

Chapter 30 Evaluating a solution

The structure of an evaluation has been outlined in Chapter 17 Evaluation of digitally authored systems (Unit 2). General practical thoughts on evaluating solutions are discussed in more detail at the start of Chapter 20 Evaluating a solution (Unit 3). The content of this chapter should be considered in conjunction with Chapter 27 Evaluation of digitally authored systems (Unit 4).

What this chapter covers

▶ Thoughts on evaluating a digitally authored solution

Thoughts on evaluating a digitally authored solution

The user requirements drive the evaluation process. At every stage the system is examined to see how the functional and non-functional requirements are being met.

Evaluation during design phase

▶ Evaluation during the design phase requires input from developers and end users.

▶ Drafts of the screen layouts (storyboards) can be shown to the end user for comment. Dialogue with the end user at this point will help improve the design of the interface.

▶ A test plan can be developed to perform both black box and white box testing. The test plan can be used to evaluate the algorithms created for the solution.

▶ The test plan can be cross referenced to the user requirements. This can be used to determine the extent to which the user requirements will be met by the proposed solution.

▶ The test plan can help predict the robustness of the system as the proposed test data can be used in trace tables and possible errors and weak points in the code can be identified.

▶ The system design can be improved or refined following this type of evaluation. Improvements at this stage are less costly.

Evaluation following the development of the system

▶ Testing occurs following the development of the code for the system and provides evidence to support any evaluation.

▶ Test data will be designed and used to trial the system. The outcome of each test will be recorded. This helps the:
  - programmer determine and evidence how well the functional user requirements have been met
  - user and programmer determine and evidence how well the non-functional requirments have been met
  - programmer assess robustness by examining the system's behaviour when invalid and unexpected data is entered.

▶ Before releasing the system to the end user, it is important to observe the system while it is being used. This gives the programmer an overview of how the system will perform when real volumes of data are used and how well the user interacts with it. Non-functional requirements can be assessed during this type of observation.

▶ The interface is evaluated to determine if it is consistent and easy to use.
  – Is the font, text size and style the same across the application?
  – Is the system easy to navigate for users? Are navigation buttons positioned in the same place on different forms?

▶ The code may be examined for efficiency.
  – Has repetition of code been kept to a minimum?
  – Have reusable sections of code been included?
  – Are the response times of the system acceptable? For example, does the system respond to user input or produce output in an acceptable amount of time?

▶ User testamonials or mini-evaluations can be used as evidence to support the findings of the evaluation.

▶ The development team may consider their own performance in terms of time management, interaction with the user and budgetary management.

Further aspects to be considered

Testing and evaluating the system can result in changes being made, for example:

▶ code may need to be corrected because of inaccurate results obtained during testing

▶ additional sections of code may need to be added because all of the user requirements have not been met. When an additional section of code is added tests for the new code need to be included

▶ error-handling proposals may need to be included because the system may have crashed when certain data values are entered.

Tasks

In Chapter 29 you created a test plan to test the Employee Take Test section of the Airtime problem. Create a structured evaluation for this section of the program using the system that you have created. Your evaluation should:

▶ contain a clear reflection on the extent to which the user requirements have been met
▶ make reference to test data to support the points being made
▶ clearly identify any refinements made during design and testing
▶ comment on the performance and robustness of the Employee Take Test sub-system and include evidence to support your comments
▶ identify strengths and weaknesses
▶ make suggestions for improvement.

Glossary / Index

Term	Description	Page
3D	Three dimensional. An image which creates the illusion of depth.	94
7-bit ASCII table	Also known as Standard ASCII, uses 7 bits to represent each character. Only 128 characters could be represented in the character set.	190
8-bit ASCII table	Also known as Extended ASCII, uses 8 bits to represent each character. A further 128 characters can be represented in the character set, totalling 256 characters.	190
A/B testing	End users are presented with different versions of a digital application; statistical analysis is carried out to determine which is most successful.	146
Absolute cell reference	An absolute cell reference is when a formula is copied to other cells; part of the cell reference does not change as the formula is modified.	29
Abstraction	Filtering out details about the problem that will not be required for the solution.	200
Accessibility	The ability to personalise digital applications to support use by any user.	86
Agile	A method of developing a system where small sections are developed, tested and reviewed by the user. Feedback from the full development team, including the user, is used to improve the small section. Development happens in short bursts called 'sprints' which could last 1–2 weeks.	216
Algorithm	A set of step-by-step instructions representing the solution to a problem.	200
Algorithm design	Creating a step-by-step set of instructions that represents a solution to the problem.	200
Alpha testing	Involves simulating the real-world environment the application has been designed for, normally carried out by a small number of users and prior to beta testing.	146
Analogue signal	A continuous varying signal that represents a physical quantity such as sound, temperature or light.	5
Anti-virus software	Software which scans files stored on a computer system looking for a virus, and compares these to a known database of viruses. It can eliminate a virus.	12
Application software	Applications software are programs designed for an end user to do a particular task, such as word-processing and spreadsheet programs.	9
ASCII code	Acronym for the American Standard Code for Information Interchange. ASCII is a code for representing English characters as numbers. Each letter is assigned a number from 0 to 127. For example, the ASCII code for the letter A is 65.	188
Attribute	Heading given to each item of data stored about a single database entity.	80
Backup	A second copy of a file made and stored on a different storage device in case the original file gets lost, or becomes corrupted or physically damaged.	12

Term	Description	Page
Bandwidth	Refers to the amount of data that can be transmitted over a network in a fixed amount of time. It is measured in bits per second.	44
Batch processing	Data is collected over a period of time such as a day and then is processed together at a later time such as overnight.	10
Beta testing	Carried out just after alpha testing and before the final version of the application is released commercially.	146
Binary digIT/bit	Has a value of 0 or 1 and is the smallest unit of computer storage.	1
Binary search	A search algorithm which works on a sorted list of data items. The target value is located by finding the mid location in the list and comparing that value to the target value. This is repeated until the target value is found or the search space has diminished to one item which is not the target value.	209
Bitmap graphic	Bitmap graphics store details about every individual element (or pixel) that makes up an image.	3
Black box testing	Where the tester is unaware of the internal structure of the application they are testing.	145
Bluetooth	A short range wireless technology which allows two devices to connect for the purpose of communication.	43
Bounded repetition	Type of loop used when we know in advance how many times the loop is to be carried out.	225
Broadband	A telecommunications link that provides a wide bandwidth communication for high-speed internet access.	42
Bubble sort	A simple sort method which repeatedly steps through a list of data items; adjacent elements are compared and swapped if they are in the wrong order.	204
Buffer	Computer memory used to store a part of the video download before it is watched.	4
Bug	Another word for error or fault, which leads to errors in the execution of a program or application.	142
Call-to-action button	A clickable link on a social media page which prompts the user to take some form of action.	93
Cascade delete/ Cascade update	Ensures that changes made in the linked table (where the foreign key is entered) are also shown in the primary table.	122, 140
Cell	Where a single piece of data is entered into a spreadsheet. The data is referred to as a piece of text, number or a formula. Each cell is referenced by a letter and a number such as C4.	23
Character	A letter, digit, punctuation mark or a control code stored in digital format as a byte.	1
Chat client	An application which supports interactive real-time chat between two participants.	93
Class	A template for creating an object. It defines the methods and properties which can be used to build an object of that class.	183

Term	Description	Page
Communications protocol	This is a set of rules used to allow different computers from different manufacturers to communicate.	42
Composite key field	A key field which consists of two or more fields.	122
Compression	The reduction of file size through the removal of unnecessary data.	88
Conditional repetition	This type of loop will run until a particular condition is true or false.	225
Contiguous	When memory locations are next to each other.	229
Cross-platform application	An application designed to operate successfully on more than one platform.	87
CSS	Cascading style sheets: a language used to describe the style of a HTML document. It describes how specified elements will be displayed.	107
Cursor	On-screen icon which moves in response to the position of an input device, such as a mouse.	35
Cyber crime	Using a computer to intentionally commit a crime, such as stealing data or money.	47
Data	Unprocessed facts or figures which, on their own, have no meaning.	1
Data compression	Used to convert digital data to as small a size as possible while still maintaining the quality of the data contained in the file. Allows data to be sent over the internet with acceptable transmission speeds.	7
Data controller	The individual in an organisation who is responsible for determining the purposes for which and the manner in which personal data is processed.	58
Data dictionary	A file containing details relating to the structure of data held in a database.	80
Data encryption	The process of scrambling data using a 'key' before it is transmitted onto a network.	49
Data integrity	The accuracy and consistency of data stored in a database.	114
Data modelling	Uses mathematical formulas and calculations on data to help predict outcomes for given situations.	30
Data portability	Transferring data from one computer to another or from one software application to another without having to re-enter the data.	5
Data recovery	Recovering data stored on a storage device which has become corrupted due to a virus or physical damage to the storage medium.	53
Data redundancy	The unnecessary repetition of data in a database.	114
Data requirements	The data that a program or system will use including data input, information output and any values to be stored temporarily during processing.	216
Data subject	An individual who is the subject of personal data.	58
Data type	When a database is created each field is allocated a data type. Different data types are used for different fields such as text or numeric. The data type will define the type of data associated with the field.	18

Term	Description	Page
Data validation	This is carried out by a computer automatically when data is input. It ensures that data is reasonable, sensible and within acceptable limits.	18
Decomposition	Breaking a complex problem down into smaller more manageable problems called sub-problems.	200
Design View	A view which allows the designer to make adjustments to the content or layout of an object created in a digital application.	116
Dry run	A paper-based exercise which allows the programmer to go through the solution step by step. The dry run will highlight any errors in the logic of the solution.	145
Dynamic page	A page where the presentation can be changed through a user's interactions with the application: they tend to end with the extensions .php, .asp, .jsp.	107
E-commerce	A means of conducting business transactions over electronic networks such as online shopping.	52
Encapsulation	An object's data is hidden so that it can only be directly accessed by the methods within the object.	183
End user	The person for whom a system is being developed.	73
Entity	An item which is represented in a database.	81
Entity-relationship diagram	A diagram used to illustrate how various entities in a database are linked together.	81
Ergonomic	The science concerned with designing safe and comfortable hardware and office furniture for humans.	64
Evaluation	A document which considers the success of a project in relation to how complete the solution is, how efficient it is, how well it meets the end user's requirements and how well it operates on specified platforms.	149
Event-driven programming	Where events such as the user's interaction with an application element can determine how the application is presented to the end user.	112
Evolutionary prototype	A prototype which is reviewed and improved and eventually forms the final system solution.	74
Extreme data	Used to test that the system can cope with very large or very small data values.	144
Fallback text	An error message in the event that a file cannot be played by the browser.	106
Feedback	Situation where input is affected by output from a digital application.	91
Fetch–execute cycle	A computer process which locates a program instruction from internal memory, decodes the instruction and carries out the action required. This process is then repeated for the rest of the program instructions.	32
Field	Part of a record that stores a single data item. In a table, each field is represented by a column.	14
Firewall	A piece of software or hardware that is used to monitor and filter data that is entering or leaving a network.	51

Term	Description	Page
Flowchart	A graphical representation which includes special symbols and flow lines to represent the solution to a problem.	201
Foreign key	A key field in one table used to create a link between data in another table.	17
Form	Used to enter a new record, modify an existing record and to view records already stored in a table.	15
Format check	Used to ensure that data entered is in the correct format. This means that the data must conform to a pattern. For example, a postcode must have the pattern XX99 9XX where X is a letter 'A' to 'Z' and 9 is a digit '0' to '9'.	20
FTP	A protocol that allows users to upload and download files from file servers using the internet.	51
Functional requirements	These describe the things that the system should be able to do.	253
Game settings	An area of a gaming application where the user can adjust game elements such as sound levels, controls and even create their own characters.	94
Gigahertz	The clock speed of a computer's processor is measured in gigahertz, whereby one GHz represents 1 billion cycles per second.	34
Graphical user interface (GUI)	A user interface which provides windows, menus, icons and pointers so that the user can operate it.	83
Hacker	A person who gains unauthorised access to a computer with the intention of corrupting data or stealing data.	47
Hexadecimal/ Hex	A numbering system which uses the base 16.	191
HTML (hypertext markup language)	The language used to define the structure of webpages. It is often combined with CSS and JavaScript to create hypermedia applications presented to users via browser software for the World Wide Web.	42
Http (hypertext transfer protocol	A protocol used by the World Wide Web that defines how messages are formatted and transmitted by web servers.	42
Https (hypertext transfer protocol secure)	A protocol used by the World Wide Web for transmitting messages securely. This is done using data encryption.	52
Human– computer interface	The use of digital technology to support communication between end users and computers.	83
Hyperlinks	Allow users to move from one HTML page to another. They can also be used to link to multimedia elements such as videos for playback, or documents for download.	42
Hypermedia	The use of media including text, graphics, video and sound elements of an application to provide links to related content in a multimedia application.	98
Hypertext	Text which can provide links to related content in a multimedia application.	98
Icon	Small image or picture on screen representing a shortcut to a tool or application.	83

Term	Description	Page
Image sources	Details of any graphic elements to be incorporated into an application. This may be in the form of file names, web location or a description of the image if it is to be created by the developer.	77
Immutable	This means that a string cannot be changed once it is created, instead a new string must be created to reflect a change.	234
Information	When data is entered into a computer system and is processed it becomes information, or 'data with meaning'.	1
Information commissioner	The title given to a government regulator who is responsible for the protection of personal data. They are responsible for enforcing the Data Protection Act.	58
Inheritance	This enables the properties of one class to be copied to another so that only the differences between the classes need to be reprogrammed.	183
Input mask	A method of controlling the format of data which is being entered into a database.	120
Insertion sort	A simple sorting algorithm that builds a sorted sub-list one item at a time. The sub-list becomes the new sorted list.	204
Integration testing	When a number of units have been tested they are combined together to form a sub-system. Integration testing ensures that all of the units work together correctly.	249
Interactive	A multimedia element of a digital application which invites input from the end user.	69
Interactive elements	Elements in a package which prompt interaction from the end user.	78
Internet	A global network that connects computers over a wide area to allow computers to communicate.	42
Intranet	A private network owned and managed by an organisation. Using usernames and passwords, it can only be accessed by people belonging to that organisation. In appearance it is similar to the internet.	42
Invalid data	Used to test that the system can process invalid data and does not crash when invalid data is entered.	251
Iteration	The use of loops and conditions to repeat sections of code.	75
Iterative development approach	A step-by-step approach taken to the development of an application. Each step sees the life-cycle of analysis, design, development, testing, installation and review being repeated, each time adding more and more to the application until it is eventually completed.	141
Key field	The field that uniquely identifies one record.	14
LAN (local area network)	A network where computers are geographically close together such as in the same building.	41
Laser beam	An intense narrow beam of light. The light from a laser is of a single colour such as red.	37
Length check	Used to ensure that the user has entered data which does not exceed or is not shorter than a particular number of characters. This type of check is commonly used when entering a password to ensure that it contains a minimum amount of characters.	19

Term	Description	Page
Linear search	A simple search algorithm that compares every data item in a list to the target value.	209
Lists and tuples	A data structure which can hold mixed data types (arrays can only hold data items of the same data type).	229
Look-up list	A list of data which can be used (or 'looked up') to provide all available values for a given data field.	119
Lossless compression	Type of data compression where the quality of an image is maintained.	7
Lossy compression	Type of data compression where the quality of an image is reduced.	7
Machine code	Instructions in binary format that can be executed directly by the computer.	186
Macro	A small program that is written to perform a repetitive task automatically.	17
Malware	Malicious software that is downloaded onto a computer unintentionally by a user.	48
Master file	The main file used to store reference data within an application on a computer system. A transaction file is used to update the master file.	10
Menu	Provides end users with a list of related options for selection.	28
Merge field	Field used to indicate the location in a document where data extracted from a database file should be inserted following the completion of a mail merge process.	136
Metadata	Data that describes other data. In a HTML document, metadata is defined inside the <head> </head> tag.	104
Methods	The behaviours that an object can perform. For example, an object may have a method which prints all of the data contained within it onto the screen.	183
Motion tracking interfaces	Interfaces which convert movement into digital signals.	85
Movie timeline	A diagrammatic representation which shows the content of a movie frame by frame.	78
Multimedia	This involves the integration of text, graphics, video, animation, and sound in a presentation.	37
Multimedia authoring	The integration of a range of media in a way that it can usefully present information to a target audience.	79
Natural language interface	A means of interacting with digital technology using everyday language.	84
Navigation structure diagram	A diagram which illustrates the various pathways a user can take through a multimedia application.	76
Network	Consists of a number of computers which are linked together either by cable or using wireless technology.	41
Network interface card (NIC)	An electronic board fitted to a computer to allow it to be connected to a network.	44

Term	Description	Page
Non-functional requirements	These describe the way in which the system should work.	250
Non-volatile	This is a type of memory that retains its content when the power is turned off.	39
Null data	Used to test that the system can cope when no data is entered.	144
Object	A self-contained element which contains the properties and methods needed to access and manipulate the data values.	183
Object-oriented paradigm	An approach to developing a solution where the focus is on data not processes. The data and the methods (program code) which operate on the data are contained within a single object class.	182
One's complement	Can be used to represent a binary number. When using one's complement, each bit is inverted, so a 1 bit changes to a 0 bit, and each 0 bit is changed to a 1 bit.	193
Operating system	A program to allow the hardware to communicate and operate with the computer's software.	9
Optimisation	When files are compressed to facilitate storage or electronic transmission.	88
Optimised	Code which uses the minimum of resources during operation and which is efficient in terms of speed of operation.	88
Overflow	Occurs when the magnitude of the number is greater than the maximum number that can be represented by the computer.	194
Parameter query	A query where the user is prompted to enter search criteria each time a query is activated.	128
Pattern recognition	Identifying patterns and trends in the data.	200
PDF	Portable document format, a piece of software which supports presentation of text, graphics and hyperlinks on a range of platforms.	88
Personal data	Data that is stored about an individual on a computer system.	57
Pixel	The smallest unit of a digital image that can be displayed and edited on a computer screen.	3
Platform	The hardware or software (or both) which supports the operation of an application.	87
Plugin	Software which adds additional features to an application once installed.	88
Pointer	On-screen icon which moves in response to the position of an input device, such as a mouse.	35
Presence check	Used to ensure that the user has entered data and has not left a value or field blank. This is commonly used in forms to ensure that all fields are completed.	19
Procedural paradigm	An approach to developing a solution where the program operates on data and is organised in self-contained blocks called procedures. The logic of the program is actioned by calling the procedures.	182
Program	A set of instructions that are written to carry out a task.	32

Term	Description	Page
Properties	Contains code which facilitates reading and writing to the data within an object.	183
Protocol	A set of rules to allow for communication between two different computer systems.	51
Prototype	A model of a system being developed; may not be fully functional.	73
Pseudo-code	A set of English-like, language-independent instructions which uses keywords and control structures to represent the solution to a problem.	200
Push technology	Allows information to be delivered automatically to recipient, for example pop-ups.	96
Qualitative user requirements	Relate to the quality of the solution, and may be subjectively assessed, i.e. not everyone may assess them equally.	151
Quantitative user requirements	Requirements which can be easily measured, for example in terms of time.	151
Query	Used to search and extract data from the database to find the answer to a question.	15
Range check	Used to ensure that the data entered by the user is in the correct range. Range checks make use of upper and lower boundaries; for example when entering percentages, the value must be in the range 0 to 100.	20
Real-time processing	Processing of data occurs immediately when data is input and updating occurs before the next input occurs.	10
Record	A number of data items related to an object or person. A record is represented as a row in a table.	14
Referential integrity	Ensures that an entry cannot be made in one table with a foreign key, if the key field does not exist in the linked table.	17
Refinement	The process of reviewing the design for a solution and making necessary changes so that the design meets the user's requirements efficiently and accurately.	74
Register	A register is a high-speed memory location used for a specific purpose such as temporarily storing the address of the next instruction to be executed.	33
Relationship	Links two tables in a database using a field that exists in each of the tables. The degree of relationship can be categorised as a one-to-one, one-to-many or a many-to-many.	17
Relative cell reference	This changes a formula's cell references to refer to the next cell(s) when the formula is copied down a column or across a row.	28
Repeater	A repeater is a network device used in a fibre optic communications system to regenerate or replicate a signal.	44
Repetition	Where select lines of code can be executed over and over again, either a set number of times or until a condition is met.	109
Report	Allows tables and results from queries to be presented in a user-friendly way to read.	16
Report View	Displays the report/form in the format which is accessible to the end user once the digital application is complete.	131

Term	Description	Page
Resolution	Measures the quality of an image in pixels. It is the total number of pixels used to display an image.	3
Robust system	A system can be considered to be robust if it does not crash when processing high levels of valid, invalid or exceptional data.	151
Robustness	A measure of the system's ability to continue to run when high volumes of valid, exceptional or invalid data is entered.	177
Role-play games (RPG)	A gaming environment where the end user plays the game in the persona of a character from the game. All interactions with the game are in that persona.	94
Router	A router is a hardware device which connects a number of networks together either by cable or wireless, to allow for data transmission.	45
Scripted elements	Extracts of code, often included as part of a HTML document, which when activated can allow the end user to interact with the application and amend the contents being displayed.	78
Secure socket layer	A protocol for transmitting private documents over the internet by creating a secure connection between the client and the web server.	52
Selection	Where only some lines of code need to be run and only if a certain condition is met. If the condition is not met, the code is not executed.	109
Sequencing	Where lines of code are designed to run one after another from the beginning to the end.	109
Social media	Digital technology application used to support content sharing and communication.	47
Software development environment	Software which provides programmers with an integrated set of programming tools to build an application from coding through to testing.	185
Software licence	A document that provides legally binding guidance for the use and distribution of software within an organisation.	58
Source code	The original program code written by the programmer.	186
SQL (structured query language)	A specialised language used to create databases and to retrieve and process data in a database.	129
Static page	A page which is presented to the user in the form it was created: they tend to end with the extension .htm, .html.	107
Storyboard	A diagrammatic illustration showing the content and layout of individual pages in a multimedia application.	77
Streaming	Process that allows video to be viewed on a website straight away, without having to wait for the full video to be downloaded.	4
Switch	A switch is a hardware device that allows a computer to connect to it using a cable to access a network.	45
Syntax	The rules, order or structure of various elements in a language.	108
Syntax error	An error in the code entered into the code editor, for example, a misspelling or the omission of a symbol.	185

Term	Description	Page
System software	Systems software includes the operating system and all utility programs that enables the computer to operate its hardware and applications software.	9
System testing	Carried out on a completed and fully integrated system to ensure correct outputs are produced in compliance with the user requirements document.	145
Table	A flat file where data is organised into a number of rows and columns.	14
Target audience	The demographic group for whom an application is being developed.	75
TCP/IP	A data transmission protocol to allow high-speed communication between different networks. It provides both the transporting and routing of data.	51
Teleworking	Using information technology (IT) and telecommunications to work from home which replaces work-related travel.	63
Template	A predefined layout containing the main elements of the document it represents. The contents and layout of the template can be edited to suit the needs of the specific user.	25
Test cases	A document which contains a set of tests to help the programmer verify that the code works as expected. It will include expected results and actual outcomes.	247
Testing evidence	Documentation which illustrates the outcome of tests applied to application software, this may be in the form of annotated screenshots.	143
The cloud	Resources and storage hosted online. The cloud can be accessed on a global scale using any device that can connect to the internet.	53
Third-party implementation	The creation of a product by someone other than the original designer.	77
Throwaway prototype	A prototype which does not become part of the final system solution.	74
Touchscreen	A device which supports interaction through the use of a stylus or fingers. Can support both input and output.	36
Trace table	Created during a dry run containing all data items and output used in the section of code being reviewed. The value of each data item is documented after each line of the solution is executed.	145
Traditional development	A model for creating a system which follows a sequential set of steps: analysis, where the user's requirements are determined; design, where the solution is designed and refined; implementation, where the design is coded; testing, where the coded solution is tested using a variety of different methods; maintenance, where the system is changed or tweaked after it has been released to the user.	216
Transaction file	This is a file that stores transactions in an application that will be used to update the master file.	11
Two's complement	A method for representing signed numbers in a computer system.	193
Type check	Used to ensure that the data entered is of the correct data type, for example, numeric, string, date.	19
Unbounded repetition	This type of loop will run until a particular condition is true or false.	226

Term	Description	Page
Unconditional repetition	Used when we know in advance how many times the loop is to be carried out.	225
Unicode	A standard for encoding characters. Unicode typically uses 16 bits to represent a character and so can represent up to 65 000 characters.	190
Unit testing	Testing one module or unit of code to ensure that it is working as expected. The logic of the code is tested.	249
URL (uniform resource locator)	The address of a website that can be entered into the address bar to locate the website.	42
USB (universal serial bus)	A manufacturer's standard that supports data transfer between different devices. A USB port on the device is used to make the connection. It supports 'plug and play'.	35
User forum	An online discussion group involving a number of users who have common interests. They use online services such as 'chatrooms' to communicate and exchange ideas.	68
User interface	Any part of the system that the user can interact with; this includes data capture forms, menus and buttons.	75
User requirements	A document which details what the end user expects the system to do. Often forms part of a contract between the developer and the end user.	73
Utility program	A program that performs a very specific task in managing system resources such as a backup program.	9
Valid data	Used to test that the system operates as expected with normal data.	25
Variable	A data value stored in memory which can change during program execution.	110
Vector-based graphic	Stores information about the components that make up an image. These components are based on mathematical objects such as lines, curves, and shapes.	4
Virtual reality	Using technology to create an artificial environment which is presented to the user in such a way that it appears and feels like a real environment.	67
Virtual space	A computer-generated representation of an environment or location designed to support end user interaction. Generally presented to the user in 3D.	97
Virus	A program which is designed to damage a computer system.	48
Virtual community	A group of individuals who communicate in an online forum.	92
Voice over internet protocol (VOIP)	Using the internet to make phone calls. These calls are free of charge, for example Skype calls.	35
Volatile	The contents of memory are lost when the power is turned off.	39
W3C	World Wide Web Consortium, a standards organisation whose focus is on ensuring accessibility of digital applications.	87

Term	Description	Page
Waterfall model	Represents a sequential approach to application development. A series of stages need to be completed in a fixed order and each stage must be completed before the next can begin.	141
Web 2.0	Second generation WWW technologies aimed at supporting user interaction and collaboration online.	92
Web browser	A piece of software used to find content from the World Wide Web.	52
Web space	An area of a host's server made available to an end user for the storage of their content.	93
White box testing	A method of testing which examines the underlying structure of the application or code which has been developed.	145
WAN (wide area network)	A network where computers are geographically far apart, such as in different cities, and are connected by telephone lines and/or radio waves.	41
Wi-Fi	A wireless medium that allows devices to connect and communicate using radio waves.	43
WIMP	Windows icon menu pointer.	83
Window	An area on screen showing the actions being carried out by an application.	83
Wireframe diagram	A tool used to show the layout of input and output screens in a digital application.	80
Wizard	Software tool which automates complex tasks for users by providing user prompts and asking questions to take the user through the task step by step.	26
Worksheet	A grid in the form of rows and columns. A spreadsheet is made up of a number of worksheets whereby each worksheet can be given a different name as a reference point.	23
World Wide Web (WWW)	The World Wide Web is a means of accessing information over the internet.	42
WYSIWYG	What you see is what you get: the content being displayed to the end user looks as it will in the final product.	79